I0819610

LOST

LOST

AMELIA EARHART'S
THREE MYSTERIOUS DEATHS
AND ONE EXTRAORDINARY LIFE

RACHEL HARTIGAN

WASHINGTON, D.C.

Published by National Geographic Partners, LLC
1145 17th Street NW Washington, DC 20036

See page 300 for text permissions.

Since 1888, the National Geographic Society has funded more than 15,000 research, conservation, education, technology, and storytelling projects around the world. National Geographic Partners distributes a portion of the funds it receives from your purchase to National Geographic Society to support their mission to illuminate and protect the wonder of our world.

Get closer to National Geographic Explorers and photographers, and connect with our global community. Join us today at nationalgeographic.org/joinus

For rights or permissions inquiries, please contact National Geographic Books Subsidiary Rights: bookrights@natgeo.com

Interior design: Nicole M. Roberts

ISBN: 978-1-4262-2254-2

The authorized representative in the EU for product safety and compliance is Disney Trading B.V., Asterweg 15S, 1031 HL, Amsterdam, The Netherlands
email: DCP.DL-EU.bookscontact@disney.com

Printed in the United States of America

26/LSCC/1

Certified Sourcing
www.forests.org
SFI-01681

Logo Applies to Text Stock Only

To my son, Will, who told me I should go,
and to Chris, who made it possible

"Women must try to do things as men have tried.
When they fail, their failure must be but a challenge to others."

—AMELIA EARHART

CONTENTS

PROLOGUE

On the afternoon of June 29, 2017, a Fijian sailor in a blue-and-white-striped shirt and wraparound sunglasses offered me his hand. I clutched it tightly as I stepped cautiously from the M.V. *Reef Endeavour,* a 63-cabin cruise ship, into a bobbing Zodiac. A bright orange life vest covered my new plaid sun shirt. A new sun hat covered my head. I was wearing lightweight hiking pants (new) and water shoes (also new).

I'd never been in the tropics before. I'd also never been on a Zodiac. I hadn't been on a cruise ship. And I'd certainly never been some 7,000 miles from home or a three-day sail from the nearest hospital.

I was terrified.

I stumbled forward on the Zodiac, groping my way to a seat on the far bench. While the boat rocked and bumped against the *Reef Endeavour,* I gripped a line and waited for the rest of my companions to board. They were a motley crew: two archaeologists, four dog handlers from the Institute for Canine Forensics, and four border collies in sky blue life vests and booties to protect their paws from the sharp coral and hot sands on which we were about to walk.

Our destination was a couple hundred yards away: the island of Nikumaroro, an uninhabited coral atoll just shy of the Equator. From where we rode the swells, the island presented a tropical vision of sandy beaches and shady trees. But we knew that between us and the sand lay a treacherous reef prepared to rip the *Reef Endeavour* apart. We'd already seen sobering evidence of its power in the wreckage of the steam freighter *Norwich City,* which had foundered on the island in a storm almost 90 years earlier and lost 11 members of its crew.

We were aiming for a roiling path of waves leading straight to the shore, a narrow landing channel colonists had blasted through the reef long ago. I didn't like what I'd heard about this channel. In a briefing the day before, John Clauss, a veteran of many expeditions to Nikumaroro, assured us he'd never seen a boat flip in these waters. But he admitted that in 2015, a wave had knocked a guy overboard; he had been pulled under the boat by the current and thrown onto the reef. The man was lucky to survive. "Things can go wrong, and go wrong in a hurry," said Clauss.

The dog handlers were even more apprehensive than I was. They'd spent considerable time and expense training their animals to detect human remains—and yet the dogs had never encountered such an environment as this. "Nothing worried me until now," said Lynne Angeloro, whose canine partner was a shy brown-and-white male named Berkeley.

The dogs were here on a gamble, and the other two people on this run of the Zodiac—National Geographic archaeologist Fred Hiebert and archaeologist Dawn Johnson—were the gamblers. Two years earlier, they had hatched the plan to bring the animals to the Phoenix Islands in the central Pacific Ocean in a long shot effort to sniff out the remains of Amelia Earhart. The missing aviator had been aiming for an island 356 nautical miles northwest of Nikumaroro when she disappeared. Dogs are among the best tools for discovering human remains; canines from the institute had located burial sites as deep as nine feet below the earth's surface, and as old as 9,000 years. But the handlers didn't know if the dogs could handle the rocking boat and the oppressive heat—or if they would detect any scent in the coral that was the island's foundational material.

I was there on a gamble, too, but a personal one. A few months earlier, an editor at National Geographic had stopped me in the hall to ask if I'd be interested in going on an expedition to search for Amelia Earhart. He wasn't sure if he could get a berth on the ship; if he did, he needed a writer to be ready. I found out later that his first choice, an unattached and adventurous young man, had a previous engagement. So the editor asked me, a married, middle-aged mother no one had ever mistaken for adventurous. Though I was a writer for National Geographic, the home of far-flung journalism, I'd never done anything like this.

I had no idea what I was getting into. I didn't know how remote the area was where Earhart disappeared—or that the Pacific's deep swells would make me horribly seasick. I didn't know that researchers had battled bitterly for decades over what had happened to her—spinning out theories that involved aerial espionage, carnivorous crabs, and fatal plunges into the sea. I didn't know that the search for the missing aviator had become the organizing principle of many of their lives.

So I said yes. I was bored with my job working on tiny morsels for the magazine, bored with my marriage to another deskbound journalist, and most of all bored with myself. I wanted to see the other side of the world. I wanted to see what I could do.

In no way did I resemble the person we were going to look for: a woman who didn't hesitate to risk her life when planes were new. Earhart had been the first woman to travel by air across the Atlantic, the first woman (and second person after Charles Lindbergh) to fly solo across the Atlantic, and the first pilot to fly alone from Hawaii to California. She'd gone up in the air in an early version of a helicopter and ventured underwater in a primitive diving suit. I had never been that bold.

Yet here I was on that skittish Zodiac, preparing to step onto an island few people had ever seen.

Once everyone was on board, the dogs clasped between their handlers' knees, we headed directly for the channel. It was easy to spot: Past the line of waves breaking against the reef was a dark swirling strip of water.

We'd been told to mind the gap between the boat and the reef as we disembarked; it would be easy to crush a foot between them or slip into the water. We'd also been told to watch our step on the reef; it was sharp and covered with slippery yellow algae. Coral wounds can take weeks to heal.

I was worried about all of these things when we set off. But as we skimmed over the waves, I tasted sea spray on my lips, and the ocean breeze pushed my new hat back and loosened my hair. The dogs lifted their noses to catch the island's scent. I couldn't help feeling exhilarated.

The sailor gunned the Zodiac, and it leaped over the surf. Cutting the motor to a gentle hum, he guided the boat to the channel's terminus, parking it parallel to the reef as neatly as a city driver.

I stepped off the boat onto the reef. Crewmen already on shore hauled the dogs over the sides and let them splash through the shallow water. I made my way carefully to the beach, where I gathered handfuls of sand to pat on my cheeks. When the island's spirits caught my scent, Clauss had explained, they would think I belonged.

I doubt they were fooled. Though I loved Nikumaroro from the moment I arrived, it was not my island. It belonged to the birds and the crabs and the fish—and to the people who had settled there many years ago, only to sail away.

The quest for Amelia Earhart wasn't mine, either; I was not capable of being an adventurer or a true believer. But the members of The International Group for Historic Aircraft Recovery (TIGHAR), which had organized a dozen expeditions to the atoll, were both. So, I learned, were the proponents of the other theories about Amelia Earhart's fate. Whether they believed Earhart had died a castaway on Nikumaroro, perished as a captive of the Japanese on Saipan, or drowned in the Pacific, these men—and the searchers were mostly men—seemed pretty sure they knew exactly what had happened. They knew the mistakes Earhart had made, whose stories to believe, and which evidence mattered. Their witnesses contradicted each other, their smoking guns were dismissed, their evidence lost—yet still they maintained their certainty. I couldn't help but wonder, Were any of them right?

I'm also not inclined to hero worship—and that's the other side to the Earhart story. Was she truly the fearless feminist hero she's now remembered as? The one who pushed women to be more daring than men, who ignored barriers to women's achievement as if they didn't exist? The keepers of that particular flame don't seem to care about how she died. Nor does her family, who mourned her long ago. Searching for her is a waste of time and money, they say. People should focus on how she lived: as a pioneer and champion of women's rights.

I could not reconcile these opposing obsessions with a legendary woman and an undying mystery—or their shared certainty. It unsettled me throughout my time on Nikumaroro—on this trip and on the second voyage I made. I couldn't let it go.

So perhaps the quest for Amelia Earhart is mine after all: to braid together her extraordinary life with the extraordinary measures searchers have taken to find out how it ended. And to discover why one person has compelled so many to such lengths.

CHAPTER ONE

1937: DISAPPEARANCE

At 10 o'clock on the morning of July 2, 1937, a silver Lockheed Electra 10-E accelerated down the longest runway at the airport in Lae, in what is now Papua New Guinea. After a thousand unpaved yards, the strip ended in a cliff overlooking the Huon Gulf. The bustling airfield had been carved out of the bush more than 10 years earlier as a jumping-off point for transporting mining equipment to southern goldfields.

The heavily loaded aircraft streaked nearly to the runway's end before it was able to lift off. As the plane became airborne, it wobbled unsteadily and dropped below the cliff's edge, dipping so close to the ocean that the propellers kicked up spray. Then the Electra gained the sky, soaring at last into the clouds.

That was the last anyone ever saw of it.

The plane's pilot was Amelia Earhart, one of the most recognizable women in the world with her direct gaze, tousled hair, and lean frame. On that tropical morning in July, she was within days of achieving her greatest triumph, "a circumnavigation of the globe as near its waistline as could be." No one had ever flown so far for so long.

Tucked into the plane's fuselage was navigator Fred Noonan. Recently married, Noonan had helped pioneer Pan American's transpacific flights and trained many of the pioneering airline's navigators. He was widely respected, even revered. Colleagues claimed he could "shoot the sun"—navigate by measuring the sun's altitude—standing on his head.

Earhart and Noonan were aiming for Howland Island. A tiny speck in the Pacific, the barely inhabited coral atoll was the third to last stop on their round-the-world flight. They'd already flown 22,000 miles over the course of a month, with 7,000 more to go—all over open water.

The 2,500-mile leg to Howland would be the most difficult one of their journey—18 or more hours across the Pacific to an island just 20 feet above sea level and a mere one and a half miles long. If they missed Howland, they had nowhere else to go.

They'd intended to leave Lae on June 30, which would have given them plenty of time to make a triumphant return to their starting point in Oakland, California, on July 4—Independence Day, with all its celebratory fireworks. Earhart's husband—and publicist—George Putnam had booked a "very important radio commitment" for July 5 with many more events to follow.

But their flight had been delayed several days. The weather wasn't cooperating: "Clouds and winds blowing wrong way," as Earhart put it in a cable to the *New York Herald Tribune*.

Meanwhile, the Lae station had been struggling to pick up radio time signals, which Noonan needed to set his chronometers. If the chronometers weren't accurate, he wouldn't be able to determine longitude. If he couldn't determine longitude, he wouldn't be able to find Howland.

Earhart reported the "radio misunderstandings" to Putnam in a telegram on June 30, informing him of the delay. She also mentioned "personnel unfitness." Perhaps she was referring to Noonan's alcoholism; that's why he'd been let go from Pan Am, or so the rumors said. And she knew he'd spent their first night in Lae carousing with local aviators at the hotel bar.

Or perhaps Earhart meant she herself wasn't well. She may have been exhausted. Photos from Lae show her looking as jaunty as ever in her mannish trousers and work shirt. Yet her eyes drooped with dark circles, and no wonder: Most days they rose well before dawn to prepare the Electra and take off on another exhausting flight. Somehow, Earhart had also managed to squeeze in writing dispatches totaling some 30,000 words for the *Herald Tribune*. Few people could keep to that grueling schedule for long. And the flight to Howland would be the lengthiest one yet.

Whatever the issue, Earhart didn't consider it serious enough to cancel the flight. She and Noonan spent June 30 reloading the Electra; it would be carrying nearly its full capacity of fuel, so they needed to jettison every ounce of extra weight. They unpacked the whole plane and set aside items they thought they wouldn't need: extra maps and spare parts, their clothes and personal belongings, tools and reference books listing marine navigational lights, broadcast stations, and coast and ship stations. Some they probably should have kept—a flare gun, smoke bombs, and the elephant hoof bracelet that Earhart wore for luck.

The next day, July 1, Earhart took the Electra out for a short test flight. She was able to establish two-way communication with the Lae station but couldn't get a bearing on it: an indication that the direction finder—a crucial tool for determining where a signal was coming from—might not be working. Earhart shrugged off the instrument's failure, attributing it to her proximity to Lae. She made plans to take off later that day, if the time signals came through. They didn't get a clear signal until 10:30 that night, when Noonan was finally able to check his chronometer. It was three seconds slow.

On July 2, 1937, Earhart and Noonan were ready. The weather forecast wasn't ideal—"partly cloudy skies with dangerous local rain squalls"—but they'd flown through worse.

At 10 a.m., the Electra, weighted down with enough fuel for this longest leg, rumbled down the runway carrying the heaviest load Earhart had ever flown. But she managed to launch the plane into the air. "The take off was hair-raising," reported James Collopy, the head of civil aviation in Lae. Even so, he said, "it was obvious that the aircraft was well handled."

They were on their way.

THE FLIGHT WOULD TAKE EARHART and Noonan on a great circle course, a route that follows the planet's curve but looks indirect on a typical two-dimensional map. They would cross the northern tip of the Solomon Islands archipelago, skirting the Nukumanu Islands. At the halfway point, the coal-burning U.S.S. *Ontario* held steady to mark their path. The Electra would then pass south of Nauru, where they would be able to see the bright lights from the island's phosphate mines. The aviators would soar over the Gilbert Islands and cross the Equator before they arrived at Howland. They would fly all day and through the night and expect to land after sunrise on July 2—the same date they'd left Lae because they'd cross the international date line.

If Noonan stuck to the navigational procedures he'd established at Pan Am, he would shoot the sun or stars every 60 minutes. Every 120 minutes, he would ask Earhart to drop the plane near the water so he could take a drift sight, measuring the wind's effect on the plane's speed and direction.

Earhart would operate the radio on a set schedule: Each hour, on the hour, she'd listen for messages from the *Itasca,* the U.S. Coast Guard cutter awaiting them at Howland; at 10 minutes after the hour, she'd listen for the *Ontario,* positioned at the halfway mark; at 15 after, she'd transmit to the *Itasca* and at 18 back to Lae; at 20 after, she listened for Lae and at 30 for the *Itasca;* and at 45 after, she'd message the *Itasca,* and then the grueling routine would start all over again.

During the day, she would transmit at 6210 kilocycles; at night, she'd switch to 3105 kilocycles. To provide a signal on which her direction finder would take bearings, the *Itasca* would transmit the Morse code letter *A* at 7500 kilocycles on the half hour. Neither Earhart nor Noonan were adept at Morse code; to communicate, they relied on voice transmissions. Those transmissions—the ones that were logged—are the only record of their last flight.

Everything went smoothly at first. Earhart and Harry Balfour, the radio operator at Lae, were in regular communication at the assigned times. But he didn't log any of her messages until five hours into the flight: "At 10,000 ft. but reducing altitude because of banks of cumulus cloud." Earhart was avoiding a storm.

Two hours later, Balfour heard, "At 7,000 ft. and making 150 mph." Twenty minutes later, she provided her only recorded position report: "Latitude: 4 degrees 33.5′ South. Longitude: 159 degrees 07′ East." They were on course about 20 miles southwest of the Nukumanu Islands. But the headwinds were stronger than predicted, 25 miles an hour rather than the forecast 12 to 15. The plane was going slower—and expending more fuel.

Eight hours into the flight, Earhart sent her final message to Balfour, telling him she was switching to her nighttime frequency. "We asked her to remain on her present frequency," he said later, "but she told me she wished to contact the American Coast Guard cutter *Itasca.* So there was nothing to do about it but pass the terminal forecast to her and the upper air report from Ocean Island."

Before she'd left Lae, Earhart had cabled the *Ontario* to request that the ship broadcast the letter *N* in Morse code for five minutes after every hour; even with her limited understanding of Morse, she'd be able to interpret that. The captain did as instructed, but never received a reply. Nor did he or his crew hear a plane overhead at the expected time.

However, a few Nauru residents picked up Earhart's signal on their radios. Some heard her say "ship in sight ahead." Others reported it as "lights in sight ahead." None of them caught the sound of the plane.

Six hours after Earhart switched to the nighttime frequency, the men waiting for her near Howland finally heard her voice. Unlike Lae, this wouldn't be a comfortable stop. Barely anyone lived on the scrub-covered atoll—only a few young Hawaiian men recruited by the U.S. government to stake a claim to this remote patch of land in the middle of the ocean.

The settlers had placed red flags along the three runways constructed especially for the round-the-world flight and used explosives to clear them of the many birds—boobies, frigates, and terns—usually swarming them. A makeshift house was swept clean for Earhart and a bed made up with fresh sheets. They'd rigged an outdoor shower for her and hung pink curtains on the windows. The *Itasca* crew set up a high-frequency direction finder in a tent near the intersection of the runways, with a radio operator ready to home in on the Electra's signal.

All was ready.

Offshore, the men on the *Itasca* began their watch early. Although the Electra wasn't expected for many more hours, in the quiet time after midnight the ship's narrow radio room became crowded with people: three radio operators; the ship's captain, Commander Warner K. Thompson, and three of his officers; Richard Black, the Department of Interior official who oversaw the colonization project; and two reporters.

Earhart and Noonan had been in the air for 14 hours and 15 minutes, together on the same aircraft but isolated from each other. Earhart sat in the cockpit, just four and half feet square with no room to stretch her legs, while Noonan stayed in the navigation area behind the fuel tanks, battling to make mathematical calculations amid the noise and fumes. They communicated by passing notes on a bamboo pole, though Noonan could scramble over the fuel tanks to sit with Earhart in the copilot's seat. Perhaps he did so toward the end.

At 2:45 a.m. local time, Leo Bellarts, the *Itasca*'s chief radioman, recorded on the radio log that he "heard Earhart plane but unreadable thru static."

Poor reception was to be expected at this stage. She was still very far away. There was no cause for concern yet.

An hour later, she was much clearer. "*Itasca* from Earhart. Overcast ... will listen on hour and half hour on 3105," according to Commander Thompson's version of the log, which often conflicts with the originals.

Bellarts responded on schedule 15 minutes later with the weather report, adding, according to Thompson's log, "What is your position? When do you expect arrive Howland? We are receiving your signals please acknowledge this message on your next schedule."

She didn't reply at her next transmission time, but more than an hour later Bellarts heard her say "partly cloudy." He didn't hear anything else for the next hour and 19 minutes.

At 6:14 a.m., her voice came through—"wants bearing on 3105 kcs, on hour, will whistle in mic"—and abruptly broke off. A minute later, the men in the room heard "about two hundred miles out. Approximately. Whistling now." The direction finder on the *Itasca* couldn't take a bearing on a frequency that high, and the battery of the one on Howland was beginning to run low. Sometime after dawn, Commander Thompson ordered the crew to make heavy black smoke that should have been visible for miles in the morning's clear skies.

Thirty minutes later, Earhart tried again: "Please take bearing on us and report in half hour. I will make noise in microphone. About one hundred miles out." This time her voice was clearer.

Nearly an hour later, Earhart's voice filled the room. She must have been close, but her message was alarming: "We must be on you but cannot see you ... gas is running low. Been unable reach you by radio. We are flying at altitude 1,000 feet."

Everyone in the cramped room realized Earhart had not acknowledged any of the *Itasca*'s messages. If she couldn't hear them, there was little they could do to help her.

At 7:58 a.m., they heard her again: "We are circling but cannot hear you. Go ahead on 7500 either now or on the schedule time on half hour." Her voice came through with a signal strength of five, the highest. Bellarts ran out on deck. "We thought she was going to be flying right down into our rigging," he said. "Oh, man, she come in like a ton of bricks."

The *Itasca* transmitted Morse code *A,* and for the first time, she responded: "We received your signals, but unable to get a minimum. Please take a bearing on us and answer 3105 with voice." The *Itasca* could not get a bearing, nor could the high-frequency direction finder on Howland. They would not be able to guide her in.

William Galten, who had taken over the radio from Bellarts, responded: "Your signals received okay. We are unable to hear you to take a bearing."

No answer.

He tried on 7500 kilocycles.

No answer.

Galten tried every frequency he thought her radio could receive.

At 8:44 a.m., the men in the room heard Amelia Earhart's voice, her words rushing and tumbling over each other: "We are on the line of position 157-337. Will repeat this message, we will repeat this message on 6210 kilocycles. Wait ... We are running north and south." Earhart was flying the Electra along a line angling 157 degrees southeast and 337 degrees northwest, hoping it would cross over Howland. It was the last message from her that they received.

For another hour, Galten and Thomas O'Hare, who operated the other radio position, tried to reach the Electra until finally, at 10:15 in the morning, more than 21 hours after Amelia Earhart and Fred Noonan had taken off from Lae, Commander Thompson told them to notify Coast Guard division headquarters in San Francisco that the fliers hadn't arrived.

IT HAD BEEN A LONG, FRAUGHT NIGHT, and Commander Thompson and his crew didn't have much to go on. They had the line of position Earhart had given; they assumed it went through Howland, but they couldn't be sure. She hadn't given a point of reference. If Howland was it, why couldn't Noonan find the island?

They also had clear skies—"unlimited ceiling," according to Thompson's message to division headquarters—except to the northwest, where a bank of cumulus clouds dimmed the horizon. Only there would Noonan have been prevented from taking the sightings telling him where they were. That left a lot of ocean to search, without any other ships nearby to help.

Thompson thought the Electra might be able to stay aloft until noon at the latest. The *Itasca* would wait to launch the search, he told his superiors in San Francisco. But the urgency to find her thrummed through the ship. At 10:15 a.m.—90 minutes after the receipt of Earhart's last message—the ship steamed northwest from Howland with every available sailor on deck to scan the waves.

Officials in the United States, conscious of public eyes on them, scrambled to organize a search. But their resources were thin: The Pacific Fleet was based in Long Beach, California; it wouldn't move to Hawaii until 1940. Only the U.S.S. *Swan,* a former minesweeper, was relatively close, camped out between Howland and Hawaii to monitor the Electra's next leg. It was ordered south to join the *Itasca*.

So was the U.S.S. *Colorado,* which had arrived in Hawaii with a boatload of Reserve Officers' Training Corps (ROTC) students and university officials on a summer goodwill tour. The battleship was told to depart for the search area as soon as it had collected its passengers from a gala and reassembled its three floatplanes from the floor of a maintenance hangar. It would take five days for it to make the voyage.

In Santa Barbara, California, the U.S.S. *Lexington* hoisted its recall flag ordering sailors to return from shore leave. The aircraft carrier, the fastest in the fleet, was also to sail for Howland, but first it had to refuel in San Diego and Honolulu. It wouldn't reach Howland until July 13.

What Thompson wanted for the search was a plane, though he came to regret the request. At 7 p.m., a single PBY Catalina took off from Hawaii with eight people on board to make the long flight to Howland—a journey nearly as grueling as the Electra's had been from Lae. But the Catalina wouldn't be landing on Howland; it was a seaplane and needed a ship nearby when it alighted on the water. The *Itasca* was recalled to Howland by daybreak the next day to meet it.

The crew on the *Itasca* didn't spot any signs of Earhart, Noonan, or the Electra during their aborted search. But radio operators across the Pacific were getting hints that someone might be out there transmitting on the Electra's two frequencies. In the evening, one of the *Itasca*'s radio operators heard a voice on 3105, so faint he couldn't understand what it said. Pan Am's Hawaii station caught a carrier signal—a tone—on the same frequency, but no voice. Later they heard voice signals, and so did an operator on Nauru to the west—strong enough to tantalize them, but too weak to indicate who it was or where they were.

The next morning, July 3, the *Itasca* received word that bad weather had forced the Catalina to return to Hawaii. The trip back to Howland had been a waste of time. Thompson immediately ordered the *Itasca* north, but he was soon diverted again. Amateur radio operators in Los Angeles reported hearing Earhart's voice on both 3105 and 6210 kilocycles, giving a position of "179 with one point six in doubt ... southwest Howland Island." The *Itasca* sailed west.

That evening, commercial stations on Hawaii with powerful transmitters broadcast messages to Earhart on 3105 kilocycles. All they got in response was a weak carrier signal—but it was heard by multiple stations, including the one on the *Itasca,* the crew remaining on Howland, and the Coast Guard, Navy, and Pan Am stations on Hawaii.

The next day was July 4, and the *Itasca* was searching west of Howland, though the commander was "reasonably certain party is not afloat in area indicated." Again, the Hawaiian radio station KGMB broadcast to Earhart:

"If you hear this broadcast, turn [your] carrier on for one minute so we can tune you in, then turn [the] carrier on and off four times." Stations across the Pacific thought they heard a response: a carrier broken in Hawaii, a man's voice on the same frequency at Midway, dashes elsewhere. One of the colonists on Howland thought he heard Earhart herself.

Early the next morning, the *Itasca* was diverted yet again. The Navy station on Hawaii had heard a message with the Electra's call signs: "281 north Howland call KHAQQ beyond north don't hold with us much longer above water shut off." It didn't make sense, but Thompson found meaning in it: The Electra was down on the water, he surmised, 281 miles north of Howland. How Earhart or Noonan would know such an exact distance to a place they hadn't been able to find was left unexplained. The *Itasca* steamed north.

Thompson assumed the Electra could float. He also assumed its radio could operate in the water—an assumption seemingly confirmed by the tantalizing radio messages. But on July 5, the Coast Guard received definitive word from Lockheed, which it passed on to the *Itasca*: "Plane radio could not function now if in water, and only if plane was on land and able to operate right motor for power."

Thompson's next assumption was that Earhart must have an emergency transmitter. That, too, proved false. "Plane carried no emergency radio equipment, except one spare battery in cabin," he was told.

Still, he kept searching in the area indicated by the mysterious message—and for a brief moment, he felt justified. At nine, a flare burst on the horizon.

"Earhart from *Itasca,*" Bellarts messaged eagerly, "Did you send up a flare? Send up another for identification."

Another flare went up, and the *Itasca* changed course toward what the crew with surging hope was sure were the surviving fliers. A Navy radio operator overheard Bellarts's transmission and notified other stations. Soon, word had flashed like lightning through newsrooms around the country.

Which is what it turned out to be—lightning, or possibly meteors. "Report in error," read the desolate message the *Itasca* sent out a short time later. But the newspapers had already gone to press with headlines about Amelia Earhart's imminent rescue. Not only was the Coast Guard embarrassed by the false report, but the *Itasca* was bombarded by media requests, offering money to Thompson and his crew for personal accounts and photographs of her safe return.

Amid the disheartening media radio traffic, Thompson received a message from the San Francisco division advising that he should be searching in the area almost exactly opposite from where his ship currently was: "All radio bearings thus far obtained on Earhart plane approximately intersect in Phoenix Island region southeast of Howland Island."

For Thompson, the new information was irrelevant. The Navy was taking over the search. The *Colorado* had arrived; its planes would survey the Phoenix Islands.

On July 9, a week after the Electra's disappearance, three floatplanes launched from the *Colorado*'s deck and soared toward McKean, the northernmost of the Phoenix Islands. The island was thick with birds, which took flight at the engine noise, forcing the planes to seek higher altitude quickly. On they flew to Gardner, as Nikumaroro was known then, where "signs of recent habitation were clearly visible," Senior Aviator Lt. John Lambrecht reported later. But, he continued, "repeated circling and zooming failed to elicit any answering wave from possible inhabitants, and it was finally taken for granted that none were there."

In the afternoon, the planes flew on to Hull, which was inhabited by colonists tending to coconut groves. Lambrecht landed in the lagoon to question the overseer. But the man knew nothing of Earhart or her flight and was flabbergasted at the Navy pilot's arrival. The island's one radio hadn't worked for weeks.

The next day, the three planes catapulted into the sky to search the remaining islands. "On any of these islands, it is not hard to believe that a forced landing could have been accomplished with no more damage than a good barrier crash or a good wetting," Lambrecht commented. They found no signs of the missing fliers or their plane.

Now the searchers began grasping at straws. Perhaps currents had taken the drifting plane west to the Gilberts, a British colony. Or maybe Earhart and Noonan were in an inflatable raft? No one knew if they'd had one on board. Some among the *Colorado* crew and its ROTC passengers speculated that they'd been picked up by a Japanese boat and taken to the Marshalls, which the Japanese controlled. The *Itasca* and *Swan* were told to sail west to search the Gilberts. Through diplomatic channels, the Japanese were asked to keep an eye out in the Marshalls.

On July 13, the *Lexington* and three destroyers arrived. Since the *Colorado* reported scouring the Phoenix Islands thoroughly—though they'd only landed at Hull—the *Lexington* aimed its 60 planes west of the northern end of the line of position. The planes swept back and forth across the ocean for five days, while the four ships hunted below. Together, they covered 262,281 square miles. "No sign nor any evidence of the Earhart plane was discovered," the captain reported.

On July 18, 16 days after Earhart and Noonan disappeared, the official search was abandoned. The unofficial one was just beginning.

CHAPTER TWO

1897–1908: "IT'S JUST LIKE FLYING!"

Amelia "always wanted to do anything new," her younger sister, Muriel, observed. And *new* is what the 1904 St. Louis World's Fair—with its motto "Nothing Impossible"—offered in splendid excess.

Within its 1,270 acres, the fair collected the world's latest inventions and many of its farthest-flung peoples. "So thoroughly does [the fair] represent the world's civilization," boasted David Francis, the exposition's president, "that if all man's other works were by some unspeakable catastrophe, blotted out, the records here established by the assembled nations would offer all necessary standards for the rebuilding of our entire civilization."

Officially a centennial celebration of the Louisiana Purchase (though a year late), the fair exulted in science and spectacle, launching what its boosters confidently assumed would be a century of American progress. With their massive grandeur and crowded displays, the palaces of transportation, agriculture, and electricity and machinery promised that advancement was inevitable and accelerating. (Never mind that the enormous plaster-built edifices would be torn down shortly after the fair closed.)

The fair brought the world to St. Louis. Visitors could climb the Alps—a version of the mountains was constructed on the grounds—travel by ship to Paris, explore the markets of Cairo, witness reenactments of Boer War battles fought by actual veterans of the conflict, or experience a miniature version of the Galveston Flood, which had killed more than 8,000 people four years earlier. The first Olympic Games in the United States, an exceedingly amateurish competition, were held at the fair (one marathon contestant ran in his street clothes, while another was chased off course by a wild dog). "Anthropology" exhibits put whole Indigenous communities—including 1,200 people brought over especially from the newly conquered Philippines—on uncomfortable display as they attempted to enact traditional ways of life before an audience of white gawkers.

Notable figures from the era graced the fairgrounds. President Theodore Roosevelt opened the exposition via telegraph from the White House in April and came to see it for himself in November, once he'd safely won election to a second term. John Philip Sousa performed his exuberant marches with his band. Thomas Edison oversaw the elaborate electrical exhibits, including the extensive fountains illuminated with underwater lights that inspired ragtime composer Scott Joplin to write "The Cascades," one of his most famous tunes.

Over the course of its seven-month run, the fair drew some 20 million visitors eager to explore the wonders of the world. Among them were a young family from Kansas City: Edwin and Amy Earhart, and their daughters, four-year-old Muriel and seven-year-old Amelia. They stayed for a week.

The whirl of invention and exploration left an impression on the girl who in a few short decades would become a symbol of American progress and derring-do. But what Amelia and her little sister, Muriel, talked about most afterward were the rides. Muriel remembered Amelia bravely mounting an elephant and being allowed to ride the observation wheel while she and her mother were relegated to watching from the ground below. That monumental conveyance—designed by George Ferris himself—lifted 36 freight car–size compartments, each holding 60 passengers, to heights few had experienced at the time. "It was scary," one fair visitor reported, "but when you were on the very top it was like you could see the whole world." Amelia wouldn't regain such heights until she flew for the first time as a young woman.

What stuck with Amelia more than the sky-skimming Ferris wheel was the attraction she wasn't allowed to board: the roller coaster. L. A. Thompson's Scenic Railway thrilled its passengers. "For three miles," one correspondent reported breathlessly, "one is borne at varying speed, up and down, back and forth, over bridges, through tunnels, into grottoes and enjoys a thousand delights." At the end, the track made three dramatic dips, which left riders giddy with excitement.

Amelia was desperate to ride it, but her mother refused. The roller coaster, she said, was too dangerous for little girls. Perhaps Amy had read the notice in her hometown newspaper reporting that six people had been injured one night on the scenic railway and "four almost had their ears torn off."

Her daughter was undaunted. When the Earharts returned home, Amelia recruited a crew—Muriel, whom she called Pidge, their friend Ralphie Martin, who had his own tool kit, and their Uncle Carl Otis, Amy's youngest brother, whom the girls called "Nicey"—to help her build a roller coaster of her own. They purloined several two-by-fours from the cellar and nailed them to the roof of the toolshed in the backyard. A makeshift trestle pitched the boards at an angle. After greasing the track with lard, Amelia was ready for the first ride, in an empty wooden crate serving as a car.

Launching from the roof, she accelerated much faster than any of them had expected, crashing into the trestle and tumbling off the track. Her dress was torn and her lip bruised, but Amelia was elated. "Oh Pidge," she said. "It's just like flying!"

AMELIA MARY EARHART WAS BORN July 24, 1897, in Atchison, Kansas. Her mother had been born there, too, in the same gracious white house on a bluff overlooking the Missouri River.

Amelia's grandfather, Alfred Otis, built the house in 1862 for his new wife, Amelia Harres, when she arrived from Philadelphia. Atchison was "really wild" then, founded shortly after the U.S. government declared Kansas a territory and began the removal of Native American tribes—Osage, Kiowa, Kansa, and many others who had already been forced out of their eastern lands. "Great piles of buffalo bones lined the newly built railroad tracks when she came and Indians in blankets were always to be seen in the town," Amelia later wrote, with a hint of envy.

Proslavery campaigners had established Atchison as an outpost in "Bleeding Kansas," where the fight over enslavement's spread had become brutal. An abolitionist and lawyer, Alfred settled in Atchison at the encouragement of the New England Emigrant Aid Company, which assured him and other like-minded pioneers that, by gaining a foothold in Kansas, they could do good and prosper at the same time. Atchison was ideally suited for the latter, situated as it was on a western bend of the wide Missouri: a convenient spot for wagon trains to cross on their way farther west.

By the time Amelia's mother, Amy, was born in 1869, Alfred had established himself as one of Atchison's leading citizens—a partner in one of the region's top law firms as well as a founder of the Atchison Savings Bank, the Atchison Gas Company, and the Atchison and Nebraska Railroad. Eventually he became a judge. Amy grew up with servants, attended private school, and rode her horse sidesaddle, like a proper young lady. In 1890, when she was 21, she had a "presentation" ball, with a wooden dance floor on the back lawn, musicians playing waltzes from the porch, and Japanese lanterns flickering over the dancing couples. It was a dreamy night Amy spoke of often, for that's when she met her future husband, Edwin Earhart.

Edwin's family background was very different from Amy's. His father, David, arrived in Kansas two years after Alfred—not in pursuit of wealth, but of souls. A Lutheran minister, David traveled the state attempting to establish churches, with limited success. David and his wife, Mary, had 12 children—Edwin was the youngest. The family often lived in dire poverty, but Edwin, bright and charming, did well in class. At 18, he became the youngest graduate from Thiel College, a Lutheran school in Pennsylvania. After a year spent teaching, he enrolled in the law school at Kansas State University in Lawrence, which is where he met Amy's brother Mark, whom he tutored. Or, as Mark put it when he introduced Edwin to his sister, "This is Edwin Earhart, the law student who has pulled me through this year's examinations!"

Although Edwin was studying law as Alfred had, Amy's father did not approve of him as a match for his daughter; he didn't seem substantial enough. But eventually Alfred relented, with one stipulation: The couple wouldn't marry until Edwin made at least $50 a month. It took him five years to reach this goal. When he and Amy finally wed, her parents presented them with a fully furnished home in Kansas City, where Edwin had established his law practice. Their marriage would soon be tested by financial—and other—woes.

Indeed, Alfred was appalled that Edwin had taken his family to the World's Fair. Just the year before, Edwin, a hobbyist inventor, used money he and Amy had set aside for taxes to fund a trip to Washington, D.C., to obtain a patent on a railway signal device. He arrived in the nation's capital only to learn that someone else had already claimed a patent for a similar apparatus. When a tax collector showed up at the house after his return, he was forced to confess to Amy where the money for the trip had come from. To pay their delinquent taxes, he sold valuable lawbooks that had been a gift from his father-in-law. Alfred was not pleased.

When Edwin earned a much needed $100 legal fee and used the money to pay for the family vacation to St. Louis, Alfred saw it as yet another example of his profligacy. But Muriel and Amelia, whom Edwin adored, remembered the trip for the rest of their lives.

AS A CHILD, AMELIA SOUGHT THRILLS and adventure wherever she could find them. "Unfortunately," she said, "I lived at a time when girls were still girls." Despite the custom of dressing girls in long, full skirts and ruffled pinafores, Amelia's mother, who encouraged vigorous activity, outfitted her daughters in gym suits—navy blue bloomers gathered at the knees. "We wore them Saturdays to play in," said Amelia. "Though we felt terribly 'free and athletic,' we also felt somewhat as outcasts among the little girls who fluttered about us in their skirts." A photo from 1906 shows her wearing the bloomers as she stands sturdily on stilts she'd built herself.

Amelia's parents were liberal in their expectations for their daughters. Amy had enjoyed adventures of her own when she was young, even climbing Pikes Peak in the Rocky Mountains when few men had made the ascent. Edwin was, for his part, "in favor of our being as much like boys as we wanted," according to Muriel. When Amelia wrote him a letter asking for a football, she and Muriel each received one.

One Christmas, he gave them two boys' sleds—a great joy, since they could ride face-first and belly-down, rather than sitting upright as one must on the slower girls' sleds. "Coasting while lying flat on the sled was considered rough for girls," said Amelia. But she claimed it once saved her life. She was racing down one of Atchison's steep hills when a junkman's cart crossed the road in front of her. It was too icy to steer, and the junkman didn't hear her cries of warning. Somehow, she slipped between the front and back legs of his horse. If she'd been sitting up, she claimed, "either my head or the horse's ribs would have suffered in contact."

Edwin also presented them with a real gun. Amelia wrote that he gave the .22-caliber Hamilton rifle to Muriel, but Muriel later said it was for Amelia. Either way, the girls used it to shoot at rats in their grandparents' barn. "We had read an article in a magazine which told about the disease spread in the Canal Zone by rats and mosquitoes," explained Muriel. "The old barn was infested with rats, and we reasoned that if rats in Panama spread bubonic plague, the rats in Kansas might do the same thing." After their rat purge, one of the servants claimed "the grain bins and side walls of the harness-room looked like a sieve."

Some of their adventures were more fantastical. Amelia led her sister and their cousins Lucy and Kathryn Challiss—otherwise known as Toot and Katch—in a game called Bogie, which deployed the old carriage in her grandparents' barn. The four girls would scramble aboard the long-retired conveyance armed with wooden pistols and set off on "hair-rising adventures without ever leaving the barn." Many times, they tried to reach the made-up town of Pearyville—Muriel remembered it as Cherryville—but inevitably were thwarted by ghosts, "hairy men," giant spiders, and other horrors. "I know I can never be so terrified by anything met with in the real world as by the shadowy play creatures which lurked in the dark corners of the hay mow to attack us, or crept up the creaking steps from the lower stalls," reported Amelia as an adult.

The girls steered their carriage and imaginary horses toward faraway places, too—places Amelia would eventually visit. "Blithely we rolled on our tongues such names as Senegal, Timbuctu, Ngami, El Fasher, and Khartoum," she recalled many years later while stopping in Dakar on her world flight. "We weighed the advantages of the River Niger and the Nile, the comparative ferociousness of the Tauregs [*sic*] and Swahili. No Livingstone, Stanley or Rhodes explored with more enthusiasm than we."

Despite her escapades, both imagined and real, Amelia was raised rather formally. She spent most of her time with her grandparents in their well-appointed Atchison mansion. "I was named for my grandmother and was lent to her for company during the winter months," she explained. The tradition began when Amelia was only three, and her grandmother was lonely and brokenhearted. Amelia Otis had recently lost both her mother and her oldest son, and her younger daughter had moved away.

Her husband, Alfred, a cold and dignified man, provided little comfort. She needed the companionship of her spirited and affectionate granddaughter.

It worked out well for Amelia too. Her cousins Toot and Katch lived next door, and she had other good friends down the street—although her grandmother forbade her from vaulting over the fence, her preferred route to visit them. To be ladylike, Amelia was told, she must walk the long way around and go through the gate.

From first grade on, she attended the College Preparatory School, a private school for the local elite, where she excelled. Her family, after all, was among the most prominent in town and was related to or friendly with other Atchison notables. Everywhere she went, she was known as the judge's granddaughter. Her childhood was happy and secure. But that was about to change.

CHAPTER THREE

CAPTURED: JOSEPHINE'S STORY

On July 5, 1937, three days after Amelia Earhart and Fred Noonan failed to arrive at Howland Island, the Japanese Embassy in Washington, D.C., received a telegram from Tokyo. Japan wished to offer the United States its assistance in the search for the missing fliers.

Tensions between the two countries had been growing. They'd both made forays into the Pacific Islands. The United States held Guam, Hawaii, Samoa, and the Philippines, while Japan controlled Palau, and the Northern Mariana Islands, Caroline Islands, and Marshall Islands—the Micronesian archipelagoes to the north of the Electra's flight path. Both countries suspected the other one of wanting more. The United States was further unsettled by Japan's 1931 occupation of Manchuria in northeastern China—and by the fact that it didn't know what was going on in the country's island territories.

In 1914, at the outset of World War I, Japan, on the side of the Allies, had seized many of Germany's northern colonies in Micronesia. After the Allies won the war, the League of Nations confirmed Japan's conquest by granting a "Class C mandate." Japan had license to rule this large Pacific swath—

some 1,400 islands—pretty much as it pleased, as long as it didn't fortify the islands militarily.

Japan kept a tight grip on what was called the South Seas Mandate. Few foreigners were allowed to visit, and were closely watched when they did. Other countries suspected Japan was indeed fortifying the islands, but visitors—including writer Willard Price, who traveled there on assignment for *National Geographic* in 1935—reported scant evidence of militarization beyond shoring up civilian infrastructure such as harbors and airfields easily adapted for use in war.

U.S. Secretary of State Cordell Hull expressed "sincere gratitude" for the offer of help. Japanese radio operators would listen for the Electra's signals, and two naval ships—the *Kamoi* and the *Koshu*—were also available for dispatch. The Japanese government broadcast a radio message to all Japanese vessels in the South Seas to keep an eye out for Amelia Earhart and her plane.

These efforts were apparently fruitless, and suspicion and paranoia between the two countries resurged, as interested parties in the region noted apprehensively. On August 25, 1937, a correspondent for the *Pacific Islands Monthly,* a publication out of Sydney, Australia, speculated that Japan had used the Earhart search to spy on American and British holdings in the Pacific. An October 16, 1937, report from another Australian publication took the opposite tack: that the United States had used Earhart's disappearance as an excuse for espionage, secretly flying over Japan's mandated islands. (And thank goodness, too, was the undertone: There could be no doubt Japan had ambitions of empire; on July 7, 1937—five days after Earhart and Noonan's disappearance—its occupation of Manchuria had turned into a war with China.)

In this tense climate, it's easy to see why many people didn't accept that Amelia Earhart's flight was simply an attempt at a world record with tragic results; someone as famous as she was, they believed, just doesn't, *couldn't*, disappear.

Japan's surprise attack on Pearl Harbor on December 7, 1941, and the U.S. entry into the Second World War fueled those suspicions. The Japanese had proved themselves villains capable of anything, the thinking went: perhaps even the capture and execution of a beloved aviator. A staff writer for the *Detroit Free Press* pronounced in 1943 that Earhart had probably been "liquidated" by the Japanese for somehow discovering evidence that their "sinister islands" were being converted into naval bases and "indestructible airplane carriers." He didn't offer any proof: just the opinion of an engineer who'd worked for the Navy in the Pacific and suffered a head wound at Pearl Harbor.

But what really seeped into the public consciousness was a film released later that year. *Flight for Freedom* starred Rosalind Russell as a daring female pilot who agrees to fake a crash in the Pacific during a round-the-world flight. The U.S. Navy would use her disappearance as an excuse to fly over the Japanese-mandated islands seeking signs of a military buildup, much as the Australian newspaper had imagined. Earhart's husband, George Putnam, reportedly had given RKO Pictures permission to produce the movie but ended up being so disturbed by it—especially the film's suggestion that the record-breaking aviatrix was in love with her navigator, played by Fred MacMurray—that he sued. But it was too late. The idea that the Japanese had something to do with Earhart's disappearance had been let loose.

In 1944, as U.S. troops were advancing from island to island across the Pacific, the Associated Press ran a story touting evidence Earhart had been taken to Japan. But it was based on a fourthhand account: A Navy officer reported that a "mission trained native" from the Marshall Islands told him that a Japanese trader told *him* that he'd *heard* that Earhart had come down between the Jaluit and Ailinglaplap Atolls, was rescued by a fishing boat, and taken to Japan. It was hearsay, but newspapers ran with it.

Also in 1944, marines on Saipan, which the Japanese had colonized, claimed they'd found a photo album filled with pictures of Earhart. They said they handed it over to authorities; no one else ever saw it. Toward the end of World War II, rumors spread that Earhart was Tokyo Rose, the name U.S. soldiers gave to the American-accented woman who spread Japanese propaganda over the Pacific airwaves; Putnam listened, but stated unequivocally that the voice was not his wife's. (After the war, investigators discovered that multiple women had voiced the broadcasts.)

None of the rumors implying that Earhart and Noonan had been captured by the Japanese were substantiated. But a lack of evidence didn't deter the speculation.

Then, years later, an eyewitness came forward.

IN 1937, THE YEAR EARHART DISAPPEARED, Josephine Blanco was 11 and, by her own admission, "a little bit of a rascal." She rode her bicycle all over the island of Saipan—"a lovely isle of billowing cane fields edged with coconut palms, breadfruit, banana, flame trees, and tree ferns," as Price, the *National Geographic* writer, described it. She often ended up in places few adults were allowed and would "sometimes get a spanking for that," according to her brother. "I was very curious," she remembered. "Very curious."

Saipan, some 1,500 miles due north of Lae, New Guinea, where Earhart and Noonan had taken off, is the largest of the Northern Mariana Islands. In Garapan, its principal town, a complicated colonial history revealed itself in the buildings: the thatched homes of the Chamorro and Carolinian people, the Spanish haciendas where well-off islanders lived, the stone houses left by the Germans, and the Japanese shops built of wood serving the current colonists, who by 1937 outnumbered the locals.

The civilian administration governing the territories when Josephine was young introduced the sugarcane industry to Saipan and brought thousands of workers to settle on the island. By the mid-1930s, more than 20,000 Japanese lived there, compared to some 3,000 Chamorro and Carolinians.

The local islanders were relegated to the bottom of the racial hierarchy. Schools were segregated, with Japanese children attending eight years and local children just two or three (five, if they showed promise, which Josephine did). Their education focused primarily on learning Japanese; most also attended Catholic school. Few local adults were allowed to attain positions of responsibility or status with the government or Japanese businesses.

Josephine's father, Juan Blanco, was the exception. He'd established himself as a cultural liaison between the Japanese government and the Chamorro population. When dignitaries visited, he provided their introduction to local cuisine by hosting dinners at the family's large home in Garapan. The family also owned a ranch on the island's southern end. Josephine remembers her childhood as "very, very happy." The youngest of seven daughters (she also had three brothers), she enjoyed more freedom to roam than most girls did.

But in the summer of 1937, after she'd finished her last year of Japanese school, Josephine was stuck at her sister Augusta's house. Augusta had given birth to a son, and Josephine had been sent by their mother to help. Augusta's husband worked at the seaplane base at Tanapag Harbor north of Garapan on the western side of the island. One day he forgot his lunch; Josephine, intrepid on her bicycle, was sent to bring it to him.

When she arrived on the base—a restricted area of docks, ramps, fuel tanks, and repair sheds, where few local people were employed—she saw a crowd gathered around two white men, who seemed to be trying to make themselves understood. "I guess they were talking in English," she remembers. "They kept moving their fingers and faces, just like at a carnival."

But it wasn't until she overheard some Japanese guards speaking nearby that she realized one of the white people wasn't a man, but a woman. The woman's hair was short and blonde, and she was wearing pants. "I'd never seen a woman in that kind of clothes," she recalls.

She hid behind a tree to watch. "I didn't want to get away," she said. "I just wanted to look and look."

But she had to leave; she wasn't really allowed to be there. Later, she reported what she'd seen to her mother, who warned her not to mention it to anyone else. "The Japanese were secretive," Josephine says, and quick to punish. "My mother didn't like us to say anything" that might get them into trouble.

This is the story Josephine told me when I spoke to her in 2021, when she was 95 years old. There have been other versions over the years—some recounted by her, some embellished by others. She'd heeded her mother's advice, she said, and hadn't told anyone what she saw until after the war had ended and the Japanese were defeated. And why should she say anything? She'd had no idea who those two white people were. But in 1946, she met someone who thought he did.

SAIPAN HAD BEEN THE SITE OF one of the most pivotal battles in the Pacific during World War II. For three weeks in 1944, American and Japanese troops grappled for every inch of the 14-mile-long island. By the time the battle was over, some 50,000 people had died—including as many as 22,000 civilians, among them hundreds who jumped to their deaths from Saipan's cliffs rather than be captured. But the war's end was in sight: Control of Saipan and the nearby island of Tinian put the U.S.'s long-range B-29 bombers within reach of Japan's home islands.

Casimir Sheft wasn't on Saipan for the battle. An unprepossessing man from New Jersey, he'd spent most of the war in dental school at the University of Maryland and arrived on Saipan in 1946. The U.S. Navy still occupied the island and would for years to come.

Sheft and a few other dentists worked at the fleet dental clinic near Tanapag Harbor. The main town was in ruins, the sugarcane industry destroyed, and the population greatly reduced—from mass casualties and the expulsion of Japanese colonists. The Chamorro and Carolinians who remained on Saipan were struggling to rebuild their lives.

The Navy employed local people when it could, including a few young Chamorro women Sheft and his colleagues had hired as assistants. "We had to train them from scratch," Sheft told an interviewer in the 1970s. "And it was difficult because there was a little bit of a language problem."

Josephine Blanco, then around 20, was one of Sheft's dental assistants. She and her entire family had miraculously survived the war, though the Japanese military had confiscated their home and the Americans used their ranchland for an internment camp. "She was a very bright, attractive girl—and willing to learn," remembered Sheft. "She picked up the work very, very quickly. You had no problem at all teaching her."

A photo from those days shows Sheft with Blanco and two other young women. He's blond, pale, with a receding hairline, wearing official-seeming khakis, though his sleeves are rolled up. He stands with a bit of a swagger, but perhaps he just doesn't know what to do with his arms. The women look fresh and pretty in modest summer dresses. While one woman retreats into the shadowy background and the other gives the photographer a side-long glance, Blanco faces the camera directly, a smile revealing the dimple on her cheek.

One day, Sheft and another dentist were chatting in the office. The subject of Amelia Earhart came up and Sheft recalled that he'd read a newspaper article during the war about something of hers being discovered on Saipan after the battle. "Josephine interrupted us with excitement in her voice," he recounted in a letter. To his astonishment, she said she remembered seeing "an American girl flyer dressed in men's khaki clothes, and with a short boyish haircut 'about nine or ten years ago.'" Blanco's description matched Earhart perfectly, Sheft thought. Who else could it be but her?

And here's where the embellishment of Blanco's story may have begun. Sheft was the first American known to have heard Blanco's story. He was also the first to spread it, though that didn't happen until later. And his recollection of what she had said was far more dramatic than what she told me.

In Sheft's version, the Japanese shot down a plane that was circling the island. In it were two people: a man and a woman. The man died, but the woman was brought ashore and put in a cell in the Garapan jail. Her cell had one small window through which people watched her humming while she darned her clothes; she also tried to speak to the children but they didn't understand English. One day, Japanese soldiers marched the woman into the woods across from the jail. Blanco heard shots, and no one ever saw the white woman flier again. Sheft said Blanco showed him where the plane went into the sea and the spot where the firing squad went into the woods.

Sheft claimed to be skeptical at first, "but the earnestness of this devoutly Catholic girl, and the verification of the story (which I received from several other natives) made me believe it to be true." Even so, Sheft didn't report what he'd learned to the American authorities, assuming that if he'd heard about this incident, then they had too.

But when he returned to civilian life, he found he was wrong. Every article he read or documentary he watched ended in the same way: "No one knows what ever befell AE to this day." The shocking story he'd been told wasn't common knowledge at all.

The *Omnibus* episode was the last straw.

Ten years after his time on Saipan, on Sunday, March 17, 1957, Sheft settled in at his Saddle River, New Jersey, home to watch television. *Omnibus* was on. Hosted by the plummy-voiced Alistair Cooke and sponsored by the Ford Foundation, the landmark program brought arts, science, and social issues to the American public. That afternoon, the show offered what Cooke called "a character study of a legend": The legend was Amelia Earhart. Actor Burgess Meredith narrated the tale while Meg Mundy, a former top model and future soap opera star, played Earhart. (Both acclaimed performers, Meredith and Mundy had run afoul of anti-communism crusades earlier in the decade and were slowly rebuilding their careers.)

Mundy looked the part of Earhart, all cheekbones and lips, and she spoke like her, too—clearly, deliberately, with a hint of Katharine Hepburn's privileged accent. Filmed live before an audience, with occasional flubs by the actors, the black-and-white production took an episodic approach to Earhart's life. The most provocative scene shows her interviewing a potential navigator for the round-the-world flight. The man tells her everything he thinks is wrong with her plan for circumnavigation: She should have a backup pilot, he says, a plane that can land on water, and a stronger radio. As for the tiny target she'd picked in Howland Island, "I think that's foolish," he concludes. She bats away all his criticisms.

After Sheft watched the show, he was irritated—not by the questioning of Earhart's judgment or her imperviousness to criticism or even by the supposed communist sympathies of the actress playing her. What annoyed him was how it ended—with the usual statement that no one knew what had happened to her.

But this time he did something about it: He wrote to the studio that produced the *Omnibus* program. "When Burgess Meredith came to the end and repeated the same thing, I just felt that I had to let him know about the information that I have," he explained later. "Maybe he or someone else could check up on it and investigate these facts out on Saipan in order to close the book finally on this mystery!"

Sheft's letter ended up in the hands of Sidney Carroll, who had written the Earhart episode (and, a few years later, the screenplay for Paul Newman's classic *The Hustler*). Carroll forwarded the letter to Captain Paul L. Briand, Jr., an Air Force officer who was writing a biography of Earhart—and unwittingly triggered a tidal wave of conspiracy theories about the flier's death.

CHAPTER FOUR

1908–16: "GREAT STRAIN AND ANXIETY"

While Amelia was blooming as the beloved granddaughter of one of Atchison's leading families, her father, Edwin, had barely been getting by as a lawyer in Kansas City, helping clients pursue claims against the railroads. But in 1908, he was offered a job on the other side of the tracks, so to speak, as a claims agent with the Chicago, Rock Island & Pacific Line. At last, he would have a regular salary and a shot at advancement.

Amy, Amelia's mother, was relieved—their finances would finally be stable—but the family would have to move north to Des Moines, Iowa. Amelia would have to go too. Des Moines was too far away to allow for the easy back-and-forth travel they'd enjoyed between Kansas City and Atchison.

For a while, everything was wonderful. Each year, Edwin earned more than the last, and they'd move to a larger house. By 1912, the family lived in the city's most fashionable neighborhood, a block away from Drake University. They purchased a piano and attended conservatory concerts dressed in silk. Amy brought the girls to art exhibits and joined a neighborhood magazine club that shared subscriptions to the nation's most sophisticated publications.

On Saturdays, when Edwin came home early from work, he would "play Indian" with his daughters and all the neighborhood children—an epic game fueled by his exuberant imagination. "He bore on his nose the marks of one raid," wrote Amelia in her book *The Fun of It,* "after some *chasee,* during the heat of the battle, had tried to push shut the sliding door to the hayloft just as the Chief Indian had poked his head through the opening." Afterward, Amy would offer everyone lemonade and cookies on their front porch. It was joyous fun.

But one Saturday, when the kids ran to greet him after he got off the streetcar, "he walked slowly, putting each foot down carefully as if to keep from stumbling," recalled Amelia's sister, Muriel. "There was no buoyancy in his stride nor in the sickly smile with which he greeted us."

When Amy opened the door, "her face became frozen," remembered Muriel. She ushered Edwin inside and closed the door. Edwin was drunk. There'd be no games that afternoon.

Although his drinking habit may have already been well established, this was the first his daughters saw of the shadow, as Muriel put it, that fell "on our gifted father." It would get worse. Soon they would experience "the loss of our material prosperity and the beginning of the disintegration of our family."

Amelia did not speak of this time, but in a biography of her sister, Muriel wrote about "the hardship and mental suffering that Amelia and I endured as adolescents." They learned they could only joke with their father in the morning; in the evening, he would come home late, raging about "the household expenses or Mother's family, the railroad, or virtually anything."

Edwin began to make mistakes at work. His stenographer covered up for him at first, but eventually, his boss at the main office in Chicago noticed. When he traveled to Des Moines to speak to Edwin about it, he found him in the office sharing a bottle with a colleague. His boss sent him home and persuaded Amy and Edwin to seek a cure for Edwin's alcoholism.

Edwin spent a month at a Keeley Institute, a popular chain of medical centers that claimed to treat alcoholism by injecting patients with bichloride of gold. Although there was no scientific basis for this supposed cure, Edwin returned home "bright-eyed and buoyant." Amy welcomed him with a carpenter's bench fully equipped with tools while Amelia and Muriel presented him with a fishing rod, purchased with money they'd earned by picking cherries for a neighbor. All seemed well.

It wasn't. Edwin soon resumed drinking and never regained his position as head of the claims department for the Rock Island line. No other railroad would hire him at a senior level. Eventually, he was offered a job as a minor clerk at the Great Northern Railway in St. Paul, Minnesota. In 1913, when Amelia was 16 and going into her junior year in high school, the Earharts moved again.

No one in the family was doing well. Muriel remembers tears rolling down her mother's face as their train pulled out of the Des Moines station. Amy, in turn, was worried about her daughters. In a letter to her brother Mark after the hurried move, she wrote, "My own girls, owing to the great strain and anxiety of the last year, are not so well and strong as they used to be." She went on to tell him that a few weeks earlier, Muriel had fainted and hit her head on a table, which "gave her such a headache she had to stay in bed for a couple of days."

Amy had lost both her parents the previous year—an emotional blow but also a financial one. Alfred and Amelia Otis bequeathed their four living children equal shares of their estate but set aside Amy's portion—as well as that of her brother Theodore, who had developmental disabilities—in a trust only accessible after 15 years. "Grandmother knew of Dad's drinking," said Muriel, "and was worried at the possibility of Dad squandering Mother's share." Insulted and humiliated, the Earharts were left with few resources.

Amy had hoped for help from her father's brother Charles, who was a prominent figure in St. Paul. At the very least, she thought he and his grown children might introduce them into St. Paul society. But no invitations came their way. The Otis relatives did not feel any obligation toward the impoverished family of an alcoholic. One frigid winter day, as Amelia and Muriel walked home from a shopping trip to the cheaper market three miles away, their great-uncle Charles passed them in his car with a wave. "He must think we're walking for exercise," Amelia said sourly to her sister.

Amelia, a strong-minded young woman, could barely tolerate her father anymore. A few months after the Minnesota move, she discovered a whiskey bottle in his traveling bag and went to empty it in the kitchen sink. When he saw what she was doing, "he leaped across the kitchen," said Muriel. "I believe he would have struck Amelia if Mother had not come running from the dining room and seized his arm from behind."

At Christmastime, Edwin promised to escort the two girls to the Twelfth Night dance at St. Clement's Episcopal Church, the center of their reduced social world. Two boys had "especially urged" them to attend; Amelia and Muriel planned to offer them refreshments after the dance. But Edwin arrived home hours after he'd promised—too late, and too drunk, to chaperone them. Muriel ran upstairs to cry, but Amelia calmly tore up the hand-painted holly napkins she'd set out and threw away the marshmallows for hot cocoa. Her father's failures no longer surprised her.

The family packed up in the fall when Edwin was offered a better job in a claims office in Springfield, Missouri. But when they arrived in the small town with all their belongings, Edwin discovered that the person who held the position he was to take had decided not to retire after all. Edwin was left with no job, and his family with no home.

That was it for Amy. She told Edwin that she and the girls would go to Chicago to stay with friends until he got settled, either back in St. Paul or in Kansas City, where he had family.

They stayed in Chicago until Amelia graduated from Hyde Park High School, the third she'd attended. She skipped the graduation ceremonies, feeling little connection to the school or her classmates. Indeed, the caption under her yearbook picture described her, somewhat melodramatically, as "the girl in brown who walks alone."

In her memoirs, Amelia described this time of upheaval jauntily, with no hint of the desperation driving each relocation. "The family rolled around a good deal during my father's railroad years," she wrote. "Kansas City, Des Moines, St. Paul, Chicago—forward and back. What we missed in continuous contacts over a long period, we gained by becoming adapted to new surroundings quickly." As late as 1932, she said she'd never lived more than four years in any one place.

After Amelia finished high school, it was time to move again—this time, back to Kansas City, where Edwin, with the help of his elderly sister Mary, whom he lived with, had landed on somewhat steady feet. After the family reunited, he directed his considerable intellect toward helping Amy gain control of her inheritance. Amy's parents intended to keep the money out of Edwin's spendthrift grasp but the trustee they'd named, Amy's younger brother Mark, was just as irresponsible and had made a series of poor investments. Edwin successfully broke the trust, and Amy put the money toward her daughters' education. Muriel enrolled at St. Margaret's College in Toronto after she graduated from high school in Kansas City, while Amelia decided to add some luster to her academic career by attending Ogontz, an exclusive finishing school outside of Philadelphia. She'd already graduated from high school but clearly felt her academic record required some burnishing before college. Her Atchison friend Virginia Park was attending nearby Bryn Mawr. In a year or two, Amelia hoped to be there too.

OGONTZ WAS THE KIND OF ELITE institution to which Amelia's status-conscious mother thought she rightfully belonged. When Amelia matriculated in 1916, Ogontz—founded in 1850 as a school for Philadelphia's well-bred young ladies—was located on the leafy estate of Jay Cooke, the banker who provided much of the financing for Union military efforts during the Civil War. One hundred girls filled his five-floor mansion, which included a library turned classroom, an "amusement room" with a stage, and a conservatory.

The young ladies were instructed in English literature, French, German, and Latin; chemistry, astronomy, history, and geography; and Bible studies, elocution, and "domestic engineering." Exercise was encouraged: Amelia especially relished basketball, hockey, and bracing walks in windy weather.

In 1888, the school had pioneered training young women in military drills, which the girls conducted in uniforms with mock weapons. "No other form of exercise is at once so complete in its demands on attention, concentration, and response to standards of posture, walking, consideration of others," declared Abby Sutherland, the principal when Amelia attended. Amelia loathed drill, mostly because the uniform made her "look like a broomstick wrapped round and round," she told her mother. "Nearly everyone looks awful. But I worst."

The instruction on concentration and posture was carried over into lessons in deportment. Amelia described one "drawing room evening" during which the teacher, a Miss Pughsey, had "us walk bow sit stand shake hands etc. etc."

"The funniest thing," Amelia wrote, "was the sitting. She put a little chair out in the middle of this huge room and we all aimed at it and tried to *clammer* on it gracefully. It was a scream. One of the girls landed with her legs crossed, on the extreme edge." Amelia was more successful: "I got on," she told her mother, "but not with noticeable grace as there was no comment made."

At 19, Amelia was older than most of the girls—and certainly poorer. But she insisted her comparative poverty wasn't a problem. "I can wear an old suit with a little alteration so it will be more reasonable," she told her mother. Five months later, she reassured Amy, "Dearie, I don't need any spring clothes so don't worry about sending me money. I have a few dollars still in the bank and I know you all need things more than I."

After her wealthy roommate tired of pumps purchased the week before, Amelia happily bought them from her for five dollars. "Her style of dressing was always simple and becoming," remembered Sutherland. "At that period, her purse as well as her innate taste required the fewest and simplest clothes. But she helped very much to impress the overindulged girls with the beauty and comfort of simple dressing."

Amelia had more on her mind than her appearance. "I don't have a minute for anything because I want to get all possible," Amelia wrote breathlessly to her mother. "Did I tell you that I have a reputation for brains?"

Unlike her dispiriting experience at Hyde Park, she threw herself into the prestigious school's activities; at Ogontz, she would not be known as the "girl in brown who walks alone." By her second year at the school, she'd been elected vice president of her class and chosen as one of five students on the honor board. Her classmates selected her to be the secretary and treasurer of Christian Endeavor, which she described as "rather an institution of torture heretofore, and not well liked but we are trying to put something into it that will make it stand for something." They even nominated her to write the class song. "The more one does the more one can do," she explained to her mother, who nevertheless worried that Amelia was taking on too much and wrote to the headmistress, much to her daughter's mortification.

"Dear hen," pleaded Amelia, "don't write Miss S. letters of advice and warning. They go thru the whole faculty and come to me and I just shrivel. I am not overdoing and all that is needed to bouncing health is plenty to eat and happiness. Consider me bursting, please."

As satisfied as Amelia was with her school life, something was missing. Although she was learning how to be a lady—and a leader and a rebel—Amelia abruptly quit Ogontz at the beginning of the semester in which she was to graduate.

CHAPTER FIVE

CAPTURED: "IT SOUNDED LIKE TRUTH"

Captain Paul L. Briand, Jr., had come to Earhart through Amelia's poetry, of all things. In 1957, he and an Air Force colleague published an edited collection of poetry and fiction about flying. The book's title—*The Sound of Wings*—came from Earhart's poem "Courage," which she wrote before her first transatlantic flight.

Courage is the price that Life exacts for granting peace.
The soul that knows it not, knows no release
From little things:

Knows not the livid loneliness of fear,
Nor mountain heights where bitter joy can hear
The sound of wings.

How can Life grant us boon of living, compensate
For dull gray ugliness and pregnant hate
Unless we dare

The soul's dominion? Each time we make a choice, we pay
With courage to behold resistless day,
And count it fair.

Although Earhart wrote poems all her life, this was the only one to be published. Briand found it deeply moving, especially given Earhart's tragic fate. It was the only piece by a woman included in the collection.

Briand wasn't a pilot himself. But in World War II, he'd served in the Army Air Corps pushing supplies out of gaping cargo doors to American troops fighting along the Western Front in Europe, including during the Battle of the Bulge. After the war ended, he attended the University of New Hampshire on the G.I. Bill, later becoming an English professor at the new Air Force Academy in Colorado.

Until he heard from Sidney Carroll, the *Omnibus* episode screenwriter, and then from dentist Casimir Sheft himself, Briand had intended to write a straightforward biography of Earhart. Surprisingly, one hadn't been published for adults since her husband, George Putnam, released *Soaring Wings,* a discursive and highly personal recounting of her life, in 1939. But the possibility of an eyewitness to her fate changed everything.

By coincidence, around the same time Sheft contacted Briand, Josephine Blanco had written to the dentist. Married now, she'd moved to the United States and was living in San Mateo, California, with her husband, Maximo Akiyama, whose name she'd taken, and their son, Edward. But she was having a difficult time finding a job in California: Would he write a reference letter for her? When Sheft replied with the requested recommendation, he asked her about the "white woman flyer" she'd seen.

Her response indicates she remembered it differently than he had. So much had happened since then, including massive air raids on her home island involving many American pilots and many American planes. She'd also just started learning English when she worked for him; misunderstandings and confused details were to be expected. Still, he'd been generous with the recommendation, and she owed him an account. "You know that I was young [at] that time," Akiyama wrote, "but I'll tell you what I remember."

There *had* been a "flying girl" on Saipan, she continued, but Sheft had misunderstood the story Akiyama told about her. Sometime around 1942, she didn't remember when exactly, a plane was shot down near Tanapag Harbor and the pilot was killed. When the body was recovered, the pilot appeared to be wearing lipstick; people thought "she is a lady," wrote Akiyama. And there *had* been an execution at Garapan jail, but three prisoners had been killed and it hadn't happened until right before the U.S. invasion in 1944.

Presented with both accounts, Briand preferred Sheft's more dramatic version, and that's the one Akiyama reverted to when he flew out to California to interview her. Perhaps she'd remembered more than she'd laid out in her letters—or perhaps her memories were guided by his line of questioning and her sense of where his interests, and her advantage, lay. Afterward, when he sent her a photograph of Amelia Earhart and Fred Noonan, she obligingly replied, "I swear that this is the couple exactly I saw in Saipan, but there cloth [*sic*] is not exactly like this when I saw specially the lady, she was dressing more like a man, but her hair is exactly like this when I saw her."

Akiyama expected something in return for her help. In a 1959 letter responding to a series of questions from Briand, she wrote, "In fairness to myself and family I do not believe I should put so much time into this matter unless it is worthwhile." She wanted to be paid. When he responded curtly that he was the one writing the book, she pointed out that her contribution "is the most important part of the story."

By the time Briand's biography, *Daughter of the Sky*, was published in April 1960, relations between the author and his source had soured. Akiyama had threatened to take her story elsewhere if she wasn't compensated. A month after the book came out, that's exactly what she did.

ON MAY 27, 1960, the *San Mateo Times* ran an eye-popping headline:

SAN MATEAN SAYS JAPANESE EXECUTED
AMELIA EARHART
Woman's Story: Aviatrix Died Before Saipan Firing Squad

Akiyama had gone to her local paper. The story, written by journalist Lin Day, offered dramatic details Akiyama had held back from Briand and Sheft—or perhaps Day had spun them himself. According to the article, Earhart and Noonan were whisked away from Tanapag Harbor in a "beautiful big black sedan." Akiyama never saw them again. But two weeks later, according to Day, she learned their fate.

One night, while she was playing outside, a Japanese military policeman came by, as he often did, to visit the older girls on her street. "They were very pretty and the nights were beautiful," Akiyama is quoted as saying. She overheard the girls ask the soldier about the "American lady pilot." He laughed. "They executed her," he said. "They shot her."

While Briand's biography had met with a muted reception, the dramatic and poignant *San Mateo Times* article was picked up by newsrooms across the country. But its most avid reader was just up the road in San Francisco: radio correspondent Fred Goerner.

With an academic background in speech and a flair for the dramatic, sonorous-voiced Goerner cohosted an afternoon news program for KCBS in San Francisco. He and his partner, Dave McElhatton, scanned the local newspapers for items to include and people to interview. Both amateur pilots, they were especially interested in anything having to do with aviation. Goerner had served on Guam with the Navy Seabees during World War II, so the tale's Pacific element intrigued him. All in all, Josephine Akiyama's story was perfect fodder for their show. Goerner, ambitious and aggressive, called her shortly after the story published to see if she'd come on the air that afternoon.

Akiyama didn't let him finish his pitch before she slammed down the phone. She'd had enough. "She was not very happy from the start," says her son, Ed Akiyama, who was seven at the time. The newspaper had printed her home address: Strangers were pounding on the front door, and the phone didn't stop ringing. She wasn't prepared for this level of attention. Worse, according to Ed, "she said she didn't say those things, that the reporter had embellished what she told him."

But Goerner was resourceful and persistent. He managed to get through to her lawyer, William Penaluna, who was representing her and her husband in a war reparations case and had penned some sharp letters to Briand about paying Akiyama for her testimony. Penaluna had been the one to reach out to the newspaper's publisher with the story. After some persuasion, Akiyama agreed to let Goerner visit her home, where she recounted her story.

It was a less florid version than what had run in the *San Mateo Times:* She was bringing lunch to her brother-in-law at Tanapag Harbor, when a two-motored plane flew overhead. When she arrived at the seaplane base, she saw two white people. She thought they were both men, until someone told her one was a woman. "They were both thin and looked very tired," she remembered. "The woman had short-cut hair like a man and she was dressed like a man. The man, I think I remember, had his head hurt some way." Guards took them away; later there were rumors they'd been executed.

This version didn't track with what Sheft remembered of her story from 1946 (in which she befriended the woman in jail and witnessed her being marched to her execution) or what she wrote in response to Sheft's questions in 1957 (a female pilot was shot down and killed in the crash, which happened sometime around 1942). But it matches what she recounted to me many decades later. It had hardened into the story she told.

Memory's a tricky thing. It doesn't unspool like video, an accurate record of what a person witnessed. Instead, it's more like patchwork pieced together from moments we recall, with the gaps filled in by what seems most likely to have happened, based on what we know now. Memories can be distorted by questions, suggestions, and social pressures. "When we are asked about whether we have experienced a particular event," wrote brain researcher Nicole Rust in *Scientific American,* "we tend to get confused by things that are similar to those that actually happened." Therefore, despite her previous contradictions, it follows that Akiyama probably believed what she was saying was true. But without further evidence, it's impossible to determine whether it actually happened in the way she said it did.

For his part, Goerner thought her story *could* be true, especially when he compared her sober tale to the overheated *San Mateo Times* article. "It sounded like truth but there was only her word," he wrote in his 1966 book, *The Search for Amelia Earhart.* If he could prove it, he would have an enormous, career-making scoop—an ambition that appears to have colored his investigation.

There was one big problem with Akiyama's account: How on Earth did Earhart and Noonan end up on Saipan? When they took off from Lae, New Guinea, their destination—Howland Island—was 2,556 miles to the east. Saipan is 1,500 miles due north. Would Noonan, a noted navigator who had helped to establish some of the first air routes across the Pacific, have made such a colossal error?

Goerner flew down to Orange County to consult Paul Mantz, a Hollywood stunt pilot and aviation entrepreneur who had served as technical adviser to Earhart on her round-the-world flight. "It's possible," said Mantz. He thought the plane would have had enough fuel to reach Saipan even if the navigational error happened mid-flight. As for going off course, if the sky was cloudy—and Earhart reported it was—Noonan couldn't take celestial readings. Compasses are reliable "to a point," Mantz said, "but there's still plenty that can happen." She never did get the radio direction finder to work. And the flight was tricky in the best of conditions.

"Howland is a peewee," Mantz continued, claiming to have warned Earhart about the route's difficulty. "It would be like our taking off from my field here at Santa Ana, flying clear across the United States without once seeing the ground or anything we could check our position by, and then trying to find the eighteenth green of a golf course in New Jersey where we're supposed to land. How would you like to try to navigate that one?"

Goerner now had confirmation from an aviation expert that it was *possible* Earhart and Noonan ended up as far north as Saipan. With that and Akiyama's eyewitness testimony, he thought he had a story worth investigating. He knew his audience was interested; the listener response to the few short features he'd already produced for the radio show was much stronger than he or his bosses at KCBS had expected. When he proposed a reporting trip to Saipan to search for evidence and additional eyewitnesses, the CBS leadership said yes. The story would be worth the expenditure.

Josephine and Maximo Akiyama offered to give Goerner the names of people who would confirm her story—but only if Max was allowed to come along on the trip. The keepers of the budget at CBS agreed to fund the whole endeavor. Fred Goerner and Max Akiyama left for Saipan on June 16, 1960, three weeks after the *San Mateo Times* first published the story about Earhart's fate.

Saipan was hard to reach. After the war, the island became part of the former United Nations Trust Territory of the Pacific Islands, which was administered by the United States. The U.S. Navy controlled Saipan and, to Goerner's puzzlement, required visitors to obtain security clearance. One of the higher-ups at KCBS had to call in a favor from an old friend to move Goerner's application along; officials at the Navy were having a difficult time believing the search for Amelia Earhart was the real reason for his request. It took him several trips to the island to figure out why.

Nevertheless, Goerner arrived on Saipan with a swagger. He was soon on a first-name basis with Commander Paul Bridwell, the Navy officer in charge. Their business was conducted over the clink of glasses of Canadian

Club whisky. An example of dialogue from *The Search for Amelia Earhart:*

"Another drink, Mr. Goerner?"

"Call me Fred ... and thank you, I will."

He declined Bridwell's invitation to stay "on the hill" with the naval officers. Max planned to stay in Chalan Kanoa village with his brother-in-law, and Goerner "had decided that Max was not going to get out of my sight and I would stay where he stayed." Max's brother-in-law was José Matsumoto, the man Josephine had been bringing lunch to when she saw the white fliers. Matsumoto hadn't seen the fliers himself, he said, but he'd heard the Japanese talk about them. When Goerner asked why he'd never said anything about it, Max translated, "He says nobody ever asked him." Goerner didn't buy it.

The next morning, Bridwell produced six men who'd worked for the Japanese in 1937. None of them knew about any white fliers, including Juan Ada, who had been a judge under the Japanese, or Juan Villa-Gomez, who had worked in the prison. "There was no white woman and man," said Villa-Gomez. "I know nothing."

Goerner distrusted their testimony. Bridwell had warned him that some people on the island "will tell you what they think you want to hear." But, thought Goerner, "there was the possibility they were telling the commander what they thought *he* wanted to hear." The Navy commander had made it clear that he thought the journalist was "out here on a wild goose chase"; Goerner suspected he was being diverted from whatever secret business the Navy was conducting on the island. Indeed, Bridwell later suggested he turn his sights on the Marshall Islands, which are closer to Howland Island.

Goerner enlisted the priests on the island, who held more sway over the devoutly Catholic residents than the Navy did. The priests helped him interview more than 200 Saipanese; 13 of them provided testimony that he said supported Josephine's. Several had seen a white woman and man at

Tanapag Harbor and remembered the Japanese saying they were pilots. None knew what ultimately happened to them, but a few thought they'd been executed. A farmer named Jesús Salas claimed a white woman had occupied the cell next to his in Garapan prison for a few hours in 1937.

Goerner asked Monsignor Oscar Calvo, a native of Guam who was part Chamorro, why none of the witnesses had previously spoken about what they'd seen. "It's been many centuries since they've had self-determination," explained the priest, and the period under the Japanese had been especially harsh. "After such experiences, you can't wonder why most of the Saipanese are not willing to become involved in something that is not really their business."

As to whether they were telling the truth, the priest claimed they would not lie to him: "Their faith in their religion is too strong."

Goerner needed something more solid than the witnesses' testimony. "All it established," he wrote, "was that a man and woman, matching the descriptions of Noonan and Earhart, supposedly American fliers and spies, had been on Saipan sometime during the latter part of 1937." To break this story, he needed concrete evidence. He needed the plane.

Goerner decided to search for wreckage in the harbor. The Japanese had begun constructing an airfield near the island's southern tip in 1934, but it probably wasn't operational by the time Earhart would have been looking for a place to land the Electra. The seaplane base at Tanapag, however, was well established.

Goerner recruited two local divers who claimed they'd seen a plane of the Electra's description underwater. But the war had littered the waters around Saipan with wreckage—aircraft and ships, of course, but "jeeps, tanks, unexploded ammunition, landing craft, rolls of wire" also lay "strewn in chaotic patterns across the sand and coral." If you travel there today, you can dive the underwater Battle of Saipan WWII Maritime Heritage Trail, which traces a path around nine wrecks in Tanapag Harbor alone.

Goerner and the two divers located a "twisted, tangled mass of junk grown over and under by coral" with no resemblance to a plane. Ignoring—or ignorant of—any standard procedures of underwater recovery, they wrenched chunks from the wreckage and brought them to the surface. One large piece appeared to be a generator. Goerner scraped off the coral and discovered a serial number: NK 17999.

With that, he decided he'd found his evidence. He sent a previously arranged message to his bosses at KCBS: "Big Hatchet Ready to Fall." (He later had the grace to be embarrassed by this overwrought code.)

The day after Goerner returned to San Francisco, KCBS held a news conference. Paul Mantz examined the wreckage with a magnifying glass before a hushed crowd, demonstrating a "sense for publicity [that] had been honed to an exceptionally sharp edge," according to Goerner.

"Well," Mantz said, very slowly for dramatic effect, "it looks exactly like the generator I put aboard AE's plane." (This, according to Goerner. Contemporary newspaper reports record Mantz as saying "it definitely could be" the generator he'd installed.)

"AMELIA EARHART KILLED ON SAIPAN: MYSTERY OF 23 YEARS IS SOLVED" screamed a headline in the *San Mateo Times*.

Evidence for Earhart's fate suddenly seemed overwhelming. And there was more.

Four days after the news broke about the generator, biographer Paul Briand reported a massive find. Two Air Force officers, Joseph Gervais and Robert Dinger, had taken up the search after reading Briand's book. Briand told the press that Gervais had conducted extensive research on Saipan, uncovering Japanese photographs of Earhart, people who witnessed her capture and execution, and the location of her grave site. "We have actual photographs of the graves, and reliable testimony from 72 witnesses who actually saw them on Saipan," he claimed. This "more than confirms" Earhart and Noonan were executed on Saipan.

It all quickly fell apart.

Bendix, the manufacturer of the generator in Earhart's plane, said the one Goerner found wasn't built by them, though it was a good copy. Serial numbers on a ball bearing indicated a Japanese company made the machine.

Meanwhile, the Air Force determined the evidence that Gervais and Dinger produced was "incomplete and inconclusive." The two officers were ordered to halt their investigation. The photographs, Gervais admitted, didn't in fact prove Earhart was executed. He also didn't have affidavits, or even testimony, from 72 people who'd witnessed Earhart and Noonan's presence on Saipan. He just had their names. He hadn't spoken to them. Indeed, he'd never made it onto the island.

In any case, the whole theory was impossible. Leo Bellarts, the chief radioman on the Coast Guard cutter *Itasca,* said there was no way he and his colleagues would have heard Earhart as clearly as they did if she'd been approaching Saipan rather than Howland.

Japanese officers involved with Saipan at the time rejected it too. "I absolutely deny it," said Zenshiro Hoshina, who was the chief of the section of the Navy Military Affairs Bureau handling executions. "No such execution could have taken place without my knowledge and approval."

Goerner, however, was still convinced he could prove that Earhart had ended up on Saipan. He believed the people who said they'd seen white fliers—not the people who said no such thing happened because they would've known if it had. And he suspected the Navy was trying to hide something from him. Perhaps it was Earhart's fate?

IN 1961 GOERNER MADE A SECOND TRIP to Saipan, again at CBS's expense. This time, he was looking for a body.

A former U.S. Army sergeant named Thomas E. Devine had written to him, claiming that when he was stationed on Saipan in 1945, an Okinawan woman had shown him a grave she said contained two white people: a man and a woman, who "came from the sky a long time ago." Devine had sent Goerner photographs of the burial ground along with detailed maps, which directed the newsman south of Garapan to a small cemetery overshadowed by jungle.

With the local Catholic priest's permission—but little if any experience in excavations—Goerner and a group of hired workers began digging. At first, all they found was an unexploded grenade, which they hurriedly dropped in the nearby lagoon. Then they unearthed an unmarked grave, pulling out skull, shoulder, and leg fragments—seven pounds of bones in all and 37 teeth—all that remained of what appeared to be two people buried head to foot. But there weren't any identifying artifacts: no clothes, identification, not even a coffin. Nothing to prove these were Americans.

Goerner wanted an expert to look at them. He gave the remains, carefully wrapped in cigar boxes, to a priest to put in the church vault and secured a promise from Saipan's commander that he'd wire for permission to remove the bones to the United States. Then he ate a sandwich, wrote up his notes, and went to sleep in the Quonset hut where he was staying.

In the middle of the night, in the midst of a terrific tropical storm, Goerner awoke with "a sense of danger." A flash of lightning revealed someone rummaging through a corner of his room. When the man turned, Goerner saw that he held a machete—and that Goerner knew him. The man was a former police officer to whom Goerner had given the pseudonym Francisco Galvan for reasons he never makes clear. Goerner suspected him of having something to do with Earhart and Noonan's deaths; others had fingered him as a cruel enforcer of Japanese authority. The man had refused to be interviewed. Now here he was in Goerner's quarters rifling through his belongings. Goerner assumed he was looking for the bones. The intruder ran off into the jungle before Goerner could stop him.

Whether the man with the machete was searching for the bones because they implicated him in the death of Amelia Earhart or in some Japanese

Mandate–era atrocity or for something else for an entirely different reason, he failed to seize anything. All he'd accomplished was to convince Goerner that he was on the right track. After some wrangling with officials, Goerner managed to get the bones off the island and into the hands of an anthropologist at the University of California, Berkeley.

I'll spare you the suspense: The bones were not those of Amelia Earhart and Fred Noonan. They belonged to at least four people—probably Pacific Islanders whose remains had been relocated to a common grave. As a reporter at a rival station put it, "It may be quite a while before Mr. Goerner makes another unfounded claim about something he's dug from a sandy beach on a Pacific isle."

CBS was certainly done supporting Goerner's fruitless investigations. "If you were merely reporting the facts of a not yet substantiated story, you would have evidenced a certain amount of skepticism yourself," his boss told him after a particularly heated news conference. Instead, "you lost objectivity."

But Goerner couldn't let it go.

CHAPTER SIX

1918–20: "GETTING EVERYTHING I CAN"

One day in 1918, during the last year of World War I, 20-year-old Amelia and a friend stood in a clearing near the Canadian National Exhibition grounds in Toronto. They'd come to the fair to see air stunts. Seeking a vantage point away from the crowd, the two young ladies watched "a small plane turn and twist in the air, black against the sky excepting when the afternoon sun caught the scarlet of its wings."

After a quarter hour or so the pilot, an ace returned from the war, became bored. "He had looped and rolled and spun and finished his little bag of tricks," recalled Amelia, "and there was nothing left to do but watch the people on the ground running as he swooped close to them."

Then he spied the two women standing apart from the others. "I remember the mingled fear and pleasure which surged over me as I watched that small plane at the top of its earthward swoop," she recalled. As the aircraft hurtled toward them, Amelia's friend darted to safety. "Common sense told me if something went wrong with the mechanism, or if the pilot lost control, he, the airplane and I would be rolled up in a ball together," Amelia later wrote.

She stood her ground. When the plane roared past, she was sure "that little red airplane said something to me." It would be several years before she understood what it was.

The United States had entered World War I on April 6, 1917, and Amelia and her fellow students at Ogontz had thrown themselves into the war effort. They set aside 45 minutes each day to knit sweaters for the troops and cut back on one item of food from each meal to send the savings to the Red Cross. Amelia had been elected secretary of the school's chapter, and she thrilled with a sense of purpose. As officers, she and her roommate took a teacher's course in surgical dressings so they could instruct their classmates. "We are subscribing to Liberty Bonds and try to do without everything else we can," she told her mother, crowing that they'd "knitted up over fifty dollars of stuff in three days. Isn't that wonderful?"

Despite the flurry of activity, Amelia didn't witness the war's human costs until she went to Toronto to spend Christmas with her mother and Muriel, who was enrolled at St. Margaret's College there. Amy and Edwin were struggling. Despite Amy's inheritance, money was tight, and Edwin continued to drink. Amy had retreated to what she called her "silent severity" and complained of loneliness, which gave Amelia "awful twinges of conscience." The trip to Toronto—Edwin stayed in Kansas City—offered a temporary reprieve.

As a British dominion, Canada had been engaged in World War I since it began in 1914, and Toronto was very much a city at war. The Canadian National Exhibition grounds had been transformed into a military training camp, while the Royal Flying Corps had taken over much of the University of Toronto campus. Three-quarters of the city's eligible male residents signed up to serve, and many young women did, too, opting to become hospital aides or even nurses shipped off to Europe. Factories spit out cars, planes, and ships. Trains chugged out of the main station overflowing with soldiers on their way to the front and into the station carrying those returning wounded from the battlefields. The streets teemed with soldiers, sailors, and pilots.

Out walking with Muriel one day on bustling King Street, Amelia encountered the scene that would knock her off her chosen path. Coming toward them were "four one-legged men at once, walking as best they could down the street together."

She was deeply shocked. "For the first time, I realized what the World War meant," she recalled. "Instead of new uniforms and brass bands, I saw only the results of a four years' desperate struggle; men without arms and legs, men who were paralyzed, and men who were blind."

Much as she'd loved Ogontz, she refused to return to the school, with its fake military drills and gossip about secret sororities, after having witnessed the devastating toll the war had exacted. "I can't bear the thought of going back to school and being so useless," she told her mother. She would stay in Toronto and become a nurse. Her mother returned to Edwin in Kansas City, and Amelia and Muriel rented an apartment at a hotel for women.

"In every life there are places at which the individual, looking back, can see he was forced to choose one of several paths," she later wrote. This was one of them. She was turning away from the well-trod route leading from finishing school to a prestigious women's college to (possibly) a decorous career and (inevitably) marriage—toward what she wasn't sure. By February 1918, she'd enrolled in a short first aid course with the Voluntary Aid Detachment of the St. John Ambulance Brigade, a leading charitable organization in Canada, learning home nursing in preparation to become a volunteer nurse's aide.

Amelia threw herself into everything, just as she had at Ogontz. She attended class at a clinic for the poor, in which the doctor asked students to diagnose patients before he set them right. "That is not compulsory of course but I am getting everything I can," she told her mother. "Also all lectures possible. I am going to see an operation if I can wheadle [*sic*] anybody into letting me." Eventually she managed to observe a tonsillectomy.

Once her brief training was complete, she was posted to Spadina Military Hospital, a Gothic building on the former Knox College campus that had been converted for the war. Her first assignment was in the ward for soldiers with shell shock, or post-traumatic stress disorder. On her first day there, someone pulled the fire alarm. If the person did it as a joke, it was a cruel one. "The result," she said, "almost killed some of the patients. They screamed and cried and rolled out of bed and we put them back and they rolled out again, begging us to give them something that would end their suffering." Such scenes transformed Amelia into a lifelong pacifist.

In her white dress and hair-covering veil, Amelia performed mostly nonmedical tasks—serving meals, massaging patients' cramping legs and backs ("some lovely ones!"), and even playing tennis with recovering patients. She also dispensed medicine from a pail and helped in the lab, where her superiors trusted her to keep away from the medicinal whiskey. But her main job, she said, was to be a "merry sunshine" for the wounded soldiers.

In a letter to her father—"Darling Pop"—written, somewhat ironically, on purloined Ogontz stationery, Amelia thanks him for the watch he'd sent her: "I never have had so much use out of anything in such a short time before," she writes. "I don't see how I managed without it so long."

"I am assisting in the Laboratory at the hospital," she explains, "and stain germs and do all kinds of tests myself besides keeping up the records of all the men who receive treatment." She started each day at nine and worked until around 4:45. Then she and a colleague headed to the diet kitchen, where they helped serve the evening meal. But, she assures her father, she is free on Sunday mornings to "cultivate the church habit that I have had instilled into me from youth up."

"I am terribly interested in my new work and am learning lots," she adds. "Your two orphans are getting along very well."

And she was. Although she was working very hard and pursuing all the medical experiences she could, she soon found her place in the social whirl of a city overwhelmed with young people living in exciting and dangerous times. A boy named Reg asked her out so frequently that she agreed to go to her first ice hockey game with him. On the weekends, she and Muriel went riding on horses from a nearby stable, where Amelia tamed a fractious horse named Dynamite with patience and apples. The steed would be her introduction to airplanes.

In 1918, Toronto, a hub for the Royal Flying Corps, buzzed with aviators. "Young, clean-cut, and splendidly fit," as one report put it, the cadets—Canadian, British, and even American—took their inaugural flights at Armour Heights aviation camp in the northern part of the city. Soon they graduated to Leaside in the east, where they learned "more intricate evolutions," including flying at high altitudes and in formation. Once they mastered more advanced skills, they were shipped off to England and the war.

With aviation so new, the inexperienced pilots risked their lives before they even saw combat. Newspapers in the United States and Canada were filled with grim reports of accidents. Cadets were killed in head-on collisions; they died when their engines stalled and the plane hit the ground. They miscalculated the angle of a turn and fell to the earth. Sometimes, planes plummeted from the sky and onlookers didn't know why. Often the pilots burned to death.

"They were terribly young," Amelia later remembered, "young and eager. Aviation was the romantic branch of the service and inevitably attracted the romanticists."

The encounter leading to her introduction to airplanes certainly had a romantic flair. One afternoon, a Royal Flying Corps officer saw her riding Dynamite and admired how she handled the dappled gray. The horse reminded him of a plane, he told her. The aircraft might fly "smooth as silk" one day, but "it flew contrary and bucked a bit" other times. He invited Amelia and Muriel to the Armour Heights airfield to watch him fly.

Approaching the airplanes—"full-sized birds that slid on the hard-packed snow and rose into the air with an extra roar"—Amelia felt her "first urge" to fly. During the war that was, of course, impossible. Yet "the memory of the planes remains clearly, and the sense of the inevitability of flying," she recalled. "It always seemed to me one of the few worth-while things that emerged from the misery of war."

Thoughts of flight were chased from her mind as the first soldiers sickened by influenza began to arrive in Toronto. Soon the pandemic was in full force, with some 150,000 people in Toronto contracting the disease. All the hospitals—military and civilian—were overwhelmed, and Amelia worked through the nights in Spadina's sick ward. Eventually, exhausted and exposed, she became a patient herself, developing pneumonia and a serious sinus infection that would plague her for the rest of her life.

On Armistice Day, she was deafened by the celebrations, which she described as "forty riots rolled into one." They disgusted her: "I didn't hear a serious word of thanksgiving in all the hullaballoo [*sic*]!" Amelia was done with the war, and she was done with Toronto. Muriel had left the city in the spring for Northampton, Massachusetts, where she was preparing to take the entrance examinations for Smith College. Amelia joined her there to convalesce.

REST WAS NOT AMELIA'S NATURAL STATE. "If only I were over there," she wrote to a friend still overseas after the war, "instead of gravitating in enforced idleness in the confines of this bally little New England village."

She and Muriel were soon tramping through the countryside around Northampton. Eventually she was able to walk the nearly six miles to the next village and to climb Mt. Tom in the Berkshires. She also began to regain what Muriel called her joie de vivre. On a whim, Amelia bought a banjo she'd spotted in the window of a pawnshop. Within a week, she'd found a local musician to give her lessons and was playing for hours at a time. She'd played the mandolin at Ogontz—another of her many activities—and mastered the instrument quickly. Both she and her father could play by ear, her sister noted enviously.

Amelia also signed up for a course at Smith aimed at teaching women how to fix automobiles—her first education in mechanics. "The incongruity of the two activities did not strike her," observed Muriel. "She had always been artistic and impractical on one hand and scientific and intensely practical on the other."

All the while, Amelia was pondering what to do next. She wanted "the life of the mind," she told a friend later, "combined with a life of purpose and action."

By summer's end, she'd found her answer. Having "acquired a yen for medicine," she would become a doctor. She moved to New York City and enrolled at Columbia University's extension program to take the prerequisite classes. She signed up for the maximum course load, impressing the professors with her curiosity and quick intelligence, and her new friend Louise de Schweinitz (the only other woman in her classes) with her fearlessness. Together, they climbed the library dome—the highest point on campus—in the period's restrictive clothing: long skirts, shirtwaists, slippery buttoned shoes, and big straw hats. Amelia also plunged into the underground passageways that snaked below campus. "I think I explored every nook and cranny possible," she recalled.

Despite the intellectual stimulation and adventurous outlet that Columbia offered, Amelia quit school after a year. Later she claimed it was to avoid a career "sitting at the bedside of a hypochondriac and handing out innocuous sugar pellets to a patient with an imaginary illness"—a callous comment that conflicted with her empathetic treatment of the soldiers in the shell-shock ward.

The real reason she left Columbia was because her parents needed her. Edwin had moved to Los Angeles, lured by the promise of the booming railroad business, and Amy had reluctantly followed. But they wanted their daughters with them to keep the peace. Amelia volunteered so Muriel wouldn't have to leave Smith.

"I'll see what I can do to keep Mother and Dad together until you finish college, Pidge," Amelia told Muriel, "but after that I'm going to come back here and live my own life."

CHAPTER SEVEN

CAPTURED: "EARHART HOUNDS"

In 1966, Fred Goerner, the KCBS radio broadcaster, published *The Search for Amelia Earhart*. It quickly became a bestseller, sharing space on the *New York Times* list with Masters and Johnson's *Human Sexual Response* and Mark Lane's *Rush to Judgment,* which promised to reveal what the Warren Commission had concealed about the John F. Kennedy assassination. An exhaustive account of Goerner's research, *The Search for Amelia Earhart* reads like a hard-boiled detective story or spy thriller, with Goerner as the square-jawed hero, astounding friends and adversaries alike with his dashing wit, investigative skills, and unimpeachable integrity. To women like Noonan's widow, he's a man to be trusted with the fate of her husband; to men like the naval station commander at Saipan, he's a worthy, if relentless, opponent. Earhart herself probably wouldn't have appreciated his description of her, however: "Under all that flying paraphernalia was a tall, slim, attractive body with enough curves to satisfy any man."

Goerner had been to Saipan four times and the Marshall Islands once by the time the book came out, and his theory had evolved. Amelia Earhart and Fred Noonan hadn't crashed at Saipan, he claimed. Instead, they went down in the Marshall Islands northwest of Howland. A man in the capital of Majuro said a Japanese friend of his had told him so. A Japanese fishing boat picked them up and handed them over to the military, who brought them to Saipan. People on both islands claimed to have seen the aviators; this new version allowed him to explain why.

There was more to Goerner's theory, an embellishment that provided a reason for the Electra to be so off course—and supplied fodder to the conspiracy minded. Earhart and Noonan ended up in the Marshalls not due to a navigational error on Noonan's part but because they were spies. The U.S. government had recruited them to fly over Truk, an atoll north of their route to Howland, where Japan was rumored to be building a massive military base. Once they'd noted the supposed airfields and vast dry docks, Goerner imagined, Earhart steered the plane toward Howland. On the way, they encountered tropical storms and headwinds, which put them off course. Low on fuel, Earhart put the Electra down on the first island she saw, which turned out to be Mili Atoll in the Marshalls.

Goerner's tale was full of mysterious tidbits. There were the numerous eyewitnesses, contrary—and uncorroborated—though their testimony was. There was the surprising secrecy around Saipan—the required top clearance and the way Bridwell, the naval commander, kept trying to steer him away from the island and toward the Marshalls with rumors of a plane stuck on a reef. Goerner did end up solving the security mystery: A substantial chunk of the island had been set aside as a Naval Technical Training Unit, a front for the CIA to train Chinese nationals in covert operations against China's communist government.

But Goerner never found the plane, in the Marshalls or anywhere else. Twenty-two tons of Japanese records were removed from Saipan after World War II was over; Goerner couldn't figure out where they went. Documents listing all the Japanese who had lived on Saipan and been returned to their homeland after the war also disappeared, preventing him from tracking down any Japanese witnesses. A military officer who pledged to help him access classified files on Earhart mysteriously went on leave. A recently retired naval public information officer told him, "You're on the right track with your Amelia Earhart investigation. Admiral Nimitz wants you to continue, and he says you're onto something that will stagger your imagination."

Admiral Chester Nimitz was Pacific Fleet commander during the war. The admiral himself purportedly told Goerner, "Fred, I want to tell you Earhart and her navigator did go down in the Marshalls and were picked up by the Japanese." Nimitz died before the book was published—and Goerner made his assertion public. Nimitz didn't leave him with any more evidence than his word.

As tantalizing as all these clues were, they were ultimately unresolvable—unless one dipped into conspiracy thinking. And Goerner certainly did. "Either I'm completely out of my mind," he told a friend, "or this thing is the damnedest coverup in the history of journalism. A lot of people are running scared for reasons I can only begin to understand." Assuming, as he did, that they were the first Americans to witness the Japanese military buildup, he wondered, "Were Amelia and Fred keys to events which led to Pearl Harbor?" Ultimately, he concluded, "There was just too much testimony from too many reputable people to draw any but one conclusion: Earhart and Noonan had gone down in the Marshalls and were captured by the Japanese."

Goerner's speculations landed on fertile ground. The American public was well aware that their government sent spy planes over hostile countries: Pilot Francis Gary Powers had been shot down over the Soviet Union on May 1, 1960, a few weeks before Josephine Akiyama's claims brought Amelia Earhart back into the news. The Eisenhower administration had lied about it, at first: Powers's U-2 was on a routine weather flight, they said; a malfunction caused him to blackout and drift into Soviet air space. The United States only admitted he was spying when the Soviets displayed the plane's wreckage and its sophisticated equipment for the world to see.

The assassination of John F. Kennedy by Lee Harvey Oswald and Jack Ruby's murder of Oswald shortly thereafter—all captured by film and photograph—further stoked Americans' beliefs in cover-ups and conspiracies. The Warren Commission, designed to defuse the talk of a far-reaching plot with an exhaustive investigation, ended up amplifying such whisperings when later investigations indicated the commission hadn't been nearly as thorough as promised. Clearly something shady was going on.

The Search for Amelia Earhart fit right in, following Lane's book on the Warren Commission up the *New York Times* bestseller list, getting paired in newspaper ads with a book called *The Second Oswald* that boasted a "startling new theory of the Kennedy assassination." Goerner had the same attractions to offer—the unanswered questions, stalling government officials, strange clues, and, of course, a legitimate mystery about what happened to the glamorous tragic figure at the center of it all. And it was as irresistible to the conspiracy-minded, launching a horde of searchers on the same quixotic quest.

Goerner abhorred these newcomers. This "pack of Earhart hounds, recent, reckless, and superficial" got in the way, he said, as the *L.A. Times* framed his critique, diminishing what he considered to be his serious reporting work. They were "a clown act," he complained: "A cottage industry. There are literally hundreds of people around this country who are pursuing answers, taking available evidence and surrounding conjecture, and fitting it to their preconceptions."

But he shared more in common with this cohort than he was willing to acknowledge. A hallmark of human thinking is projection, and that applies to conspiracy thinking as much as anything. Indeed, conspiracy theorists employ common practices of the human mind, as psychologist Rob Brotherton explains in his book *Suspicious Minds.* He cites our tendency to make tenuous, unproven connections; ascribe malign intentions to accidental or innocuous occurrences; believe that the "official story" of significant events (such as the disappearance of a celebrity pilot) is rarely the true one; and refuse to accept evidence that contradicts our chosen narrative. Even so, one research team has argued that extreme cases should be designated a personality disorder. Yet if that were true, most Americans would receive a diagnosis, since recent polls show that the majority of us still believe a conspiracy was behind Kennedy's assassination.

But what makes certain individuals immerse themselves in a conspiracy theory, when most people are content to read about it and move on? A 2025 meta-analysis led by Mikey Biddlestone at the University of Kent examines what the researchers call the "psychological motives" that draw people to conspiracy theories. Although their beliefs might seem outlandish to others, the desires that drive them—"security, certainty, and social belonging"—are deeply human. Pursuing an unsolved mystery provides community, purpose, and a sense that this unstable world is ultimately comprehensible—and that they are just the people to make it so. "A conspiracy theory," writes Brotherton, "is an invitation to join an enlightened but embattled minority."

THOMAS DEVINE WAS ONE OF THE "Earhart hounds." His testimony had been the basis for three of Goerner's expeditions to Saipan—and the reason CBS stopped funding his reporting trips. The former serviceman claimed that a local woman had shown him the grave site where two aviators were buried; Goerner dug there on his second and third trips, unearthing the bones that proved *not* to be Earhart and Noonan during the first excavation. All he found during the second was detritus from the war—"50-caliber machine-gun ammunition, clips of Japanese rifle cartridges, rotted fabric, shirt buttons, combat goggles, and a broken sake cup."

Devine had pushed Goerner to take him along on his investigations but wasn't able to travel to the island until the CIA shuttered its spy school and the island opened up to visitors. In the meantime, a California newspaper syndicate agreed to back Goerner's research and fund Devine's travel. The two men met for the first time in San Francisco at the beginning of their expedition. Devine was "a pleasant-faced Irish-appearing man in his mid-forties," Goerner later wrote, "armed with maps, photos and absolute confidence."

Devine didn't record his impressions of Goerner in his book, *Eyewitness: The Amelia Earhart Incident,* which came out much later, in 1987, and to much less acclaim than Goerner's. Instead, he recounted his own attempts to assert his dominance among the other researchers the journalist was consulting. By the time the party—which included Matthew Katz, Goerner's business manager—arrived on Saipan, Devine was burning with resentment. Katz and Goerner wouldn't listen to his arguments that they'd been excavating at the wrong cemetery. They wouldn't read what he called his protocols for how the search should be conducted (though he had no expertise), and they never gave him enough time to search—even deserting him in the jungle at one point, leaving him to walk the three miles back to their quarters in town.

The expedition proved fruitless, though Devine later claimed he'd located the "stone-encircled" tree that served as a marker for the grave site he'd been shown, but "decided to keep my discoveries quiet" due to his "strong misgivings as to how my information might be handled." When a typhoon loomed, the team was forced to cut their trip short, leaving Saipan with little to show for their troubles. To save face with Goerner, Devine offered him a fantastical tale of a cover-up that, of course, went nearly to the top of the U.S. government.

Devine had served with the Army's not-yet-activated 244th Postal Unit, he said, and had come ashore on Saipan on July 6, 1944, before U.S. forces had achieved complete control of the island from the Japanese. When his unit arrived on the southern tip of Saipan, Devine claimed his commanding officer ordered him to drive him to Aslito Field, the Japanese air base that had been a primary target of the U.S. invasion. When they drove up to a hangar, a man in a white shirt told them the area was off-limits.

A marine officer yelled angrily, recounted Devine in his book: "What do you mean it's off-limits? We know Earhart's plane is in there! What are you trying to pull? Our men laid their lives on the line, and now they won't even get credit for finding the plane!"

Devine was stunned. The man in the white shirt looked familiar to him, but he didn't know from where. When a marine told Devine to move the jeep away from the forbidden hangar, Devine asked if it was true Amelia Earhart's plane was inside.

"Yes," the marine replied, "but for the love of God don't say I said so! I don't know why the hell they want to keep it a secret."

Devine didn't see the plane then, he said, but later that day a twin-engine civilian aircraft with the identification number NR 16020 (the registration for Earhart's Electra) roared over his camp. Despite multiple warnings from his commanding officer and various marines to stay away, he and a buddy sneaked back to Aslito that night. There, out in the open on the runway was the civilian plane he'd seen earlier. They tried to get a closer look—but then they saw the man in the white shirt, this time with a bandolier of ammunition slung across his shoulder. Spooked by the man and a photographer who stealthily snapped their picture and ran away, Devine and his friend crept back to their camp. Not too much later, an explosion rocked the airfield. When Devine caught sight of what was burning, he later wrote, "I was aghast! The twin-engine plane was engulfed in flames!"

The mystery continued. Devine wrote down the plane's registration mark and put the piece of paper in his wallet and slipped it into his pants pocket. Two days later, the pants disappeared.

He also learned that the person who had supposedly identified the plane was Marine Col. Wallace Greene. In 1963—at the time Devine shared this story with Goerner—Greene was about to be sworn in as commandant of the Marine Corps. And the man in the white shirt? James Forrestal, appointed Secretary of the Navy in May 1944—and the subject of many conspiracy theories after he jumped to his death in 1949 at the National Naval Medical Center in Bethesda, Maryland, where he was being treated for "a psycho-neurotic disorder."

Despite the many unbelievable details, Goerner found Devine's story compelling enough that he eventually finagled a brief interview with Greene, whose response wasn't encouraging: "I want to make it quite clear at the beginning of this meeting that I had nothing to do with identifying either her or her plane on Saipan as has been alleged," said the general. "I have nothing to offer that could help you."

Why would the secretary of the Navy get personally involved in destroying Amelia Earhart's plane? Devine claimed Forrestal was looking ahead to postwar relations with Japan. "The discovery of Amelia Earhart or her Electra could have hindered peace efforts and post-war international relations," argued Devine. (Note that the United States had captured Saipan and its neighboring island Tinian specifically as jumping-off points for long-range bombers to obliterate Japanese cities—a greater hindrance, one would think, to future friendship between the two countries than the reappearance of a missing flier's aircraft.)

There are other holes in Devine's story. Units from the Army's 165th Infantry, 27th Division, captured Aslito field on June 18, 1944, with Army Air Force units arriving four days later. The Marines never controlled the airfield. Even if they had, the hangars were so damaged by the fighting—"skeletonized" in the words of one observer—that nothing could be hidden within their shattered walls. Several researchers claim Devine wasn't even on the island until 1945.

After returning home from Saipan and still hoarding the "secret" location of Earhart and Noonan's grave, Devine took steps toward planning his own expeditions. He pestered Muriel Morrissey, Earhart's sister, and Mary Beatrice Ireland, Noonan's widow, for permission to bring back any human remains he thought might belong to their loved ones. And he sought funding for the trip from anyone he could think of. But Morrissey refused his request, and Ireland never responded—and no one with the means to support further jaunts to Saipan found his story credible. Devine never returned to Saipan, but he kept pushing his version of events until shortly before his death in 2003.

JOSEPH GERVAIS, ANOTHER "EARHART HOUND," had an even wilder tale than Thomas Devine's—one that eventually got him into serious legal trouble. Gervais, an Air Force officer stationed in Okinawa, had been on the Earhart hunt since reading Paul Briand's 1960 biography featuring Josephine Blanco Akiyama's version of the aviator's end. After Gervais's claim to have found 72 eyewitnesses to Earhart's presence on Saipan was very publicly refuted—he hadn't spoken with these people or even made it onto the island—he'd been told by his superiors to halt his research. He left the Air Force instead, eventually ending up in Las Vegas, where he worked for the school district. He continued his investigation, later claiming he'd examined every wreck in the Pacific islands. But none of them were Earhart's Lockheed Electra 10-E.

Gervais got his big break, as he saw it, in 1965, when Viola Gentry, a friend of one of his relatives, invited him to speak about his quest at a meeting of the Long Island Early Fliers Club. Known as "the flying cashier" due to her day job, Gentry had gained instant celebrity when she flew under the Brooklyn and Manhattan Bridges in New York in 1926. Two years later, she set a solo endurance record, unofficially the first for a woman. In 1929, when she tried to break another one, her plane crashed, killing her copilot and grievously injuring herself.

When the Long Island Early Fliers Club gathered at the Sea Spray Inn, Gervais, an experienced pilot with thousands of hours of flight time under his belt, was almost giddy. Only people who had flown in the first 30 years after the Wright brothers took to the air at Kitty Hawk on December 17, 1903, belonged to this illustrious group. Here were the aviators who'd started it all: daredevils who'd barnstormed in open-cockpit biplanes. Many of them were members of the Ninety-Nines, the organization for women pilots co-founded by Earhart in 1929. Some, including Gentry, a charter member, had known her personally. Gervais brought his camera and eagerly snapped pictures of these pioneers. "I was thrilled and extremely happy," he recalled later.

Then, across the sun-bright room of chattering aviators, Gervais caught sight of a woman who sent a chill through his body. Later, he struggled to explain her effect on him to Joe Klaas, the Boswell to his Samuel Johnson: "For five years I had been living with this Earhart thing. I had been reading about Earhart, asking about Earhart, speculating about Earhart, studying photographs of Earhart ... and then, all of a sudden, right there across a room in the Sea Spray Inn, I thought I recognized her."

The woman's name was Irene Bolam. "Was this the same face that I had studied in so many photographs?" Gervais wondered. "The same face twenty-eight years older than in her last pictures? The hair was silver now ... but shaped the same way, short around her head. It was even parted the same way. But this was ridiculous. It was too much to believe."

And yet he did believe, although he felt compelled to notice that "her bosom ... was much fuller than the younger Amelia Earhart's." After an awkward conversation in which he made leading statements such as "I'll bet you knew Amelia rather well" and "I'll bet you made a lot of flights with Amelia Earhart," Bolam's husband led her away. But not before Gervais snapped her picture.

In it, Bolam is standing with her husband, Guy, a spry-looking older man with a thin mustache and a bow tie. She wears a light-colored skirt suit with the jacket thrown over her shoulders. Reading glasses and a medallion-like necklace hang from her neck. A pin adorns her blouse. Her short gray hair is thick and upswept. It resembles Earhart's, but her comfortably padded body does not. Of course, people often thicken with age. Irene smiles graciously at Gervais, unaware of how the retired Air Force major would change her life.

Gervais later claimed she invited him to dinner the next day, but he didn't accept because he had to pick up his children and catch a plane. As Klaas wrote, "Gervais had the depressing feeling that he would regret for a long time not having accepted Mrs. Guy Bolam's invitation. And he was right." Gervais's "fanatical hunt"—Klaas's words—was about to become frenzied.

Soon, Gervais was wondering whether the medallion Bolam wore was the same as the medal Earhart received for her solo transatlantic flight. And the pin on her blouse? He was sure it was a major's oak leaf insignia. He thought he'd spied a miniature Distinguished Flying Cross ribbon on her as well; Earhart had been awarded one for the transatlantic flight.

When Gervais tried to contact Bolam again, no one answered the phone. When he traveled to her home in Bedford village, New York, the house was empty. He finally reached her at the home of a friend in North Carolina. When he asked her to meet with them to discuss "the old days and Amelia Earhart," she insisted the interview had to be outside the country. They made a date to rendezvous in Montréal. Irene never showed. He contacted her husband and arranged to fly from Newark to North Carolina with him. Guy never showed. Gervais flew south anyway, only to discover that Irene and her friend had recently driven north. It's possible one of them was going mad, but her mysterious elusiveness only added to Gervais's conviction that she was hiding her true identity.

At last, he got her on the phone. She told him to "put exactly what you want from me into writing."

He and Klaas did. "If you are not Amelia Earhart," they wrote, "please let us know enough about your background so that we may be certain that you really are someone else." And if she admitted to being the lost flier, they pleaded, who could tell her story better than they, the men who'd devoted "all this effort to her memory and then [had] the amazing luck to rejoice in her survival?"

Bolam's response was courteous yet brief. After expressing "great surprise" at their claims, she informed them that their "quest has not ended, for I am not she." She provided the names of two people who knew both her and Earhart. They confirmed that the two women were not the same, although their lives intersected.

Irene Bolam was born October 1, 1904, in Newark, New Jersey. Like Earhart, she attended Columbia University. Like Earhart, she was a flier. But she didn't make her first solo flight until 1933. Her first husband, Charles Craigmile, died in 1931, in their third year of marriage. Two years later she married Alvin Heller, her flight instructor. They had a son together and later divorced; she had the marriage annulled in 1940. She married Guy Bolam in 1958; they were together until he died in 1970. For many years she worked as a banker: A 1950 newspaper announcement of her promotion includes a round-faced photograph with little resemblance to Earhart.

All of which is to say she that had a full and well-documented life.

Gervais was not convinced.

In 1970 Klaas, serving as Gervais's faithful amanuensis, published *Amelia Earhart Lives,* which explained how Earhart made it from Lae, New Guinea, in 1937 to a meeting of the Long Island Early Fliers Club in 1965, where Gervais met her under the guise of Irene Bolam. Earhart had been a spy, Klaas and Gervais argued, assigned by President Roosevelt to fly over the Pacific island of Truk, where the Japanese were rumored to be building a heavily fortified base. Instead, she crashed on Hull, one of the Phoenix Islands, and was captured by the Japanese, flown to Saipan (where, to explain sightings of her there, Klaas and Gervais had her crashing a second time), and then shipped off to Tokyo, where she spent World War II living in the emperor's palace, possibly serving as the propagandist Tokyo Rose or as a hostage to guarantee that Hirohito would not be tried as a war criminal. With General MacArthur's help after the war, she was dressed as a nun and spirited back to the United States, where she assumed the identity of Irene Bolam.

Gervais's evidence for these head-spinning claims included footage taken during the Navy's search for Earhart: On the island of Hull, flocks of seabirds separate for the briefest of moments to reveal what Gervais claimed was the Japanese flag. He also argued that, if stacked a certain way, the names of the Phoenix Islands at the time—*G*ardner, Enderb*u*ry, S*y*dney, *B*irnie, Ph*o*enix, Hu*l*l, C*a*nton, and *M*cKean—spelled out the name of Guy Bolam, Irene's husband. Furthermore, that name, when translated into numbers, gave the coordinates of Hull's lagoon. Also, he knew what happened to Earhart's Lockheed Electra: It had crashed in California in 1961.

Irene Bolam was not pleased. Within a day of the book's publication, she'd hired a lawyer and called a press conference. "I am not a mystery woman," she said. "I am not Amelia Earhart." She called the book "a hoax" and "utter nonsense."

Bolam filed a $1.5 million defamation suit against Gervais, Klaas, and McGraw Hill, the book's publisher, saying the book implied she was a spy, a traitor, and a bigamist. The publisher eventually withdrew the book and the suit was settled. But Bolam would be known for the rest of her life as the woman who might be Amelia Earhart.

LES KINNEY THINKS HE KNOWS THE real story—and he has photographic evidence for it. The former investigator first got interested in Amelia Earhart when he started out as a junior agent in the Office of Naval Intelligence (ONI) in Chicago in the late 1960s.

One day he came into work to find the other men—they were all men then—gathered around the assistant special agent in charge. He was regaling them with stories from his early days, including how he'd once investigated claims that Amelia Earhart had ended up on Saipan. A 1960 report for U.S. Naval Intelligence discredited the testimony of Akiyama and Devine and dismantled Goerner's theories. "A preponderance of hearsay evidence, and the statements of persons who were in the area in 1937," the report concluded, "failed to indicate that Subject [Earhart] crash landed her airplane at Saipan, or that she was buried at Saipan."

Kinney had just read Fred Goerner's book, and he couldn't help himself. He blurted out a question. "Frankly, I don't quite remember exactly what I asked him because I just kind of threw it out there," says Kinney. "It took him by surprise." The agent's answer, whatever it was, didn't seem honest to Kinney: "I thought to myself, Gee, there's got to be something more to this thing." That feeling has driven him ever since.

Kinney—who sprinkles his conversations with a generous dose of the words *accurate, corroborate,* and *credible*—began investigating Earhart's disappearance on his vacations. When he retired from a federal law enforcement career that included travel to the Marshall Islands, Saipan, and Guam for drug interdiction, he dove into the mystery full time. "I've spent, I don't know, hundreds of hours in the two archives in Washington, D.C.," he says. "I've been to every holding site in the United States." He's guided by an old adage: "'Where there's smoke, there's fire' is usually very accurate. And if you see a lot of smoke, there's probably going to be some fires."

Kinney's standard practice when researching in archives was to take photographs of the documents he uncovered and examine them later. The photograph he believes is incontrovertible proof Earhart was captured by the Japanese had been in his possession for several years before he took a look at it and realized what it was.

He'd found it loose in a file at the National Archives facility in College Park, Maryland. The photograph depicts people standing on a dock with boats moored nearby, and the caption reads "Marshall Islands, Jaluit Atoll,

Jaluit Island, Jaluit Harbor." The image had been assigned an ONI number (14381), but not a year.

When Kinney expanded the photo to peer at the people, he was astonished. There, leaning against a pole was Fred Noonan. Sitting on the dock, with her back to the photographer, was Amelia Earhart. And at the edge of the frame was an airplane being towed by a Japanese military vessel.

Here's what Kinney thinks happened. Earhart and Noonan lost their way and went down on Mili, a coral atoll in the Marshall Islands, which was under the Japanese Mandate. They were picked up by the Japanese and brought to Jaluit, where the photo was taken, Kinney thinks, by a German Australian missionary operating as a spy. The missionary and his wife were killed by the Japanese several years later.

After Jaluit, Earhart and Noonan were transferred to Kwajalein, which came to be known as "Execution Island" during World War II, after the brutal treatment of Allied prisoners of war. But that's not where Earhart and Noonan died, according to Kinney. He believes Goerner's collection of eyewitnesses, as contradictory as they may be: Earhart and Noonan met their end on Saipan.

In 2017, Kinney presented his case on a History Channel documentary. His evidence included the testimony of a young medical aide who said that sometime around 1937, he treated a white man with a gash on his knee on a ship in Jaluit Harbor while a white woman looked on. A marine named William Jackson who took part in the invasion of Kwajalein in 1944 claims he found a suitcase filled with "women's effects," as well as a diary embossed with the title "The Ten-year Diary of Amelia Earhart." He handed the suitcase and diary over to intelligence, where it seems to have disappeared, though Kinney says he's confirmed Jackson's story in the archives. "It's just three or four lines but it's total corroboration," he says.

The documentary was received with great fanfare and coverage in all the major news outlets. Days later, the edifice of evidence Kinney had constructed collapsed.

A Japanese blogger did an image search and discovered the photograph in a travel photo book published in 1935, two years before Earhart and Noonan made their attempt across the Pacific. Another one of "Earhart's hounds" had failed to catch their quarry.

Kinney's response? "Well, that's baloney." The book was "nothing more than a scrapbook" in which photos could easily have been added or removed after publication. "I do firmly believe that that picture is accurate."

CHAPTER EIGHT

1920–24: "I WANT TO FLY!"

When Amelia arrived in Los Angeles in May 1920 after the long journey from the East Coast, she may not have realized the balmy city was fast becoming "America's aviation capital." In 1910, the country's first public air meet was held at Dominguez Field, just south of Los Angeles. Featuring planes, balloons, and dirigibles, the Los Angeles International Aviation Meet attracted more than 20,000 spectators each day of its 11-day run, with visitors coming from all over the state and beyond. The meet's organizers were astonished by its success, especially since only 16 of the promised 43 planes showed up and not all of them managed to get off the ground. Still, the *Los Angeles Times* Sunday paper declared the air meet "one of the greatest public events in the history of the West."

Newspaper magnate William Randolph Hearst, a key booster of the event, flew for the first time with French pilot Louis Paulhan (Paulhan's participation allowed the meet's backers to add "International" to the title). A 13-year-old named Jimmy Doolittle—who as an adult would lead a pivotal air raid against the Japanese in World War II—saw his first planes there.

William Boeing, already wealthy from his timber holdings, desperately tried to get someone to take him up in a plane, but no one would. (When he experienced his first flight a few years later, in a rattletrap Curtiss hydroplane, he decided to go into the plane-building business himself.)

The air meet occurred during construction of the 233-mile aqueduct that promised to solve the city's water woes—and just after the annexation of San Pedro, which had a port ready to welcome the new Panama Canal shipping traffic. Like those infrastructure projects, the event underscored that Los Angeles had the makings of a booming city: one that could support such cutting-edge industries as aviation.

By the time Amelia arrived in 1920, many of the men who would build some of aviation's most influential companies had gravitated to Southern California, where the weather was conducive to year-round flight. In 1912, self-taught Glenn Martin constructed his first plane in an abandoned church and demonstrated its fitness by flying from Newport Harbor to Catalina Island. His employee Donald Douglas, the only trained engineer among this group of founders, started his own aircraft company in 1920. In 1916, brothers Malcolm and Allan Loughead moved their aircraft manufacturing business from San Francisco to a Santa Barbara garage. A mechanic named Jack Northrop who worked next door soon joined them. The business eventually folded, but in 1926 a new company emerged with an easier-to-pronounce spelling of the brothers' name: Lockheed, the future manufacturer of Amelia's Electra 10-E.

But you didn't have to be a future aviation titan to access the world of flight. With some 20 airfields dotting Los Angeles and more beyond the city's limits, flying was everywhere, and air meets were a common weekend activity. In the winter of 1920, Amelia attended her first in California at Daugherty Field in Long Beach, where "the fastest planes the army, navy, and individuals in the western country can muster will compete ... [on] one of the most perfect aviation fields in existence," according to the *Long Beach Press,* which devoted its entire Christmas Eve front page to the first national Winter Air Tournament. It featured a hundred-mile free-for-all race where speeds were expected to reach 130 miles an hour, as well as blimp flights, a dirigible balloon race, and formation flights by U.S. Army pilots.

Amelia attended with Edwin, who was less thrilled about airplanes than she was. "As the dust blew in his eyes and his collar wilted, I think his enthusiasm for aviation, such as it was, waned," she observed. Nevertheless, he agreed to ask an official at the meet about instruction. "I felt suddenly shy about making inquiries myself," said Amelia, "lest the idea of a woman's being interested in trying to fly be too hilarious a thought for the official."

Unlike in wartime Toronto, flights were available to anyone who would pay. Soon Amelia was scheduled for "a trial hop" at nearby Rogers Airport. Her father, optimistic about the family's financial future after starting a new law firm, covered the $10 fee. Frank Hawks, a former Army officer who went on to set numerous speed records, took her up in a three-seated plane. The third seat was filled by a friend of his, whose sole job, Amelia realized, was to grab her if she got scared and attempted to jump out. "It was no use to explain I had seen airplanes before and wasn't excitable," she recalled.

Afterward, she didn't remember being frightened, though the motor seemed very loud. "I was surprised to be able to see the sea after a few moments of climbing," she wrote later. She lost all track of time and, she realized, space. When they made their descent, she could not spot the airfield; the ground below "looked totally unfamiliar." She hadn't realized populated areas were divided into "hundreds of little squares." It never occurred to her to jump.

That evening, she mentioned casually to her family that she was thinking of learning to fly, "knowing full well I'd die if I didn't." Her parents put up surprisingly little fuss. When she returned a few days later with more information about lessons, she realized why: They hadn't taken her seriously. "I thought you were just wishing," her father said. "I can't afford to let you have instruction."

To Amelia, that hurdle was easily surmountable. She went out and got her first paying job—in the back room of the telephone company. And she started to look for a woman to teach her. Hawks's sexist assumption that she'd panic in the air had offended her, and she worried his view would be prevalent among the many ex-servicemen who populated the fields. She wanted to learn, and she didn't want to be distracted by an instructor with false ideas of what a woman could do.

She found Neta Snook.

At 24, Snook was a year older than Amelia and a good deal shorter, with bright red hair and a singular drive. She'd dropped out of Iowa State University to attend a local flying school. When the school went out of business, she made her way by foot, train (freight cars), and car (hitchhiking) to the Curtiss School of Aviation in Newport News, Virginia, where she convinced the instructors to take her on as the only female student. When the Curtiss School closed during World War I, she bought a wrecked Curtiss Canuck and fixed it up herself. She'd discovered at an early age "that many of the things I wanted weren't to be given to me," she said many years later. "I found out I had to make them for myself."

Snook's first test flight with the Canuck was also her first time soloing. She wasn't scared: "I knew I could fly."

Like many pilots, Snook had moved to Southern California so she could fly year-round. She made Kinner Field, situated among the farms south of Los Angeles, her headquarters, from which she offered tours (loftily titled "The Orange Empire Air Voyage"), lessons, and aerial advertising. The male pilots called her Snooky: "We were not quite sure as to whether Snooky was a man or a woman, as few of us ever saw her except in a pair of dirty coveralls," said one.

Indifferent in her single-mindedness to such commentary, Snook nevertheless recognized the contrast she made with "well-groomed and cultured" Amelia, who arrived at the field to make inquiries about lessons in a well-cut brown skirted suit, scarf, and gloves, with her still-long hair braided around her head. Edwin was with her, and Amelia's question was direct: "I want to fly. Will you teach me?"

Snook would. She charged one dollar a minute, the same amount it cost her to fly. Amelia paid in Liberty bonds and signed a release acknowledging she understood "that being transported through the air by so-called Flying Machines is a dangerous thing, and that the machines themselves are a dangerous instrumentality." On January 3, 1921, Amelia had her first lesson. She showed up for it with a book on aerodynamics under her arm.

Amelia learned on Snook's Canuck, an underpowered biplane with two open cockpits, each with a set of rudimentary controls that were connected during instruction. The foot-powered rudder bar directed the plane's nose left or right, while the stick pushed the plane's nose up or down and tipped the wings. "Every movement made by the instructor is duplicated in the student's cockpit and vice versa," she would later write in one of her many evangelizations for learning to fly. "Obviously, therefore, the experienced pilot is master of the situation at all times, and can correct any mistakes made by the pupil, or show how maneuvers should be executed." It was a sensible system.

Amelia sat in the front cockpit and Snook in the back. After instruction on the ground, Snook took them up and made circles around the field: "For what seemed a long time but was actually only about twenty minutes, I watched the movements of the controls," said Amelia. When Snook pushed the foot-powered rudder bar to steer the plane left, Amelia's rudder bar moved as well. Later, when Amelia was learning to turn and climbed a little too high—as she tended to do—Snook would nudge her own stick forward to prevent a stall.

But Snook didn't need to correct Amelia often. "She was a natural pilot and as an instructor, there wasn't very much for me to do," Snook observed. "She just seemed to take over and do it."

Snook put Amelia through the basics. Once her student could fly fairly level in a mostly straight line toward a landmark, she was allowed "the exciting experiment of trying to make a turn." Eventually she learned to land, "most difficult of all and requiring the most practice."

Perhaps inevitably, the two women crashed. Once, they ran out of gas (the plane had no fuel gauge). Another time, due to an engine malfunction during takeoff, they didn't gain enough altitude to clear a stand of trees. Amelia put the plane into a stall.

"If you haven't experienced a stall at low altitude, it's really interesting," said Snook in a characteristic understatement. "Instead of going ahead, we were just gradually settling back on the tail. And as soon as it made ground contact, Amelia cut the switch, and the front end dropped, and one wing kind of dropped to one side. I think the undercarriage was probably broken. It evidently was a harder ground contact than we really realized because it seemed that we were so gradually sliding back."

"But anyway, it was a good wreck."

Neither of them was hurt. When Snook looked back, Amelia was powdering her nose. "She says we have to look good when the reporters come," remembered Snook. "Then there was always reporters, looking for accidents."

Snook and Amelia were lucky; many early fliers lost their lives in crashes. In the summer of 1920, when Amelia moved to Los Angeles, two acclaimed pilots—one of them a woman—died within weeks of each other. Laura Bromwell's plane plummeted to the earth during a loop, while Owen Locklear, the first stunt pilot for the new movie industry, went into a tailspin and crashed. That year, 15 aerial mail pilots were killed on the job.

Despite the danger, Kinner Field had become the center of Amelia's life in Los Angeles. She spent every weekend there, bringing a picnic that included her mother's chocolate cake. With the other pilots, she would patch the fabric serving as the planes' skin, mend wooden struts, and perform whatever other maintenance needed doing. She also eyed the Kinner Airster, Bert Kinner's experimental aircraft. The little plane had an air-cooled engine, which made it much lighter than Snook's unwieldy Canuck.

After watching it for several months, she "realized that the small plane took off more quickly, climbed more steeply, was faster and easier to handle than its bigger brothers with their greater horsepower and wing spread." The Airster had a range of 200 miles compared to the Canuck's 100, a top speed of 90 miles an hour to the Canuck's 75, and the ability to ascend as high as 13,000 feet compared to the Canuck's 10,000.

She wanted it.

And against Snook's advice, she bought it.

The Airster fell short in one comparison: the price tag, which was $2,000 compared to $1,000 for surplus World War I Canucks. Edwin had offered to help cover the cost, but changed his mind. Counteracting her husband, Amy stepped in with funds from her inheritance. "I realized that if she wanted to be a flyer someone in the family had to be interested and had to go with her and help her out," Amy later wrote in response to questions from a correspondent. Although her mother could be difficult, Amelia was wise enough to appreciate her support. "If Mother was worried during this period, she did not show it," she later commented. "She could have done nothing more helpful."

Amelia owned a plane before she'd ever soloed. After nine hours of flight time, Snook thought Amelia was ready, yet she resisted. Amelia wanted to learn stunts first—not to show off, but to know how to get out of perilous situations. "It seemed foolhardy to try to go up alone without the ability to recognize and recover quickly from any position the plane might assume, a reaction only possible through practice," Amelia recalled.

She found a former war pilot to teach her the "three S's" of stunt flying—slips, stalls, and spins—as well as vertical banks, loops, and barrel rolls. Slips mean the plane is moving sideways against the airflow; stalls are a sudden reduction in lift; and spins are stalls around the plane's vertical axis leading to a steep corkscrew descent. "Side slips sometimes come in handy in landing in a short field; stalls and spins in knowing what to avoid in normal flying," Amelia later explained. "A vertical bank is necessary in a very short turn and loops and barrel rolls and their relatives and friends are mostly for fun."

Only when she'd mastered the stunts did she agree to solo. But after all that preparation, the experience was anticlimactic. A shock absorber broke as she was taking off, forcing her to abort the flight. After it was fixed, she tried once more—this time making it 5,000 feet into the sky on her own and returning to the earth with a "thoroughly rotten landing."

Soon Amelia—hair now trimmed into a fashionable bob—and her nimble plane were familiar sights at the area's air meets, where she was becoming a featured attraction. In December 1921, she and Aloysia McLintic, another female student of Snook's, performed stunts together at the Pacific Coast Ladies Derby in the second ever air rodeo. *The Ace* magazine reported in that month's issue that she had managed to reach a height of 10,200 feet. In 1922, she flew higher than 14,000 feet, establishing a record for female pilots: her first. Newspapers described her as "beautiful and young" and a "society girl-student aviatrix."

She had a "very disquieting" experience during another attempt a little while later. The skies appeared clear, but she encountered clouds at 10,000 feet, and sleet at 11,000. At 12,000 feet, she flew into dense fog and could not see her way out. Instruments had not yet been developed that allowed pilots to fly blind; she didn't know which direction she was headed or if she was right side up. "It was extraordinarily confusing and, realizing I could not go farther, I kicked the ship into a tail spin and came down to 3,000 feet where I emerged from the fog and landed."

Her satisfaction at landing safely was deflated by a more experienced pilot, who pointed out she would surely have crashed if the fog had gone any lower.

By the end of 1923, Amelia had earned licenses from two aviation associations—the first woman to do so with the National Aeronautic Association and the 16th with the Fédération Aéronautique Internationale. She'd even been admitted to the Aeronautical Hall of Fame as someone "influential in advancing aeronautics."

Amelia was soaring but, as had happened before, family and financial troubles brought her down. The family's prospects in Los Angeles had been promising at first. Edwin's law practice was doing fairly well. And, more important, he had stopped drinking with the help of a colleague and his Christian Science congregation.

The family had moved to a larger house in 1921 and taken in borders, including a young engineer named Sam Chapman. Amelia and Sam began spending time together, playing tennis and attending a meeting of the Industrial Workers of the World. Sam was intelligent and curious, if more traditionally minded than Amelia. In the spring of 1923, nearly two years after they first met, they became engaged.

But the family fault lines had just been papered over. Edwin, spending more time with the Christian Scientists whom he felt had saved his life, was increasingly disenchanted with Amy. And their financial situation remained unstable. To earn money, Amelia worked at the telephone company and a photography studio, and even drove a sand and gravel truck—although she declined an offer from someone she assumed was a bootlegger "to make some easy money bringing some stuff across the border."

Amy's dwindling inheritance hadn't been invested, so when a friend bought a gypsum mine in Nevada, Amelia suggested her parents back it. Having learned to trust their daughter's judgment more than their own, they put their entire savings into the mine. It was a disaster. When Amelia and Edwin went to visit, they arrived as a flash flood ripped through the site and watched helplessly as their friend was submerged in his truck. "Peter is drowned, the mine seems irreparably flooded, and all of mother's investment is gone," Amelia wrote to Muriel. "We are still reeling from the blow." Muriel left Smith that semester.

The Earharts never did recover from the blow. In 1924, Edwin divorced Amy, and Amelia, with her sister and mother, returned to the East, leaving sunny Los Angeles and her jaunty little plane behind.

CHAPTER NINE

CASTAWAY: THE DESERTED ISLAND

When Richard "Ric" Gillespie founded The International Group for Historic Aircraft Recovery (TIGHAR) in 1985, he had no intention of getting into the Amelia Earhart business. Gillespie had quit his job the year before as an aviation crash investigator for an insurance company. "I'm not a very good employee," he said. "I can't keep my mouth shut, and we reached a point where you can't fire me because I just quit."

At the same time, Gillespie was going through a financially ruinous divorce. Nearing 40 years old, he found himself bankrupt and unemployed. It was time to start over and do what he wanted with his life.

Unlike many people in similar situations, he already knew what that was: "I love history. I love aviation," Gillespie thought. "I hate aviation accidents, and I'm a pretty good investigator." He decided to start a nonprofit organization that would treat aviation historical investigations and recoveries as a real science and discipline. He also remarried. Together, he and Patricia Thrasher, his new wife, launched TIGHAR: He's the executive director and spokesperson, while she runs background operations.

From the beginning, Gillespie was asked whether TIGHAR would tackle the most famous historical aviation mystery of all. By that time, the Japanese capture theory had been coursing through the culture for more than two decades. Plenty of debunking articles had been written, but few plausible alternative theories had been proposed. Gillespie wasn't tempted to join the discussion. "My response was always, look, she probably just ran out of gas," he said. "There's nothing substantive that can be done. The whole thing's a media circus, and I don't want any part of it."

Instead, TIGHAR focused on historic planes with some hope of recovery, such as the *L'Oiseau Blanc*, a French aircraft that disappeared in a transatlantic attempt 12 days before Charles Lindbergh's record-breaking flight in 1927. Gillespie calls the French flight "a hinge pin in history." If pilots Charles Nungesser and François Coli had been successful, he says, Lindbergh wouldn't have made his flight, rocketed to worldwide fame, inspired the burgeoning U.S. aviation industry, or made promoters like George Putnam ecstatic when they found a "Lady Lindbergh" in Amelia Earhart. All that energy would have shifted to France. Rumor and folklore had the plane crashing in Maine, so that's where Gillespie, Thrasher, and the growing roster of TIGHAR members looked (they are still looking, though now in Newfoundland).

But Earhart turned out to be unavoidable for a group focused on aircraft recovery. In 1988, one of the organization's new members, a Florida man named Tom Gannon, asked for an audience at TIGHAR headquarters in Delaware. He and a friend, Tom Willi, had a theory about Amelia Earhart that needed to be explained in person.

When the Toms (as fellow members subsequently dubbed them) arrived, they spread out maps and navigational charts on Gillespie and Thrasher's kitchen table (TIGHAR headquarters was their split-level home in Wilmington). "And to my surprise," said Gillespie, "they're not telling me tales of the South Pacific about what some marine saw on Saipan. They're talking about navigation. Celestial aerial navigation." Both men had been navigators during World War II, trained in the same methods Fred Noonan had used. They'd homed in on Earhart's last officially confirmed message—"We are on the line of position 157-337. We will repeat this message on 6210 kilocycles. Wait ... We are running north and south."

To the Toms, that communication meant Noonan had calculated a line of position bearing 157 degrees to the south-southeast and 337 degrees to north-northwest, and that it crossed through where he thought Howland Island should be. When it wasn't there, he assumed they'd flown too far south or too far north and directed Earhart to fly the plane along the line. Eventually they'd hit the island. But the Toms pointed out that flying north along the line was risky: If they missed Howland, they'd have no other place to land for thousands of miles. Flying south was the better bet, because the Phoenix Islands lay less than 400 miles away, with two of them—McKean and Gardner—not far off the line. Neither island was inhabited, but perhaps the beach or surrounding reef served as an emergency landing strip. An island would be a whole lot easier to search than an ocean.

"Oh man," thought Gillespie. "We've got to look into this." And so began an odyssey that would lure him and his TIGHAR colleagues into a search of more than three decades for Earhart and Noonan, clue after tantalizing clue leading them on.

Gillespie and Thrasher soon learned that, despite Gardner's isolation, many people had passed through the island. In 1929, the British steamer S.S. *Norwich City* ran aground on the island's reef during a tropical storm and burst into flames. Eleven crewmen were killed, though only three bodies were recovered and buried on the beach; 24 survivors were rescued four days later. The wreckage still looms over the island's northwestern reef.

In October 1937—three months after Earhart and Noonan disappeared—British colonial officers Harry Maude and Eric Bevington accompanied 19 Gilbertese and Ellice Islanders to Gardner Island. The team was scouting the uninhabited Phoenix Islands to see if they'd be fit for human settlement as part of the Phoenix Islands Settlement Scheme—dubbed PISS in a hint of English boarding school humor. The scheme's purpose was twofold: first, to ease overpopulation on the Gilbert and Ellice Islands (now Kiribati and Tuvalu, respectively) by arranging the colonization of uninhabited islands; and second, to develop a profitable copra, or dried coconut meat, industry. Expanding the British Empire was an added bonus.

The group spent three days on Gardner, walking its circumference. "Everywhere were fish, birds, and teeming life," wrote Bevington in his journal. "Overhead thousands of seabirds wheeled and soared—there were terns, frigates, boobies, and many other. The natives added to the general excitement; here were their own natural foods, in masses and easily caught." The soil was richer than that of their home islands: "The universal decision was that this island was paradise and ideal for habitation." And Bevington agreed with them: "There was truly the most amazing romantic feeling—an uninhabited coral island."

The first settlers arrived on Gardner in 1938, a few days before Christmas. A year later, some 60 people lived there. In 1944, in the midst of World War II, they were joined by the U.S. Coast Guard, which set up a long-range navigation (or LORAN) station on the island's southern tip. The Guardsmen left after the war ended, but the colonists stayed until 1963.

The TIGHAR founders also discovered that the Toms' theory was not a new one; indeed, it had been considered shortly after Earhart and Noonan disappeared. On July 7, 1937, the U.S.S. *Colorado* launched three planes from the ship's quarterdeck to survey the Phoenix Islands from the air. In choosing the search area, the ship's captain, Wilhelm Friedell, followed the same reasoning the Toms would decades later: "To the Air navigator with position in doubt and flying a land plane it is apparent that the thing to do would be to steer down the line toward the most probable land ... logical deduction pointed to the southeast quadrant" in relation to Howland.

And they did spot *something*. From the air over Gardner, one pilot saw what he described as signs of recent habitation. But despite "repeated circling and zooming," Senior Aviator Lt. John Lambrecht later wrote in a

Navy newsletter, "we were unable to elicit an answering wave." However, he never recorded what exactly he had seen, and Friedell didn't put personnel ashore to investigate further.

Other signs also pointed to the Phoenix Islands as a potential haven for the doomed plane. In the days after Earhart and Noonan disappeared, people around the world claimed to have heard Earhart's distress calls on their radio. Some of these were hoax reports, some the product of wishful thinking, and at least one the result of mishearing the radio program March of Time's dramatization of "an imaginary two-way conversation between Miss Earhart and the *Itasca,*" according to a contemporary report in the *New York Times*.

But a few signals appeared plausible. While the Electra's radio was able to transmit several hundred miles, depending on the frequency and time of day, harmonics—multiples of the transmission's frequency—send transmissions skipping across the ionosphere, far beyond its usual range. Pan Am, with its high-powered radio direction finders, could pinpoint where those signals came from. The credible ones tracked by the airline converged on the Phoenix Islands close to Gardner and McKean, 60 nautical miles to the northeast. The battery powering the radio would be inoperable if submerged; if those signals were Earhart's, the Electra must have been on land.

Then there was the Floyd Kilts story. After the roar of publicity from Fred Goerner's Saipan visits in 1960, Kilts piped up with a countertheory. He'd served in the Coast Guard, dismantling LORAN stations across the Pacific after World War II. In 1946, he was working on Gardner when a colonist told him that in 1938, a work crew had discovered a skeleton in the bush near the shoreline. Next to the bones lay a pair of women's shoes and a cognac bottle filled with fresh water. According to Kilts, the colonist said the young Irishman leading the crew had "thought of Amelia Earhart right away."

To Gillespie, Thrasher, and their fellow TIGHAR members, this assemblage of clues was enough to justify an expedition, and they began to make plans. Their biggest hurdle was raising money, but Gillespie had some ideas. On her final journey, Earhart was carrying in the Electra's nose thousands of souvenir covers—signed envelopes with stamps canceled at her stops. She sold them in advance to collectors via Gimbels department stores for five bucks a pop (more than $100 in today's dollars) to defray flight expenses. If the Electra was on Gardner, maybe the covers were there too. As proof that one of the world's greatest mysteries had been solved, they'd be worth considerably more than Earhart's original asking price.

Gillespie wasn't sure about the ethics of selling such a discovery. He called Tom King, an archaeologist he knew at the Advisory Council on Historic Preservation, a federal agency in Washington, D.C. King, a specialist in cultural resource management, was fine with the ethics (although he admitted that many in his field did not share his position on selling artifacts). But he advised Gillespie that paper was unlikely to survive very long on a tropical island.

Although he didn't give Gillespie the answer he wanted, King—restless at his desk job and intrigued by the proposed expedition—offered him something else: his considerable expertise. King's father had been in the U.S. Navy during World War II and played poker with a couple of guys involved in the search for Earhart. They all thought she'd crashed in the ocean; his dad referred to her as that "dizzy dame." King himself had conducted fieldwork throughout Micronesia, as well as on Saipan. If the expedition needed an archaeologist, he'd be delighted to go.

By 1989, Gillespie and Thrasher had assembled a 17-person team, including divers, archaeologists, and a doctor who brought a body bag. They'd chartered the *Pacific Nomad*, a dive boat that, somewhat ominously, had run aground on a reef in a previous incarnation. They'd obtained permission from the government of Kiribati to visit and excavate on the islands; an official named Kotuna Kaitara would accompany the TIGHAR team on the voyage. Kiribati had achieved independence from British colonial rule in 1979 and had given Gardner Island a new name: Nikumaroro.

The TIGHAR team planned to scout out Nikumaroro and nearby McKean, looking for the Electra or perhaps Earhart and Noonan's remains. The other islands in the Phoenix archipelago were too far from the 157-337 line of position, they thought, to be worth a visit. The explorers had 20 days to conduct their search; all they had to guide them were a few indistinct aerial photos and maps dating from a 1939 survey. But the island was small—four and a half miles long, and a mile and a half wide. "We should be able to go in there and walk all over it," thought King.

On September 18, 1989, they saw it: a low-lying island topped with a tangled wall of vegetation. Scores of seabirds rode the air currents above. The TIGHAR members experienced the terrain very differently than the colonial scouting party had more than 50 years earlier. To most of them (King was a notable exception), this wasn't a place to flourish. Rather, it guarded its secrets with fecundity: its dense forests, its skies laden with birds, and its hordes of crabs—legions of strawberry hermit crabs swarming on the beaches and football-size coconut crabs watching from among, and occasionally in, the trees.

"I still remember standing up on the fo'c'sle of the *Pacific Nomad* ... with Ric as we came up on Nikumaroro," said King, "and just looking at each other and saying, 'Oh, shit.'"

The *Pacific Nomad* anchored on the *Norwich City,* its wreckage a further warning of the island's implacability. The reef that had doomed the British encircled Nikumaroro, but the group found the rough landing channel the colonists had blasted through the coral and took their first steps on the island. "An occasional bird called; the crabs scuttled; otherwise the silence was total but for our footsteps," wrote King in his journal. "What a strange thing for a twentieth-century person to be somewhere where no one lives but that's full of life and the whispering ghosts of prior human habitants."

They began their search north of the colonial village ruins, near the Tatiman Passage, a mudflat between the ocean and lagoon. It seemed a likely place for a plane to land; perhaps a storm surge drove it into the foliage, where it remained hidden from the villagers. Gillespie and King directed the team to cut lines through the green mass every 15 feet, spending hours, then days, hacking away at scaevola and Tournefortia, the dense shrubs blanketing the island.

To entertain themselves during this grueling monotony, they began composing songs; if nothing else, King and Gillespie share a dexterity with words:

Scaevola 'n Tournefortia, I don't care which is which.
One's tall, the other's shortia; together they're a bitch.
They grab you by the throat and then they fall upon your head.
They clutch you by the crotch and make you wish that you were dead.
Oh, scaevola, oh won't you part for me?
'Cause if I don't find Amelia, Ric will never set me free.
[Sung to the tune of "Oh! Susanna" by Stephen Foster]

DESPITE THESE MINOR AMUSEMENTS, THE SITUATION began to seem dire. The temperature soared to 110 degrees, with no breeze among the trees. King became convinced that someone was going to die from heat exhaustion. After days of hot, futile effort, they hadn't found anything and tempers were frayed.

Victor Jione, the *Pacific Nomad*'s Rotuman captain, and Kaitara, the Kiribati representative, were becoming increasingly concerned. But the two men thought they knew what had made everything go wrong. When TIGHAR had disembarked, they hadn't paid their respects to the island's spirits. Nikumaroro had been named for the home of a legendary figure in Kiribati culture: Nei Manganibuka, a goddess of navigation who came from an island thick with towering buka trees, like this one. Perhaps they'd offended her. In any case, they needed to start over.

Six days after they'd landed, the TIGHAR team and the *Pacific Nomad*'s crew gathered on the beach. A crew member, the son of a Fiji island chieftain, asked the spirits for forgiveness. They passed around a bowl of *yagona,* or kava, a mildly narcotic drink common throughout the Pacific islands. Afterward, Kaitara instructed everyone to press wet sand into their cheeks so the island spirits would know they belonged—a practice TIGHAR continues to follow whenever visiting Nikumaroro.

Whether from spiritual intervention or an injection of humility, morale improved somewhat, though the group was no closer to solving the mystery of Earhart's disappearance. A small, isolated grave midway down the island piqued Gillespie's interest as possibly containing Noonan's or Earhart's remains; King thought it probably belonged to a Kiribati child, because it was marked by coral slabs similar to those they'd discovered in the colonial village. Among the settlement's ruins, they found aluminum parts that might have come from a plane: a flattened box, a rectangular riveted piece, a wheel, bits of a radio, and other fragments. But nothing showed that any of it came from the Electra rather than the copious World War II aviation wreckage across the Pacific. And they saw no sign of the plane itself.

McKean Island, a former site for guano mining (the seabird excrement is a valuable source of fertilizer), proved no better; in fact, it was a great deal worse. The passengers on the *Pacific Nomad* encountered the atoll's stench before it came into view. When they went ashore, recalled King, "we were completely enveloped in birds, riding the wind all around us, keeping pace, and shrieking at the top of their tiny but collectively quite powerful lungs ... tens of thousands blackening the sky and filling the air with their cries and the beating of their wings." The lagoon itself was a "noisome ooze" of guano. The island was practically barren, and the beach that appeared as a possible landing site on the charts had eroded irrevocably.

McKean was dismissed as Earhart and Noonan's final resting place. But Gillespie and the rest of the TIGHAR team hadn't given up on

Nikumaroro. It took them two years to raise the money for a return, but on October 1, 1991, TIGHAR's second Earhart expedition left Honolulu for a second attempt.

They'd learned some things since the last expedition. The flattened aluminum box they'd found in the colonial village had a part number on it, which allowed them to identify it as an air navigator's case for storing charts and books. Originally designed for a PBY flying boat, it showed signs of modification—perhaps for a Lockheed Electra. Was it Noonan's?

Meanwhile, publicity from their initial search had drawn out other servicemen who'd been stationed on the island. A PBY pilot remembered seeing colonists using an airplane control cable as fishing tackle; the fishermen told him the cable had come from plane wreckage that had been there when they first arrived. Two Coast Guardsmen recalled coming across a curious structure not far from their station at the island's southern tip: a cloth rigged on poles over a metal tank. They assumed some colonists had rigged it to catch rainwater—but the colonists said it wasn't them. Nearby was a campfire site, a pile of bird bones, and a five-gallon can. To the TIGHAR researchers, it sounded like a possible castaway camp.

The challenge for Gillespie and his team was investigating these leads—the water catcher, the small grave they'd discovered on the first expedition, the airplane parts in the village ruins—on an island that resisted easy exploration. King wasn't there to help; he and Gillespie had nearly come to blows on the last trip. King thought Gillespie was abrasive and haughty, while Gillespie thought King purposefully undermined him. According to Gillespie, the two men didn't speak for five years. Yet they are similar: Neither appreciates authority that isn't his own, and both are skilled storytellers. Janus-like, they would become the two public faces of TIGHAR.

Gillespie divided the team in half, directing one group to search for the water catcher on the island's windward side and the other to excavate the grave near the south end of the lagoon. The first group didn't find anything—not yet, not on this expedition—but those disinterring the grave uncovered something else entirely.

Manikaa Teuatabo, this expedition's Kiribati representative, oversaw the excavation, with the understanding that if the remains very clearly didn't belong to Earhart or Noonan, they would quickly and respectfully be reburied and the coral monuments restored. Tommy Love, a doctor and veteran of the previous expedition, oversaw the digging. But before he got started, he sat down to change his shoes, which had become drenched in the passage from their ship to the island. In doing so, he disturbed a crab that, in its rush to get away, upset a leaf, revealing something black. Love picked it up. It was a sliver of rubber imprinted with the name Cat's Paw Rubber Co USA.

"There's the heel of an old shoe over here," he announced. As the only medical personnel, Love went to work on the grave, while Gillespie scoured the area where he'd found the heel, recovering eight items—some rubber and some leather—that when pieced together sure resembled a shoe. The next day, another heel was found—this one, from someone with a bigger foot. One shoe from Earhart and a larger one from Noonan? It was the natural assumption to make.

Over in the village, Pat Thrasher, Gillespie's wife, stumbled on another promising find: a piece of aluminum punctured with rivet holes that looked like airplane skin to Gillespie and the other aviators on the trip. Once they got home, they could compare the rivet pattern to an image of the Lockheed Electra.

But before they left, they'd have to rebury the bones they'd unearthed. They weren't Earhart's. Or Noonan's. They belonged to a very small child. The coffin, the size of a small box, must have rotted long ago, leaving a space for the baby's remains to be cradled by roots of the island's trees.

THE TIGHAR TEAM MADE TWO MORE trips to Nikumaroro that decade. In 1996, they found the water-catcher site and an intriguing clearing shaped like the number seven; in 1997, a cyclone chased them off the island. But their biggest breakthroughs in the 1990s didn't happen on the island at all.

In the April 1992 issue of *Life* magazine, based on the tenuous evidence of the shoe heels, the aluminum panel, and the navigator's bookcase, Gillespie had declared the mystery solved: "Every possibility has been checked, every alternative eliminated. There is only one possible conclusion: we found a piece of Amelia Earhart's aircraft."

At first, the statement only generated disagreement and ridicule, and he soon let it drop. But the article was successful in flushing out an important source: Eric Bevington, who'd been on the colonial scouting trip in 1937. Although Bevington was highly skeptical of Gillespie's claim—after all, he'd been all around the island three months after Earhart disappeared and hadn't seen a plane—he offered to share what he knew.

Gillespie and Thrasher traveled to the cottage in the south of England where Bevington and his wife, Enid, had retired after a life in the British Empire's employ. They read Bevington's journals, and Thrasher took pictures of the images in his photo album. Their interest flared when they learned Bevington had encountered signs of previous inhabitation, but waned when he couldn't remember the details so many years later. Maybe it was a bivouac. Maybe he saw it at Aukaraime South, where they'd discovered the shoe. But he couldn't be sure. They wouldn't recognize the significance of what he'd shared with them for 18 years.

Peter McQuarrie's discovery offered more immediate gratification. In 1997, the TIGHAR member had traveled to Tarawa, the island capital of Kiribati, to do research for a separate World War II project. Fiji had been the seat of Britain's colonial power in the Pacific, but after the empire's breakup, documents related to the Gilbert and Phoenix Islands ended up in the Kiribati National Archives. What McQuarrie found there appeared to echo Coast Guardsman Kilts's story—and justify TIGHAR's fixation on the coral atoll.

In a series of telegrams, Gerald Gallagher, the PISS officer in charge on Gardner, recounted a strange tale. It began on September 23, 1940, when he sent a puzzling message to a British colonial officer on Tarawa: "Please obtain from Koata (Native Magistrate Gardner on way to Central Hospital) a certain bottle alleged to have been found near skull discovered on Gardner Island. Grateful you retain bottle in safe place for present and ask Koata not to talk about skull which is just possibly that of Amelia Earhardt [*sic*]."

Later that day, Gallagher sent a report filling in the details for the resident commissioner of the Gilbert and Ellice Islands Colony. Workers had discovered the skull a few months earlier, he said, and hurriedly buried it. When Gallagher found out, he had the area searched and discovered more bones (including teeth and a lower jaw), part of a shoe, and a sextant box. He thought the skeleton was probably female—he did not say why—and that the shoe definitely belonged to a woman.

Gallagher elaborated further in a telegram sent October 6: Coconut crabs had scattered the bones, which were found 100 feet from the high tide line. The shoe, which was really just part of a sole, appeared to have been a "stoutish walking shoe or heavy sandal." The person must have been alive when cast ashore because they'd found evidence of fire and birds being killed and eaten. Eleven days later, he added that the bones had been found on the island's southeast corner. "Body had obviously been lying under a 'ren' tree," he reported. "Remains of fire, turtle and dead birds appear to indicate life." (Ren refers to the low-growing Tournefortia tree that so tormented the TIGHAR teams.)

Nothing else—neither additional bones nor personal effects—had been found. Gallagher and his work crew had encountered the same difficulties that the TIGHAR teams would face decades later: "Organised search of area for remaining bones would take several weeks as crabs move considerable distances and this part of island is not yet cleared." Instead, he had a coffin built from the easily worked wood of a kanawa tree that had grown "on the edge of the lagoon, not very far from the spot where the deceased was found." On December 27, the coffin and the sextant box were loaded onto the R.C.S. *Nimanoa,* destined for the High Commission office in Suva.

But the voyage of the Gardner bones didn't end there.

Engineer and dogged TIGHAR member Kenton Spading traced a path from the Tarawa records through New Zealand's national archives to the Foreign and Commonwealth Office records center in Hanslope Park, northwest of London. There, a helpful librarian tracked down a file called "Skeleton. Human: - Finding of, on Gardner Island." Inside was the report of a Dr. Hoodless, a colonial medical officer on Fiji who examined the bones.

"All the bones are very weather-beaten," Hoodless wrote, "and have been exposed to the open air for a considerable time." He counted 13 of them: skull; mandible, with four teeth; part of the right scapula; the first thoracic vertebra; part of a rib; left humerus; right radius; right innominate (hip) bone; right femur; left femur; right tibia; right fibula; and the right scaphoid bone of the foot. They belonged to a middle-aged person, he thought, "probably not that of a pure South Sea Islander." Perhaps they came from a "short, stocky, muscular European, or even a half-caste." But one thing was certain, he claimed: "From the half sub-pubic angle of the right innominate bone, the 'set' of the two femora, and the ratio of the circumferences of the long bones to their individual lengths it may be definitely stated that the skeleton is that of a MALE."

The all caps hit like a deliberate insult, given how close the TIGHAR members thought they were to solving this decades-old mystery. Rather than feeling deflated, though, TIGHAR's single-minded researchers began to question Hoodless's qualifications. He was a doctor, sure, but his specialty was in tropical medicine, and "the forensic study of human skeletons wasn't a terribly advanced science in 1940," King wrote. But Hoodless's conclusions soon became irrelevant. Tucked away in the Hanslope archives was another gold mine: the doctor's original handwritten measurements of the cranium and the long bones. Running those measurements through a modern analysis would provide a much stronger sense of who those bones belonged to.

In 1999, University of Georgia forensic anthropologist Karen Burns was recruited to examine the measurements using Fordisc, a software program that estimates the race, sex, and stature of unknown human skeletons by comparing the remains to a database of skeletal measurements whose origins are known. But even this sophisticated program would not be as definitive as Hoodless claimed to be. It only offers probabilities that the unknown bones match the characteristics of known ones.

When Burns got the results, she called Gillespie and asked if he was sitting down. He sat. The best match for the skull, she told him, was a female of northern European ethnic origin. Her colleague Richard Jantz, who had co-created Fordisc, confirmed her analysis. "The bones," King wrote later, were "more likely female than male, more likely of European than of Pacific Island origin, and most likely somewhere between 5 feet 6 inches and 5 feet 9 inches tall." Earhart was five feet and seven or eight inches.

Of course, they still didn't have the bones. Nor did they know whether Hoodless measured them accurately or from the same points as modern forensic scientists. But presumably the rest of the bones—193 or so of them—lay somewhere on Nikumaroro. They just had to figure out where.

IN 1996, A SMALL TEAM FROM TIGHAR, including Gillespie, had investigated the seven-shaped clearing on the island's windward side that they'd spotted in early aerial photos. Nearby, they'd discovered the water catcher the Coast Guardsmen had mentioned: a rectangular steel tank, with the faint words TARAWA POLICE painted on it. Scattered around it were coconut shells, halved apparently to serve as drinking vessels. Ten feet away in one direction was a ren tree with bird bones scattered beneath;

20 feet in the other direction was a two-foot-deep hole with a .30 caliber rifle cartridge at the bottom. The cartridge probably came from the Coast Guard—the young men had entertained themselves with target practice—and the tank from the colonists. The site, Gillespie thought, wasn't relevant to their search.

After the discovery of Gallagher's bone records, Gillespie and King, who'd negotiated a truce, decided to revisit the clearing, which they'd christened the Seven Site. Nikumaroro, roughly lozenge-shaped, runs at an angle from the northwest to the southeast. The Seven Site was situated on the northern side of the island's southeastern tip, where Gallagher had said the bones were found, and some 100 feet from the high tide line, where he said they were positioned. There was a hole there—maybe not a well, but a place where the skull might have been buried and later unearthed. And they themselves had found bird bones there, under a ren tree. They needed to go back.

In 2001, a TIGHAR team returned to the site, focusing at first on what they dubbed the Skull Hole and retreating to the relatively cool ridge above to rest. One day while taking a break, King—sweaty, thirsty, and tired—plopped his backpack to the ground. Only it wasn't on the ground; it was on something strange: a strip of bony material that opened up into four points at the end. Upon closer inspection, he realized it was part of the shell of a sea turtle. Gallagher's account said the bones were discovered near the "remains of fire, turtle and dead birds." They'd already found the dead birds. Now they had the turtle.

The rest area became an excavation site. They soon discovered five patches of burned coral rubble, the fire remains Gallagher had mentioned. They excavated three of them. They found animal bones there too. The fish bones turned out to come from reef fish, which are relatively easy to catch by hand. The bird bones came from frigate birds, which nested in nearby trees. And the shell came from a green turtle, which lay their eggs on the adjacent beach. They also found two piles of clamshells mixed with charcoal. Some had been smashed, apparently to get at the meat, while others were chipped along the edges. Pacific Islanders don't open clams this way; they slit the adductor muscles while the shellfish are still gape-mouthed in the water. It probably wasn't a local who smashed those shells.

They'd found a campsite, possibly of a non-native castaway. But they hadn't found any bones.

Over the next 14 years, whenever they could raise enough money, a TIGHAR team returned to Nikumaroro, discovering several suggestive 1930s-era American artifacts at the Seven Site. In 2007, they found a Talon zipper pull, glass from a compact mirror with a wafer of rouge, the broken end of a pocketknife, and two partially melted bottles upright among the traces of a fire. Perhaps the castaway had used them to boil water. In 2010, they did an extensive excavation, recovering shards from a nearly complete small glass jar, which TIGHAR researchers tentatively traced to Dr. C. H. Berry's Freckle Ointment. Earhart *hated* her freckles, it was said; the salve used mercury to fade them. What they didn't find, despite all their work, were bones or teeth.

They needed to try something new.

CHAPTER TEN

1924–28: "A CONSUMING VOCATION"

Amelia's move back to Boston in 1924 had started as a grand adventure: She'd wanted to fly across the country in her plane. But the sinus infection that periodically plagued her since a bout of pneumonia in Toronto at the war's end thwarted her plans; altitude changes would be too painful. Plus her mother, reeling from the divorce from Edwin, was coming with her, and didn't relish the long, uncomfortable flight.

Instead, Amelia sold the plane and bought a bright yellow Kissel Kar. She and Amy set out for a road trip across the country—a novel (and dusty) thing to do in the 1920s. When her mother asked her which way they would go, Amelia replied, "I am going to surprise you." Driving mostly on unpaved roads, they visited many of the continent's new national parks—heading north to Sequoia, Yosemite, and Crater Lake, into Canada to see Lake Louise and Banff, and then south to Yellowstone.

By the time they reached Medford, the Boston suburb where Muriel had settled into a teaching job at a junior high, they'd covered some 7,000 miles and Amelia was in agony from her sinuses. She'd had an operation in Los Angeles to drain them, but it didn't work (and she didn't pay for it). Within days of their arrival, she'd checked in to Massachusetts General Hospital for a procedure to remove a piece of bone from the troublesome sinus passage. Her recovery was long, but, her sister noted, for the first time in four years she was "entirely free from headache and nasal discomfort."

Meanwhile, she was casting about for what to do next. She'd dismissed medicine as a career, but she wanted to return to Columbia, where she'd been so intellectually satisfied and successful. This time, with the mechanical experience she'd gained from piloting and her exposure to her fiancé Sam Chapman's career, she thought she'd study engineering. In the spring semester of 1925, she enrolled in two classes: algebra and physics. But by April, she'd withdrawn from Columbia and moved back to Boston. She'd run out of money.

That summer, she tried college again, signing up for a trigonometry class at Harvard, which allowed women to attend during summer school. In the fall, she hoped to attend the more egalitarian Massachusetts Institute of Technology, which was developing an aeronautical engineering department. But her application for a scholarship was rejected; she couldn't afford to go without it.

"No, I did not get into M.I.T. as planned, owing to financial difficulties," she wrote to a friend. "No, I cannot come to New York, much, ah, much as I should like owing to when I leave Boston I think I'll never come back."

Aviation had opened up the world to her in Los Angeles; without it, she'd lost her sense of purpose. Further education and flight seemed to be out of reach. All she could hope for was a job to ease her money woes.

She didn't appear to consider one option. Sam, Amelia's faithful fiancé, had followed her back to Massachusetts, to his hometown of Marblehead, where he took a job at the Boston Edison electric company. She could have remedied her financial situation—and, in many people's eyes, her aimlessness—by marrying him. He was eager, she loved him, and society expected women to eschew careers for marriage and motherhood. But Amelia had witnessed the dangers of dependency in her parents' relationship and refused such a scenario, even if it appeared to offer stability. She wanted a life of purpose, and she couldn't imagine finding it in a purely domestic existence.

Instead, she took a job teaching English through the state's university extension program, which served some 28,000 immigrants in cities across Massachusetts. Her classes were scheduled all over the Boston area, costing her a good deal of time and money to get to them: "She didn't enjoy it too much," Muriel recalled. "The meager pay and transportation allowance barely allowed her to break even."

Amelia sought a teaching position limited to one location and found one at an Amesbury automobile body manufacturing plant, where she taught "an office class in the Miller Course of Correct English" to the company's many foreign workers. She only lasted a few weeks.

Next, she tried working as a nurse companion at a mental hospital. Although her sympathies for those with mental illness had improved, she was not suited for a menial job with little hope for advancement. And again, the pay was poor.

In 1926, at 29 years old, she found her way to the Women's Educational and Industrial Union (WEIU), which had been founded the previous century "to increase fellowship among women and to promote the best practical methods for securing their educational, industrial, and social advancement." Staffed entirely by women, WEIU offered social services, including legal advice and job training, as well as an appointment bureau with career counseling and placement services in business and professional positions.

In what may have been a mark of her desperation, Amelia lied extensively on her application, according to one biographer—claiming four years at Hyde Park High School in Chicago instead of one, three years at Columbia University instead of three semesters, and "five years of tutoring experience as well as class work," when she'd taught for only one. She also took two years off her age. Sam contributed an ambivalent character reference, describing the woman he'd been engaged to for three years as "all right." He continued, "I have known her four years and she is a very dear friend of mine." He declared she was "a good scholar and is capable in any field that she may claim."

Nevertheless, Amelia charmed her WEIU interviewer, who jotted in her notes that she was "an extremely interesting girl—very unusual vocabulary; is a philosopher—wants to write—does write." Separately, across the top of the application, the interviewer scrawled "Holds a sky pilots license?" This fascinating young woman was someone the WEIU would be very happy to help.

When asked on the application to list "Work Desired," Amelia had written, "Teaching English to Foreigners, Hostess, Anything connected with an Aeronautical Concern." The WEIU appointment bureau sent her to Denison House.

DENISON HOUSE WAS A SETTLEMENT HOUSE, so called because it was part of a movement—beginning with Toynbee Hall in London and including Hull House in Chicago—that sought to expose immigrants and the poor to middle-class values by having college-educated people "settle" in their neighborhoods. The movement's leaders soon recognized that their new neighbors needed more concrete help than mere proximity to privileged people, and switched to offering social services instead. Denison House primarily served Boston's Chinese and Syrian communities by providing education, medical care, and citizenship preparation, as well as culture, arts, and sports activities, especially for the children.

Amelia loved it.

Marion Perkins, Denison's "head worker," put Amelia—despite her lack of experience—in charge of adult education, which included English and citizenship classes. Soon Amelia had started a club for Syrian mothers and taken over the girls' program. She began driving children to their medical appointments in her yellow Kissel Kar. She brought teenagers home to her mother and sister in West Medford for suburban picnics. She oversaw the kindergarten. She organized a basketball team for Chinese girls and learned to fence alongside them. Within the year, she'd moved into Denison as a full-time worker.

Sam was dismayed that social work was taking Amelia further away from his hopes for marriage, though the couple was still engaged. However, the women in Amelia's life heartily approved. "It was obvious to Miss Perkins, as it was to Mother and me, that Amelia had found a consuming vocation," wrote Muriel. "Amelia gave of herself as she did at the hospital in Toronto. Her payment was the devotion of the children and the respect and friendship of their parents."

Two years into her new career as a social worker, Amelia joined the board of Denison House and served as a delegate to the Conference of the National Federation of Settlements, where she was received "as one of the most thoughtful and promising of the younger group." When she was asked what kept her in this particular line of work, she answered "self-preservation." Rejecting "old ideas of the inevitability of suffering" and embracing "the satisfaction of any scientific work which opens unexplored fields and presents problems to solve," she declared, "what shuts out the happiness for some does so for me and mine." Amelia had found her purpose.

She'd also found her way back to flying. Bert Kinner, proprietor of the Los Angeles field where she learned to fly and designer of her beloved Kinner Airster, asked her to be his East Coast representative, demonstrating his plane to customers in exchange for the use of it. Through him, she met an architect who was building his own airfield near Boston. With a small purchase of stock, she joined the new operation's board. "As a reawakening of my active interest in aviation," she signed up for the Boston chapter of the National Aeronautic Association, where she became a vocal advocate for making the city more "air-minded." For her pains, they made her vice president.

Amelia wrote about flying for *Bostonian* magazine—completely charming the Brahmin editor—and blanketed the city with passes to a carnival fundraiser for Denison House that she dropped from the sky. Soon, her sister reported, she became known around town "as a woman who could not only fly well, but who also knew about engine performance, tensile strengths, and something about instrument flying."

When she got the call that would change her life, she was as content as she'd ever been.

CHAPTER ELEVEN

CASTAWAY: TIGHAR BRINGS IN THE DOGS

By 2015, the TIGHAR team still hadn't found Earhart's bones or plane on Nikumaroro.* Ric Gillespie continued to put forward TIGHAR's theory—or as he and his colleagues preferred to call it, the "Nikumaroro hypothesis"—as the most logical explanation for what happened to Amelia Earhart and Fred Noonan. The aviators flew south on the line 157-337 looking for Howland Island, he argued. When they spotted Nikumaroro instead, Earhart landed the Electra on the deceptively flat reef near the island's northern tip. The plane was likely

* In 2013, Timothy Mellon—heir to the Mellon family banking fortune—sued TIGHAR and Gillespie, claiming they'd located the Electra on a 2010 expedition. TIGHAR hid the discovery, Mellon charged, to secure funding for more expeditions, including the 2012 voyage to which he'd donated more than $1 million in stocks. The U.S. District Court dismissed the case after "Mr. Mellon's own experts would not confirm that the footage [from the 2010 expedition] proved the plane had been found." Mellon's appeal was denied.

damaged by the rough coral, but the fliers were able to broadcast from the radio until rising tides floated the plane away, leaving them marooned on the coral atoll where they died as castaways, at least one of them at the Seven Site on the other end of the island. That's what happened, he insisted.

Yet, despite decades of research, 12 expeditions, and a substantial collection of suggestive evidence, TIGHAR had no proof. But Gillespie and his team wouldn't give up. They knew they were right; all they needed was something tangible to persuade the doubting public. Like gamblers on a losing streak convinced their luck was about to turn, they'd gotten too close too many times to walk away.

Tom King had an idea. Well, two ideas. The first: TIGHAR should join forces with an adventure travel group to bring the first ever large cruise ship to Nikumaroro. He wanted other people to have the chance to experience the deserted island he loved. As a bonus, the passengers would cover most of the cost of chartering the boat—and serve as enthusiastic, if inexperienced, free labor. In June 2015, 60-plus passengers and TIGHAR members boarded the *Fiji Princess* for a voyage to Nikumaroro, arranged by Betchart Expeditions. They were on the island for four days: long enough to participate in some amateur archaeology and to see where Earhart and Noonan died, maybe—and for King to lay the groundwork for his second idea.

He wanted to bring dogs.

Actually, it wasn't his idea, though he eagerly seized upon it. Archaeologist Dawn Johnson had come up with it the previous year, when she was working with the Institute for Canine Forensics (ICF) to locate Indigenous burial grounds in northern California. She'd been impressed, if not awestruck, by how the organization's historic human remains–detecting dogs had sniffed out centuries-old sites without disturbing the burials. A TIGHAR member since she'd recovered her uncle's remains from a World War II fighter plane crash in Belgium, Johnson wondered if the dogs could do the same with the missing bones on Nikumaroro.

But she wasn't sure how well the dogs, who are trained to detect volatile organic compounds (VOCs) released by the decomposition of buried human remains, would function amid the island's tropical conditions. Weather, temperature, and the environment determine how detectable those VOCs are. Scent is strongest in moist soil, when the ground temperature is relatively mild—between 40 and 85 degrees Fahrenheit—and weakest when bones have been exposed to sun, wind, and heat. On Nikumaroro, the ground temperature soars well past 100 degrees, and dry coral rubble forms the foundation of its soil.

Johnson decided she needed to test the dogs before ICF went to the considerable trouble of transporting them to the isolated island. At the end of the cruise, which saw enthusiastic passenger participation but no mystery-solving discoveries, she collected 13 soil samples from locations across Nikumaroro: six from known colonial-era graves, four from the Seven Site, and the rest from areas too close to water to be burial sites. In August 2015, after her return, Johnson invited four certified teams of dogs (mostly border collies) and handlers to gather at a shuttered summer camp in the Santa Cruz Mountains. Johnson had poured small piles from each soil sample throughout the camp's cafeteria; two human ribs were placed in the middle, a macabre control to make sure the dogs could catch the scent of human remains in the drafty room. One by one, the handlers brought in their dogs.

The results were mixed: Several dogs followed eddies of scent into the cafeteria's corners, away from the soil. One dog "alerted"—a conditioned response exhibited when it has identified a trained-for odor—on soil from a known grave, nosing the pile thoroughly, then sitting and looking at her handler expectantly. Two others detected scent on separate Seven Site samples. The test wasn't definitive, yet it wasn't a total failure either. For Johnson and King, it was enough. On the next expedition to Nikumaroro, the dogs were coming too.

ON JUNE 28, 2017, PASSENGERS ON the M.V. *Reef Endeavour* saw a blur on the horizon: a scribble marring the infinite line bounding the Pacific. But as the cruise ship drew nearer, Nikumaroro's outline sharpened into swaying trees and birds banking in the sea breezes. The group hadn't seen land in days.

The *Reef Endeavour* was a thousand miles off its usual course of ferrying holidaymakers around the lush isles of Fiji. But for many passengers, this was a vacation. They'd signed up for a three-week voyage to one of the most remote areas in the Pacific, where they would try to solve, as Betchart's brochure for this second expedition put it, "One of the Greatest Mysteries of the 20th Century." They were a well-heeled bunch—many of them retired, all well traveled and eager to spend steamy tropical days scrabbling through coral rubble for clues to Amelia Earhart's fate.

This trip would be longer and more ambitious than the 2015 cruise. Four dog teams were on board: an alert pack of border collies who weathered the ocean voyage with better spirits than some passengers. The ship would anchor offshore for eight days, to allow enough time for the dogs to work their noses across the Seven Site and—if they found anything—for the archaeologists and tourist volunteers to excavate the spots where they'd scented human remains. Tom King would lead the archaeologists, along with Fred Hiebert, the National Geographic Society's archaeologist in residence. Two National Geographic videographers and a writer for *National Geographic* magazine (that would be me) had joined the expedition as well, ready to capture the big discovery in what was being billed as the best chance yet to finally solve this alluring riddle.

Watching the ship's approach from an upper deck, King and Hiebert were subdued—Hiebert because he was gazing upon Nikumaroro for the first time, and King because he knew what challenges lay ahead. Over the years, TIGHAR had developed a protocol for arriving at the island. The only relatively safe place to go ashore was the landing channel, where the colonists had blasted a motorboat-wide cut through the reef. From there, expedition veterans John Clauss and Andrew McKenna led machete-wielding members of the ship's crew in clearing a path from the shore to the lagoon. There, small boats would be stashed to transport teams to the Seven Site.

Meanwhile, the dogs—outfitted in blue life jackets and booties to protect their paws from the sharp reef and hot sand—were loaded onto a tender, one of the small boats that would ferry passengers between the island (where they explored) and the ship (where they ate and slept). Johnson wanted to take them to the small cluster of graves where she'd gathered soil samples during the 2015 trip. If the dogs alerted on these known burials, they could work in tropical conditions. If they didn't, their handlers had brought them on this long voyage for nothing.

As the tender bumped over the waves to the landing channel, the dogs thrust their noses into the air, nostrils flaring with the onslaught of new odors. Their handlers were more apprehensive, clamping their knees around their dogs' slim bodies and holding tight to the handles on the back of their life jackets. These dogs were their babies, their work partners, their multiyear investments (the dogs flew first-class to Fiji; no way would their handlers put them in a plane's hold). "This is way beyond anything we've ever done," said Lynne Engelbert, whose border collie, Piper, had quickly become the ship's lapdog.

The cemetery was 20 or so meters into the jungle north of the landing channel; Clauss and McKenna's team had come through earlier to clear a path. John Grebenkemper, ICF's field coordinator, measured the ground temperature: It was 107 degrees Fahrenheit. Scent begins to dissipate at around 80 degrees, and the dogs, with their thick coats, had never experienced anything like this heavy, wet tropical heat. Despite quick splashes in the surf along the reef, their tongues were lolling.

At least there was a breeze on the beach. Within the tiny cemetery, the air was thick and close. The handlers went into the newly opened space with their dogs one by one: Engelbert with Piper, Grebenkemper with his dog Kayle, Lynne Angeloro with Berkeley, and Miranda Krebs with Marcy. The grave sites—marked traditionally by coral slabs—were barely discernible beneath piles of branches slashed from the surrounding brush to clear space.

But all four dogs alerted on the hidden grave sites, sitting or lying down where they sniffed human remains buried beneath them. "We've solved one problem," said Grebenkemper. "Scent survives in coral."

The dogs' first foray onto Nikumaroro had gone smoothly. The return to the *Reef Endeavour* amid the Pacific's deep swells was another story. As skilled as the tender's pilot was, he could not align the small boat with the ship's dive platform; the ship would rise with the crest of each wave while the tender sank into the trough.

Krebs, an experienced rescue worker, took charge. Balancing at the prow of the boat, she grabbed each dog in turn to hand them—toss them, really—over to the crew on the ship during the brief moments when ship and boat met at the same point on the swell. The rest of the passengers—myself included—had to leap across the gap between ship and boat, trusting in the sea legs and strong arms of the crew to pull us on board if we came up short. Miraculously, everyone made it—the three other handlers, the videographers with all their camera gear, the archaeologists, and me. I wasn't frightened until afterward, when the image of wiry, dark-haired Krebs bracing herself on the boat resurfaced. The height of the swells could be measured by whether her head or feet matched the level of the ship's diving platform.

The next day, the first party going ashore dutifully stepped in a bucket of disinfectant on the lower deck of the *Reef Endeavour* to prevent any foreign biology (beyond humans and dogs) from invading Nikumaroro's pristine shores. The coral atoll is part of the Phoenix Islands Protected Area (PIPA), one of the largest marine sanctuaries in the world; PIPA representative Kaono Koura had come along to make sure the expedition didn't do anything to harm the environment. Next, the island-bound group boarded one of the ship's tenders perched on the boat lift—a safer alternative to the diving platform—and waited to be lowered into the water.

After landing, the team—Clauss, King, Hiebert, Johnson, and dog handlers Grebenkemper and Angeloro with Kayle and Berkeley, as well as the National Geographic journalists—adjusted their packs and plunged into the forest's shade. We followed a trail through the buka trees that TIGHAR members had dubbed the Gallagher Highway, after Gerald Gallagher, the colonial administrator who'd reported the discovery of bones in 1940 "on South East corner of island ... under a 'ren' tree." For the dog handler and National Geographic teams, it was their first immersion into the life of the island.

Nikumaroro is cacophonous. The surf is audible throughout the island, though among the trees it resonates in your bones like a bass, playing a clef below the wind riffing across the tops of the buka trees and coconut fronds. As we wound our way through the buka forest toward the lagoon, pairs of fairy terns—snowy white in a place that had never seen such precipitation—hovered in the air above, scolding the trespassers. They knew humans didn't belong, but they weren't afraid.

The new arrivals, on the other hand, weren't sure what the fauna would do. Would those beautiful birds swoop down if people neared their nests? And what about the crabs? There were so many of them. On the beach, swarms (tens and even hundreds) of strawberry hermits picked their way among discarded palm fronds or anything else left on the ground. Coconut crabs, the island's giants, haunted the path; TIGHAR lore has it that team members on an early expedition saw one in a tree, peeling a rat like an orange.

After some 20 minutes of trekking, we made it through the forest unscathed. When we reached the lagoon, the sky opened up—or so it seemed, because its blue waters matched the Pacific heavens above. Boobies nested under palm trees with their chicks—fuzzy, black-footed, awkward. The group stepped carefully through the warm water to board the dinghies

Clauss and his team had ported over the day before. (The lagoon is a blacktip shark nursery, but no one mentioned that until later; the silty water near the shore camouflaged their fins.)

From the lagoon's shore, Nikumaroro's volcanic origins are clear. The waters fill the caldera while the scant hills (just a few meters tall) mark the pinnacle of the submerged mountain, which plummets thousands of feet to the ocean floor. The island is a mile and a half wide, but the lagoon, at more than two miles long, takes up most of it. You'd think the relatively narrow strip encircling the water could be quickly searched for a plane or bones, but the place bursts with life—life that tends to overwhelm and undermine anything left behind.

As the dinghies zoomed toward the island's southeastern corner—weaving around the coral heads Clauss had marked with inflatable water toys—several birds, mostly boobies, flew behind, surfing whatever air the boats were leaving in their wake. Or perhaps they thought the people were fishing and might toss scraps overboard. They can't have encountered many humans.

The sun, up perhaps an hour or two, was gentle, softly burnishing palm fronds in the forest that edged the lagoon. The water was pale, and the sky was too. No one spoke.

The landing on the lagoon's far end was far more prosaic. For reasons known only to the tides and currents, much of the island's guano collected here, making it a squelchy, stinky walk from the shallow water where the tenders anchored at the narrow beach leading to the Seven Site.

A path had been cleared to the site's antechamber—a shady spot in the buka forest on the edge of the unforgiving scaevola bush's territory. It was like being at the entrance to a cave: You had shelter but also fresh air, a view, and a clear way out. But once you entered the cave, it became your entire world.

The Seven Site lay up a small rise from the encampment along a single-file path slashed through scaevola. At the center was a ren tree more wide than tall, and looming on all sides was the impenetrable green wall of scaevola. The sky was visible through the ren tree's branches, but the air was still. It seemed a miserable place to die.

But this is where King, Gillespie, and the rest of the TIGHAR team believed Amelia Earhart passed away—under the tree, marooned on a deserted island, starving, dehydrated, and possibly injured. And this is where the dogs were going to search for her bones.

"THE IDEA IS TO LET THE DOGS follow their noses," said King. Each dog and handler team would work the site separately to avoid biasing the others: Angeloro and Grebenkemper with their dogs on this first day, Krebs and Engelbert on the next.

Angeloro, a garrulous woman, brought shy Berkeley into the site first, taking off his leash and collar so he wouldn't get caught in the brush.

"Show me," she said, and Berkeley went to work, nose down and ears forward, intent on following an erratic trail invisible to humans. It brought him closer and closer to the ren tree. Finally, at its trunk, he lay down, looking expectantly at Angeloro.

"Show me," she said again. He got up and lay down in the same spot. He'd alerted right under the ren tree, the location that appears similar to what Gallagher described so long ago.

Susanne Martin, the expedition's doctor and a dog handler in training, logged the time, temperature, and GPS location and planted a bright orange flag on the spot.

"I took him away four times," said Angeloro, "but he kept coming back. That's 1 to 2 on the scale."

The handlers rate alerts on a scale of 1 to 4. One is the strongest—the dog goes back to it—while 4 means the dog doesn't officially alert, but seems to have smelled something based on its body language.

Grebenkemper, a retired physicist, brought in his dog, little Kayle. She sat down right under the ren tree.

King and Johnson were waiting impatiently outside the site when Grebenkemper officially delivered the news. "Under the big ren tree, we've had three solid alerts," he told them.

The team was elated. Johnson and Hiebert broke into song, while King kept repeating, "Well, that is fantastic."

Grebenkemper hurried to caution them. "Alerts may not be as precise as we would like," he said. "I would not dig where the flags are." Scent travels along strange, convoluted paths, following roots and fissures in the ground. And dogs can detect the lingering scent of human bones long after the bones themselves have decomposed. There was no guarantee that digging under the ren tree would uncover anything. Nevertheless, now they knew that a human—whether Amelia Earhart, Fred Noonan, or someone else—had died or been buried nearby.

However, the alerts needed to be confirmed. The next day, Krebs brought Marcy to the site, where she let her roam. Marcy also alerted at the base of the ren tree.

"Find another," said Krebs.

Marcy alerted behind the ren, at the same spot where Kayle had. Krebs, who'd maintained an air of skepticism about the whole Earhart project, was satisfied: "That was a lot of nose and a solid down." She entered the flag locations into the GPS and brought Marcy back to the antechamber for water and her reward—a vigorous game of tug-of-war.

Next, Engelbert brought in Piper. She gave her dog water before letting her loose at the site. "That's to get the mucus membranes nice and moist," she explained. Piper alerted at the same spots.

All four dogs signaled that human remains had lain somewhere near the ren tree.

Now it was up to the TIGHAR team to find the bones.

"WE BROUGHT IN NEW TECHNOLOGY—the dogs—but now we need to rely on old technology: human eyes, fallible human eyes connected to human brains," said King.

The excavation's leaders were also relying on their understanding of the island's most fearsome occupants: coconut crabs. As the largest land invertebrates on the planet, the crabs can measure up to three feet across and weigh in at more than nine pounds; their claws exert more force than most animals' bites. During the day, when the TIGHAR team did most of its work, the crabs were easily avoided. Those that emerge from their burrows into the intense tropical heat spend their time in the shade of coconut palms or among the branches of ren trees.

But at night? "The crabs close in on you," said Clauss, who has spent several nights on the island. "If you shine a flashlight, outside the shadow ring there are a thousand crabs." Or so it can seem. He learned not to sleep on the ground. The castaway may have had no other option.

When Gallagher described the bone discovery site, he observed that "coconut crabs had scattered many bones." The omnivorous crustaceans—who earned their nickname of "robber crabs"—eat coconuts, fallen fruit, birds, rodents, other crabs, and carrion. TIGHAR teams have performed several experiments to see if the crabs would drag bones back to their burrows. In one, they brought a lamb carcass to the island and used time-lapse photography to show what happened to it. Crabs—coconut crabs plus the smaller, more numerous strawberry hermit variety—swarmed the body, removing most of the flesh within a week and carting off the bones.

"This tells us crabs drag bones," said King, "but it doesn't tell us how far." A year after the experiment, they discovered some bones had been dragged 60 feet from the body. They never accounted for all the remains.

King hypothesized that after Earhart died, the crabs consumed her flesh and dragged her bones into their burrows—except, of course, the 13 bones Gallagher's team discovered.

The primary hurdle to recovering the remaining bones was the composition of the island itself. The pieces of coral rubble underlying everything looked an awful lot like bone fragments, a fact that frustrated the searchers beyond measure. "We're looking literally for a finger in a haystack," said Nancy Farrell, an archaeologist specializing in the Pacific who always wore purple, despite the tropical heat.

The team—a rotating cast of cruise passengers, ship's crew in their nautical striped shirts and blue shorts, and professional archaeologists—sat with legs splayed near each flag marking the dogs' alerts. With hands and trowels, they went through the soil, which was flecked with tiny brown ren seeds and riddled with coral rubble.

Farrell and Clauss sifted the material with screens. When something looked vaguely bone-like, they tapped it with a big knife (Clauss) or a trowel (Farrell). If it clinked, it was coral. If it didn't, it was bone. It always clinked.

Johnson tried using water. She had people gather bucketfuls from the reef on the far side of the ridge. Then she dumped shovelfuls of earth into the buckets. She removed anything that floated—coral and other organic materials—and sifted through the sediment at the bottom. She also came up empty.

The amateurs optimistically brought any suggestive material to the experts, which included Dave Grant, a gruff osteologist who favored Hawaiian shirts. He soon reduced his verdict to one grumpy grunt: "coral."

By the last day, after three days of searching, they hadn't found anything, and King was getting increasingly desperate. His hopes had been so high when the dogs alerted; he wanted to bring them back to see what else they might find. The handlers resisted. "The issue is that dogs have memory," Engelbert told him. "Think of the dog's thought process: 'I've already shown them this, so I'll show them something else like a rock or a stick.'" Whatever they alerted on now would be tainted.

Hiebert, ever the optimist, suggested bringing soil back to the United States for DNA analysis. Earlier that year, scientists had announced they'd extracted Neanderthal mitochondrial DNA from sediment in four caves in Europe and Russia. Why not extract DNA from the soil and compare it to DNA from Earhart's closest living relative? he argued.

Shortly before the *Reef Endeavour* sailed away from Nikumaroro on July 6, Johnson and Kim Zimmerman, a doctor with a passion for Earhart, donned masks and plastic gloves to collect soil from each spot where the dogs alerted. Human eyes may not have solved the mystery. Perhaps cutting-edge science would.

CHAPTER TWELVE

1928: FLIGHT OF THE *FRIENDSHIP*

On May 21, 1927, Charles Lindbergh became the first person to fly solo nonstop across the Atlantic. Taking off from Roosevelt Field on Long Island, New York, he flew more than 33 hours without sleep to Paris, where he landed at Le Bourget Aerodrome to ecstatic crowds. He wasn't the first airplane pilot to cross the Atlantic: In May 1919, a U.S. Navy six-man crew had steered a Curtiss plane across the ocean, stopping midway on São Miguel Island in the Azores. A month later, British pilots John William Alcock and Arthur Whitten Brown flew nonstop from Newfoundland to Ireland.

Still, Lindbergh's solitary feat captivated the public and set off a frenzy of competition. He won $25,000 in prize money, made $50,000 on a goodwill tour, and earned $125,000 from the *New York Times* for his story, as well as the adulation of what seemed to be the entire world. In those days, there were few quicker paths to fame than daring feats of aviation. Other records remained to be broken, and more prize money—offered by cities, newspapers, and wealthy backers—remained to be won. Before the year was out, 18 planes carrying 55 fliers had attempted to cross the Atlantic: some from the west, as Lindbergh had, and some from the east, a harder journey against the wind. Fourteen of those fliers died.

Five women were among the strivers. On August 31, 1927, Anne of Lowenstein-Wertheim-Freudenberg, a 63-year-old widowed princess, took off in a plane piloted by her old friend Captain Leslie Hamilton and Lt. Col. Frederick F. Minchin, who aimed to be the first pilots to cross the Atlantic from east to west. Their Fokker was last seen off the Irish coast, making the princess the first woman to die in the race to cross the Atlantic—but not the last.

Viennese actress Lilly Dillenz made the next attempt, but her seaplane, after a days-long layover in the Azores, was too heavy to lift off from the water. Glamorous pilot Ruth Elder led the charge from the Atlantic's western side, but she and her copilot were forced to ditch about 350 miles short of the Azores when their plane lost oil pressure. Lucky for them, a ship was nearby and they were rescued from their watery landing.

Frances Grayson, a niece of Woodrow Wilson, wasn't so fortunate. Her plane disappeared on the way to its Newfoundland jumping-off point. The elegant aristocrat Elsie Mackay and her copilot, one-eyed ace Walter Hinchliffe, tried the route from the east. Thousands of people waited at the Long Island field where they were scheduled to land on March 13, 1928. They never arrived. Several days later, parts of their plane washed up on the northwestern coast of Ireland.

Despite the fatalities, more women waited in the wings to fly that spring. Mabel Boll, a self-made socialite known as the "Queen of Diamonds" based on a million-dollar wedding gift from her third husband, planned to make the eastern hop. She preferred to be known as the "Queen of the Air," she proclaimed. Thea Rasche, an accomplished German pilot, promised a flight all the way to Berlin. Amy Phipps Guest, a 55-year-old Pittsburgh heiress married to Britain's former air minister, had secretly bought a trimotor Fokker plane from the explorer Richard Byrd, who agreed to outfit it for a London-bound flight.

Guest didn't plan to fly herself. She was to be a passenger while Wilmer "Bill" Stultz, a respected pilot Byrd had recommended, piloted the plane. (She'd managed to lure him away from Boll, whom the old-moneyed Guest considered a tacky upstart.) She knew her family wouldn't approve such a dangerous endeavor, so she told only her younger brother. The secret weighed on him, though; he soon revealed his sister's transatlantic scheme to her son Winston (named, incidentally, after her husband's good friend Mr. Churchill). A law student at Columbia University, Winston claimed he'd be so worried about his mother's reckless plan that he'd fail his exams. Also, her daughter Diana was due to be presented at the British royal court; that would hardly go well if her mother was lost at sea. The rest of her family joined the chorus of objection, and Amy, formidable as she was, backed down.

But not entirely. She owned the plane, and she was determined that a proper American woman—*not* Mabel Boll—would be the first one to make it across the ocean. She ordered her attorney David Layman to find "someone nice who will do us proud." The family lawyer was entirely out of his depth. Luckily for him, George P. Putnam hijacked the expedition.

Soon after Layman received his extralegal assignment, Putnam and his instinct for publicity encountered Bernt Balchen, a Norwegian aviator who often worked with Byrd, on the Staten Island Ferry. Putnam seized the opportunity to ask about Byrd's upcoming Antarctic expedition. Under Putnam's shrewd questioning, Balchen let slip that Byrd had sold the plane he was originally planning to use to a woman for a transatlantic flight. (He'd been offered a Ford Trimotor free of charge.) "I had stumbled on an adventure-in-the-making which, once completed, certainly should provide a book," Putnam later crowed, anticipating a bestseller.

Byrd was based in Boston. By day's end, Putnam had recruited his friend Hilton Railey, a well-known Boston publicist and fundraiser, to uncover information on this transatlantic attempt. By midnight, Railey had learned that Stultz was the pilot and tracked him down at a hotel bar, where Stultz drunkenly spilled the whole plan. The next day Putnam "dropped from the clouds and introduced myself," as he put it, to Layman, who "was wondering what to do next." The transatlantic flight became Putnam's show.

Putnam set Railey to finding a woman for the attempt. Per Amy Guest's instructions, the woman had to be educated, a lady, and, preferably, a pilot, though the former requirements took precedence over the latter. Railey consulted his friend Reginald Belknap, a retired admiral and a member of the Boston chapter of the National Aeronautic Association. Belknap swore he had the perfect candidate: "a young social worker who flies."

"I'm not sure how many hours she's had, but I do know that she's deeply interested in aviation—and a thoroughly fine person," the admiral assured Railey. "Call Denison House and ask for Amelia Earhart."

Amelia wouldn't take Railey's call at first. School had just let out, and Denison House was flooded with children. Tell whomever it was to call back, she said, "unless the message was more important than entertaining many little Chinese and Syrian children."

It was more important, she was told.

When Amelia picked up the receiver, Railey got right to the point. Was she "interested in doing something aeronautic which might be hazardous?" he asked.

She assumed he was a bootlegger. Fliers were popular with rumrunners during those days of Prohibition, and she'd been approached several times before. She demanded that Railey give her names of people who would vouch for him. Somewhat taken aback, Railey did and quickly passed muster. Amelia agreed to meet him at his office that day.

Still wary, she arrived at the scheduled time with a friend in tow. Despite her cautious behavior, or perhaps because of it, Railey found her perfect for the project he represented. "I asked forthwith 'How would you like to be the first woman to fly the Atlantic?'"

Amelia, with little hesitation, said she'd like that very much.

Amy Guest wanted a young lady with the qualities of the ideal American woman. Amelia, Railey thought, was "not their norm but their sublimation." He sent her to Putnam, who was less visibly enthralled—at least at first. He'd made Amelia wait several tense weeks before he summoned her to New York City for an interview; when she arrived for the long-delayed meeting, he made her wait outside his office several hours more. "She was as sore as a wet hen!" he later recalled. "She didn't like me one little bit, and she didn't take much pains to conceal her dislike."

But Putnam, Layman, and John Phipps, Amy Guest's brother, quickly recognized that Amelia—with her finishing school manners, social work–confirmed moral character, and well-established piloting experience—was ideal. Amelia herself found the interview harrowing. "I was being weighed," she said. "If I were found wanting on too many counts I should be deprived of a trip. On the other hand, if I were just too fascinating the gallant gentlemen might be loath to drown me." They didn't interview anyone else.

After the interview, Putnam brought her to the train station, talking the whole time. Her initial annoyance had quickly transformed to fascination. Amelia told her sister, Muriel, that she wished the ride to the station had been longer: "He was so interesting," she confided.

And he was. Putnam had crammed several lifetimes into his 40 years. Born in a New York suburb to an illustrious publishing family—his grandfather had published James Fenimore Cooper, Edgar Allan Poe, and Nathaniel Hawthorne—he dropped out of Harvard to head west. Settling in Bend, Oregon, he took over the local newspaper as editor and publisher; later, he became the town's mayor when the previous officeholder resigned. The Oregon governor then tapped him to be his private secretary, a powerful role in a state without a lieutenant governor. When the United States entered World War I, Putnam enlisted, serving in field artillery. After the armistice, he returned to the East Coast. His father and older brother had both died, and the family business needed him. As a publisher, he favored adventure stories, bringing out expedition accounts by Richard Byrd and Charles Lindbergh. (Lindbergh's book, *We,* became a huge bestseller when it came out a mere month after the pilot's historic flight.) Putnam, Amelia quickly learned, was a man in a hurry.

But this time, Putnam had to wait on other people. Amy Guest's approval was required. After a flurry of cables to London, where Guest was preparing to present her daughter to the king and queen, he and family attorney Layman had it.

"You may make this flight if you wish under the agreed conditions," Layman told Amelia. The conditions were parsimonious. She would not be paid, nor was she allowed to endorse commercial products. Any profits she made afterward from speaking tours or publications would go toward defraying the flight's expenses.

Amelia would not be reaping a Lindberghian windfall from this life-risking flight. But then, she would not be doing the actual flying. Bill Stultz would, earning $20,000 (mechanic Louis "Slim" Gordon received $10,000). Yet, once the plane set out from Boston, she would be named its captain.

PREPARATION FOR THE FLIGHT WAS INTENSE and secret, and Amelia was involved in very little of it. Indeed, she only saw the plane twice before takeoff and never flew in it until their first attempted launch from Boston Harbor. "I was pretty well known at the landing fields and obviously it might provoke comment if I seemed too interested in the plane," she later wrote in her account of the flight. She knew Boll and Rasche were planning transatlantic flights; a media frenzy would make it much harder to get ready quickly enough to beat them.

The plane in question was a trimotored Fokker F7 dubbed *Friendship* by Amy Guest in homage to the close relationship between the United States and the United Kingdom. "Strong and exquisitely fashioned," according to Amelia, its golden wings spanned 72 feet. Its fuselage was reddish orange—the better to stand out to rescuers if the plane were to go down. Its three air-cooled engines had been designed by Charles Lawrance, the same man who'd created the revolutionary engine that powered Amelia's Kinner Airster.

Byrd outfitted the *Friendship*. He'd been one of the aviators racing to cross the Atlantic before Lindbergh, but he and his crew had become lost, run low on fuel, and ditched in French waters in the foggy night near what would become known less than two decades later as Omaha Beach. Based on this "most terrible experience," Byrd judged that the only safe way to cross such a wide expanse of ocean was in a plane equipped with pontoons. Accordingly, the wheels were removed from the Fokker and 29-foot-long pontoons constructed of superlight duralumin attached. Each had nine airtight compartments, which would purportedly keep the plane afloat for weeks.

The problem was getting off the water. Rough waves doused the engines, while a smooth sea exerted hydrodynamic drag on the pontoons, making them "stick to water much as a dime sticks to a wet table," as one of Byrd's colleagues put it. The team would have to keep the plane's load as light as possible—no small task when the *Friendship* needed to carry four crew members and 5,300 pounds of fuel.

In addition to the four 95-gallon tanks in the airship's wings, two 246-gallon tanks were installed in the passenger cabin for a total fuel capacity of 872 gallons. To reduce the distance covered, Byrd recommended that the *Friendship* launch its transatlantic hop from Trepassey, the easternmost harbor in Newfoundland.

By mid-May, Byrd's team declared the *Friendship* "the safest and best equipped airplane ever to attempt an ocean flight."

Amelia, meanwhile, acted as if she had nothing momentous planned. Denison director Marion Perkins, who was in on the secret, put her in charge of the settlement house's summer program, as Amelia only expected to be away for two weeks. Of Amelia's family, only her fiancé Sam Chapman knew about the flight. She gave him the sensitive task of informing her mother and sister when the plane finally took off, but the news made the papers before he could tell them.

Amelia understood how hazardous this jaunt would be. She left a will and what she called her "popping off letters"—to be given to her mother and father if she died in the attempt. In her letter to her mother, she attempted some comfort: "My life has really been very happy, and I didn't mind contemplating its end in the midst of it." To her father, she was more celebratory: "Hooray for the last grand adventure! I wish I had won, but it was worth while anyway."

Her estate (the Kissel Kar, a treasury bond, and stock in Kinner Airplane and Dennison Airport) was to go to her mother once her debts ($1,000 or so, including $140 for a fur coat at Filene's department store) were paid off. "My regret is that I leave just now," added Amelia in a postscript. "In a few years, I feel I could have laid by something substantial for so many new things were opening for me."

She packed very little for the flight. "The men on the *Friendship* took no 'extras.' Pounds—even ounces—can count desperately. Obviously I should not load up with unessentials if they didn't," she later explained. Her only luggage was a small Army knapsack loaded with a camera, field glasses, a logbook, and "little rubber ear stops" (recommended by Byrd's wife to block the engine noise), as well as personal toiletries: a toothbrush, comb, fresh handkerchiefs, and a tube of cold cream. She wore high-laced boots, brown broadcloth breeches, a white silk shirt with a red necktie, a "homely" brown sweater, a leather helmet and goggles, and the battered leather coat she bought when she first started flying. Her "single elegance" was a brown-and-white silk scarf. To guard against the high-altitude chill, she borrowed an enormous fur-lined flying suit from a friend who had no idea what she'd be using it for.

She was ready, and so was the *Friendship*. The team had hoped to take off in mid-May 1928, but the weather wouldn't cooperate. When it was clear in Boston, it was foggy in Trepassey, their first destination. And vice versa. They waited through "long grey days, which had a way of dampening our spirits against our best efforts to be cheerful."

On June 1, the weather improved. They awoke at 3:30 in the morning, breakfasted at an all-night restaurant, filled thermoses (a large one with coffee for the men, and a small one with hot chocolate for Amelia, who abstained from coffee and alcohol), packed sandwiches, and boarded the tugboat that would take them across Boston Harbor to the *Friendship*'s mooring at the Jeffries Yacht Club. Amelia and Stultz scrambled on board the plane, while Slim Gordon stood on the pontoons to get the motors running. Once the propellers whirred, Gordon climbed aboard and took a seat in the cockpit beside Stultz. Amelia and backup pilot Lou Gower settled among the fuel tanks in the cabin. Stultz aimed the *Friendship* into the wind and gunned the motors. The plane zipped across the water. But that's all it did. There wasn't enough wind to lift it into the air.

The next day, they went through the same routine, down to filling thermoses and packing sandwiches. This time, the fog thwarted them.

June 3 promised to be clear. Again, they awoke at 3:30, made their appearance at the diner, and replaced their coffee, hot chocolate, and sandwiches. When they tugged over to the *Friendship,* conditions were perfect, with just enough wind but not too much. Even so, in their first run across the water, "the drag of the pontoons held us down." Stultz opened the throttle: "Still the water wouldn't let us go."

They couldn't hope for better weather conditions so they kept trying. To lighten the load, they dumped six of their eight five-gallon gas cans. It didn't work. Amelia, Gordon, and Gower moved to the back of the plane to force the nose up, "to no avail." With that, Gower packed up his things and "bade us adieu very quietly." The plane couldn't bear the weight of an extra pilot. "For the first time then I felt the *Friendship* really lighten on the water and knew the difference of a few pounds had made her a bird."

On the plane's fifth attempt at takeoff, the *Friendship* became airborne. But the flight nearly ended in calamity right then. The cabin door's spring lock was broken, and Amelia had secured it to a gas can. But during takeoff, the door started inching open; she tried to hold it closed herself while Gordon fixed it. "Slim came within inches of falling out when the door suddenly slid open. And when I dived for that gasoline can, edging towards the opening door, I, too, had a narrow escape," she wrote. Eventually, they secured the door to a brace in the cabin.

Once the door was secured, and all crew members accounted for, Amelia enjoyed the flight. "The motors are humming sweetly," she recorded in her log. "One can see deeply into the water and mark shoals and currents. What an easy way to see what are bugaboos for surface craft."

About halfway to Trepassey, they encountered fog, which forced them to land in Halifax, Nova Scotia. Amelia stayed on board the moored plane while Stultz and Gordon figured out how to get her to lodgings without anyone seeing her. They'd hoped to keep the flight—and Amelia's involvement—secret until they left Trepassey, but reporters in Halifax soon realized a transatlantic jump was in the works. By morning, they'd learned a woman was on board. The crew had "many encounters with newspaper men" at breakfast, fielding questions and posing for photographs. When they finally managed to escape—an easy launch from a "perfectly calm sea"—they carried "a sheaf of Halifax newspapers with strange assertions about us all ... strange reading matter," reported Amelia.

Their arrival in Trepassey proved to be the highlight of what would become an interminable stay. They were greeted by a "rodeo," as Amelia dubbed it. "A dozen small boats began to circle madly about us, the local motto seeming to be that the early boat catches the plane." Although Putnam had already arranged a mooring, fishermen raced to claim the soon-to-be-famous plane for their own patch of dock or buoy. "Poised in the bows of the launches each maritime cowboy whirled aloft a coil of rope, attempting to cast it at us," Amelia recounted. Gordon, frantic that the ropes would get tangled in the propellers, was out on the pontoons "to ward them off." A wildly thrown coil hit him, nearly knocking him into the water. "I was convulsed with laughter," Amelia wrote afterward. "Truly, I've never had a more entertaining half hour."

Once the *Friendship* had been safely moored, Amelia, Stultz, and Gordon settled in with the Devereaux family, whose home doubled as the general store for the rustic fishing village. Each of them took a child's bed, the children having been sent to stay with relatives. The house lacked indoor plumbing or a bathtub, but Amelia thought she could manage without those luxuries for the one night they planned to stay.

For the next four days, a strong wind riled the sea, making the waves too rough to load the gas tanks on board the plane. On the fourth day, they tried to take off. "In vain we tried three times and had to give up." They were lucky: Gordon found a hole in the oil tank that would have drained the plane mid-flight. He soldered the crack shut and repaired a leaking pontoon.

By this time, Amelia, Stultz, and Gordon were getting heartily sick of the 600-person town. Food was limited: canned rabbit, canned fish, and eggs tasting of the hens' fishy diet. "Once we were in Trepassey, we were trapped," Amelia wrote.

Meanwhile, they were getting word about Mabel Boll's and Thea Rasche's accelerating preparations for their own transatlantic flights. The race was on, and the *Friendship* crew was stuck in an isolated town with dodgy weather and a narrow harbor that only allowed them to take off in one direction. Amelia and Gordon became obsessed with playing rummy, while Bill discovered a "guitar harp," which he taught himself to play.

On the sixth day, they were invited to go "eeling," and Amelia washed her hair. "I wish I had manicuring facilities and a bathtub," she wrote in her logbook.

On the seventh day, Atlantic weather reports looked good, but Trepassey was submerged in a "thick and woolly" fog. "I wish we'd have a break," Amelia had written the day before, but things were about to take a turn for the worse. That night, the men all got drunk. Some reporters who had followed them to Trepassey brought liquor. "The boys went after bad booze and got it last night," raged Amelia. "I could choke Frazer [one of the reporters]. It doesn't matter if *he* drinks."

From then on, she was locked in a losing battle with Stultz to keep him sober.

The next day dawned fair in Trepassey, but the Atlantic was stormy. The team visited a 200-year-old cannon and tried their hand at puzzles. "Oh, if only we can get away soon. It is hard indeed to remain *sans* books, *sans* contact with one's interests and withal on a terrific strain," Amelia observed.

On the ninth day, she wrote, "This has been the worst day." The wind was at last in their favor, but they could not get airborne. The spray from the waves was "thrown so high that it drowned the outboard motors. As we gathered speed, the motors would cut and we'd lose the precious pull necessary." They unloaded everything they could, but the pontoons would not release their grip on the water.

On the 10th day, they removed 300 pounds of gas from the plane, but still couldn't take off. To add to their misery, while Gordon and Stultz were tinkering with the motor, the tide went out, leaving the plane on a sandy ledge from which they had to be rescued. "None of us are sleeping much any more and we need all we can get. We are on the ragged edge," Amelia wrote. Sensing her growing despair, Putnam sent her a telegram: "DARN SORRY BUT YOU WILL EMERGE ON TOP WE ALL KNOW YOU ARE DOING YOUR BEST."

Finally, on June 16, their 13th day in Trepassey, they received a cautious go-ahead to fly the next day. Despite the potential departure—or perhaps because of it—Stultz spent the whole day drinking. "Just now the boys are at Paddy Mortons and I know liquor flows," reported Amelia in her diary. "I loathe watching men. Why can't they be more responsible?"

In what Putnam later described as "either the bravest or silliest act of her whole career," Amelia decided they would depart on June 17 no matter what state Stultz was in. She rousted him out of bed and filled him with coffee. "We have a dandy breeze behind us," she told him, "and we are going in spite of everything."

It took them three tries. To lighten the load, they jettisoned their canned gas, the motion picture camera, flotation cushions, a rubber raft, and the large thermos. The *Friendship* was left with 700 gallons of fuel on board, which would get them to London, but barely. They would have to rely on sodden Stultz not to make any mistakes. Although Gordon and Amelia were both pilots, neither had Stultz's navigational skills, and Amelia had never flown a trimotor. Their lives depended on Stultz.

Once they were airborne, the anxieties plaguing them in Trepassey fell away. As they flew at 1,000 feet over Newfoundland, Amelia sketched the shapes of lakes in her logbook, asking herself of one long-tailed, long-necked form, "Is this a pleseosaurus [*sic*]?" At 2,500 feet, they skimmed the "fluffy top of the fog." At 5,000 feet they escaped the fog but encountered a storm—the "heaviest storm I have ever been in, in the air, and had to go through."

Amelia spent most of the flight in the cabin, kneeling at the navigation table to peer out the window. The temperature dropped as low as 42 degrees. Despite the nearly daylong flight, she napped only briefly, and barely ate. Their rations, as she described them, were "eccentric": 2.5 gallons of mineral water, three "elephantine" egg sandwiches, eight or nine oranges, tins of Drake's Oatmeal Cookies, pemmican, a bottle of Horlicks Malted Milk tablets, and some Hershey's chocolate.

When they were more than a thousand miles out, she wrote in the logbook, "The view is too vast and lovely for words. I think I am happy—sad admission of scant intellectual equipment. I am getting housemaid's knee kneeling here at the table gulping beauty."

Her belief that Stultz's legendary skills would overcome the alcohol once he was in the cockpit seemed to have been justified. During the "night of stars ... Bill sits up alone," she observed. "Every muscle and nerve alert."

Throughout the flight, they were either in or above the clouds; rarely did they spy the ocean. Stultz was flying using rhumb line navigation, which meant he was keeping to the same compass bearing for the entire flight. Gordon had rigged a flashlight to shine on the compass so Stultz could see it in the dark.

As the night progressed and they began to get closer to their destination—and to the end of their fuel—Amelia became nervous. Stultz brought the plane through the clouds to a lower altitude. "Awfully wet," she reported. "Water dripping in window. Port motor coughing. Sounds as if all motors were cutting. Stultz opens her wide to try to clear. Sounds rotten on the right."

At 3,000 feet, the radio stopped working. "We are going to go into, under or over a storm. I don't like to, with one motor acting the way it is," Amelia commented.

They should've been close to Ireland, but without the radio they couldn't communicate with nearby ships to find out. Amelia's notes became increasingly terse: "Try to get bearing. Radio won't. One hr's gas. Mess. All craft cutting our course. Why?" They assumed any ships they spotted would be heading east, as they were; instead, the two they saw were cutting across their path. She worried that the plane was off course.

In a desperate measure, they tried to drop a message onto one of the steamers; ships had been known to paint their coordinates on deck for planes in need. Stultz wrote a note and Amelia tied it in a bag with an orange as weight, which they lofted from the hatch. It missed. "The combination of our speed, the movement of the vessel, the wind and the lightness of the missile was too much for our marksmanship," according to Amelia. A second attempt also failed. They considered landing near the steamer, but whitecaps on the waves indicated that the rough seas would make landing dangerous and takeoff impossible.

At this point, all the *Friendship* crew could do was assume they were on the correct course and fly on. Gordon handled the tension by eating his egg sandwich. Before he finished it, a fleet of small boats appeared before them on a course parallel to theirs. A blue shadow grew in the distance.

"It was land! I think Slim yelled. I know the sandwich went flying out the window. Bill permitted himself a smile," Amelia reported. He found a harbor near what looked like a factory town and landed, completing an extraordinary feat of navigation. Flying mostly by instruments—and with a mind-befuddling hangover—Bill Stultz had kept within a mile of his chosen course.

But he wasn't the one whom this flight would make famous. Amelia Earhart had become the first woman to cross the Atlantic. When they went ashore in Burry Port, Wales—where they later discovered they were—thousands of people had gathered to greet them and nearly tore off the fliers' clothes. When they arrived in London the following day, to be cheered by crowds of many more thousands, all attention was on Amelia, much to her embarrassment.

"The accident of sex—the fact that I happened to be the first woman to have made the Atlantic flight—made me the chief performer in our particular sideshow," she observed. She was the one whom Lady Astor hosted, the one who sipped tea with the prime minister, the one who was invited to give a speech alongside Winston Churchill, the one who received the congratulatory telegram from President Calvin Coolidge. She was the one who, for the rest of her life, would never again be able to walk down a street unrecognized.*

---

* Bill Stultz died in a plane crash on July 1, 1929. An autopsy found he was intoxicated, but witnesses said he appeared sober. The *New York Times* reported that Amelia collapsed at his funeral. Lou Gordon quit flying in 1938 and had a long career at Trans World Airlines as a senior mechanic.

CHAPTER THIRTEEN

CASTAWAY: WHERE'S THE PLANE?

In 1992, Ric Gillespie and his wife, Pat Thrasher, visited Eric Bevington, the colonial officer who'd explored Nikumaroro (then Gardner Island) in 1937. They wanted to know what he'd seen. He didn't remember much that was useful but he invited Thrasher to photograph some of his snapshots, including one showing the *Norwich City*'s wreckage. Gillespie enlarged the image to more closely examine the damage the surf had done to the freighter. In doing so, he cropped the photo's left side. And that's how it remained for 18 years.

But in 2010, a TIGHAR member suggested that forensic imaging specialist Jeff Glickman revisit the historic photos TIGHAR had collected over the years. When Glickman developed the negative of the *Norwich City* photo, he immediately spotted something sticking out of the water. It wasn't a flaw in the photo, he told Gillespie. It was the wrong shape to be a chunk of coral and in the wrong spot to be the ship's wreckage. Could it be part of a plane? Gillespie sent the image to the U.S. Department of State's Bureau of Intelligence and Research for analysis.

Two years later, celebrated explorer Robert Ballard went to the Pentagon to give a presentation. A marine geologist by training, he had made his name with blockbuster scientific and historic discoveries: hydrothermal vents and so-called "black smokers" on the seafloor; John F. Kennedy's World War II patrol boat in the Solomon Islands; the Nazis' largest battleship, the *Bismarck,* off France's western tip; and most momentous of all, the wreck of the *Titanic* in the North Atlantic. Ballard also has had a long-standing and mostly top secret relationship with the military; the U.S. Navy funded his development of remote operated vehicles (ROVs) with the understanding that, on occasion, he'd deploy them on the service's behalf. He found the *Titanic* in 1985, in the time remaining after surveying the secret wreckage of two nuclear submarines that sunk in cold Atlantic waters in the 1960s.

He's still coy about the 2012 briefing. But afterward, the friend who'd organized it suggested he pay a visit to Kurt Campbell at the Department of State. Ballard knew Campbell; they'd worked together when Campbell had been a naval intelligence officer. Now he was assistant secretary of state for East Asian and Pacific affairs, and he had something to show Ballard.

When Ballard strode into Campbell's office, the diplomat shut the door behind him and handed him a black-and-white photo. The image was unremarkable: a sky with scudding clouds, a thin line of vegetation and sand, a stretch of calm waters. Offshore lay a large ship, its stern drooping.

It was the Bevington photograph.

"Looks like an old shipwreck resting on a reef off a small island," said Ballard.

Look closely, Campbell told him. On the frame's left side, Ballard spotted something indistinct—a smudge, maybe—sticking out of the water.

Campbell handed him a second photograph, an enhanced version of the first. The blurry object, he said, "is the landing gear of a Lockheed Electra."

Ballard was stunned. "That's her plane," he said. He'd been convinced it would never be found.

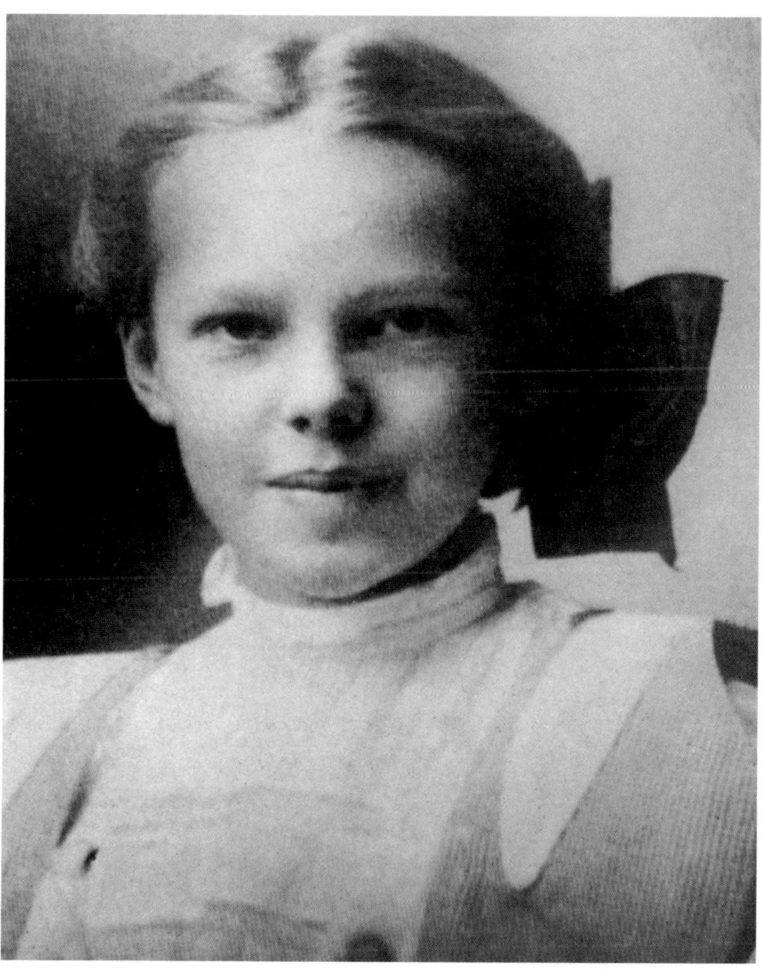

Amelia Earhart, pictured here in 1904, spent most of her early childhood in Atchison, Kansas, where her grandparents were prominent citizens. Despite her grandparents' formal expectations, Amelia sought adventure however she could—building a roller coaster, sledding down steep hills, and hunting rats in the barn. (Bettmann/Getty Images)

Visiting her sister in Toronto over Christmas in 191 Amelia encountered numerous wounded soldiers. "Fo the first time, I realized what the World War meant," s wrote later. Shocked, she quit school to become a nurs staying in Toronto until the war ended. (Provided by Harvard University)

In Atchison, Kansas, Amelia (center) was surround by family: (from left) younger sister, Muriel; uncle Ca Otis; grandmother Amelia Otis; aunt Anna Otis; mother, Amy Earhart; and father, Edwin Earhart. Am and Edwin struggled throughout their marriage over limited finances and Edwin's excessive drinking. (Provided by Harvard University)

Amelia got her first taste of fame when she arrived in Southampton, England, after the *Friendship*'s transatlantic flight 1928. Mrs. Frederick Guest (left) sponsored the flight; Wilmer Stultz (second from right) piloted the plane. Although ıelia was the first woman to cross the Atlantic, she was only a passenger on this flight. (Bettmann/Getty Images)

ꜰour years later, in 1932, Amelia made the transatlantic flight alone in her "little red bus," a Lockheed Vega. After a rough ssing—a storm knocked her off course, the altimeter failed, and the manifold ring cracked—she landed in a field outside ᴇrry in Northern Ireland. (Scherl/Süddeutsche Zeitung Photo/Alamy Stock Photo)

nelia learned to fly in California, and she started her first attempt at circumnavigating the globe from Oakland, California, March 17, 1937. She flew west over the new Golden Gate Bridge, pictured here, to Hawaii, but wrecked the plane during :eoff for the second leg to Howland Island. (Keystone/Hulton Archive/Getty Images)

◀ Amelia met Samuel Chapman, a young engineer from Marblehead, Massachusetts, when he moved into her parents' Los Angeles house as a boarder. Like her, he was intelligent and curious, and in 1923, they became engaged. (Bettmann/Getty Images)

▼ Publisher and promoter George Palmer Putnam orchestrated the *Friendship* flight that introduced Amelia to the public. He then served as her manager for the rest of her life. The couple, shown here examining maps for the world flight, married in 1931. (Corbis Historical via Getty Images)

Amelia called her Lockheed Electra 10-E a "flying laboratory." Purdue University bought it for her to pursue aeronautical search. But first she'd use the dual-engine plane—larger and faster than any she'd had before—to fly around the world. F-(sdasm2)/Alamy Stock Photo)

A late addition to the world flight in July 1937, Fred Noonan was known as the best navigator in aviation. He'd recently t Pan American, where he'd charted the airline's Pacific routes, crossing that ocean 18 times. But he was rumored to have a inking problem. (Topical Press Agency/Hulton Archive/Getty Images)

tish colonial officer Eric Bevington took this photo in October 1937 during a scouting trip to Gardner Island (Nikuma-o). On the right is the S.S. *Norwich City*'s wreckage; on the far left is an indistinct object that some suggest is the landing r of a Lockheed Electra 10-E. (Courtesy of TIGHAR)

▲Josephine Blanco (far right), pictured here in 1946, had never heard of Amelia Earhart when she told her employer, Navy dentist Casimir Sheft (center), that she saw Japanese soldiers seize a white woman pilot on Saipan before World War II. (Courtesy of Edward Akiyama)

▼Researcher Les Kinney argued that this photo from Jaluit Atoll in the Marshall Islands depicts Earhart (sitting, with bac to camera) and Noonan (leaning against a pole) in 1937 in the custody of the Japanese. But the photo was discovered in a Japanese travelogue published two years before their disappearance. (U.S. National Archives)

ne Bolam, a recent widow who'd worked as a banker, held a news conference on November 10, 1970, to state unequivocally at she was not Amelia Earhart, despite claims made by Joseph Gervais and Joe Klaas in the book *Amelia Earhart Lives.* ettmann/Getty Images)

➤ In 1960, Paul Mantz, Earhart's technical adviser, examines an airplane generator that CBS radioman Fred Goerner (right) retrieved from Tanapag Harbor on Saipan that same year. Mantz declared it looked like the one he'd installed on the Electra, but the manufacturer disagreed. (Bettmann/Getty Images)

➤ Richard "Ric" Gillespie, executive director of The International Group for Historic Aircraft Recovery (TIGHAR), has spent three decades pursuing the theory that Earhart and Noonan landed on Nikumaroro. Pictured here in 2015 on his final expedition there, he has found many tantalizing clues, but none have been directly linked to the fliers. (TIGHAR)

When Elgen Long flew around the world at the poles in 1971, he found Howland Island easily. After he returned, he and his wife, Marie, pictured here that same year, set their sights on discovering why Earhart and Noonan never made it there. (Barry James Gilmour/Fairfax Media via Getty Images)

While scanning the waters west of Howland Island in November 2023, a new ocean exploration company called Deep Sea Vision captured this sonar image that, they announced on January 27, 2024, "appears to be Earhart's Lockheed 10-E Electra." Ten months later, they returned for a closer look. (Deep Sea Vision)

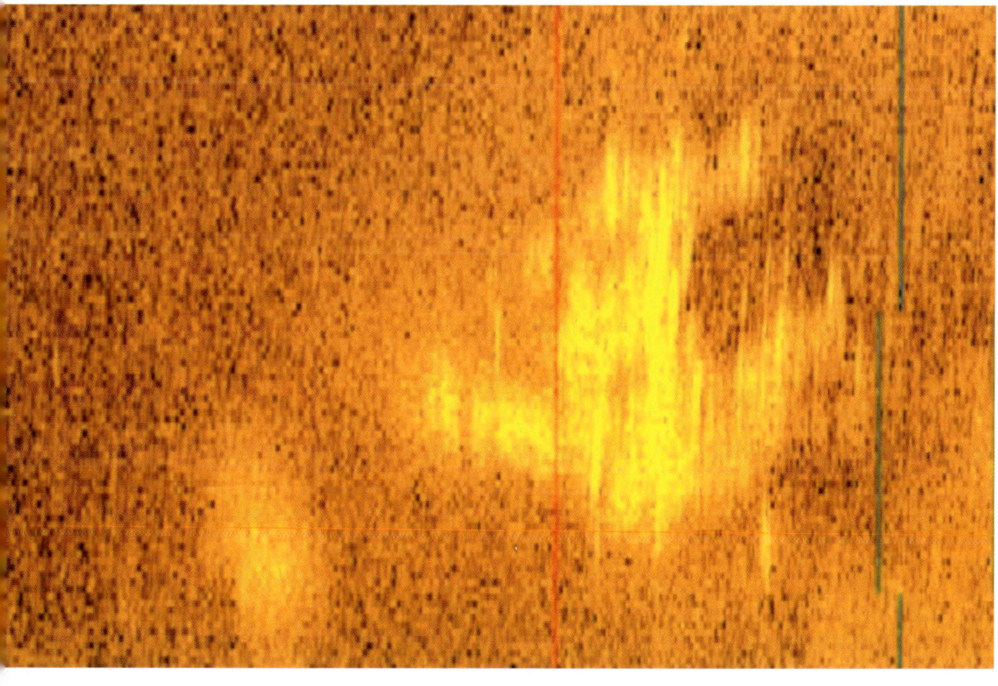

▲According to TIGHAR, the reef around Nikumaroro, pictured here, is wide and smooth enough for a plane to land at low tide. In 2001, members of the organization found what they believe to be a castaway's campsite near the far end of the lagoon. (TIGHAR)

▼Before archaeologist Tom King arrived on Nikumaroro for the first time in 1989, he assumed the four-and-a-half-mile-long island would be easy to survey. Its tangled vegetation proved him wrong. But in 2017, he and his colleagues brought forensic dogs to sniff for human remains. (Gabriel Scarlett)

Amy Kleppner, photographed in 2019 at the Amelia Earhart Birthplace Museum, was about to turn six when her aunt Amelia disappeared. Although she provided a genetic sample to compare with any remains thought to be Earhart's, she didn't believe "one penny" should be spent on searching for her. (Gabriel Scarlett)

When Amelia Earhart disappeared somewhere between Lae, New Guinea, and Howland Island on July 2, 1937, she was 39 years old. And so she'll remain, even—and especially—if the world never learns what happened to her. (Bettmann/Getty Images)

Campbell was dangling this photo in front of Ballard for a reason. TIGHAR was planning its 10th expedition to Nikumaroro, and then secretary of state Hillary Clinton wanted to endorse it. The 75th anniversary of the pilot's disappearance was approaching, and Clinton had long been an admirer of Amelia Earhart. Ballard's support would give the mission credibility—and Bevington's photo suggested there might actually be a plane to find.

Standing at a podium in the Benjamin Franklin Room of the Department of State on March 20, 2012, with Clinton attentive behind him, Ballard endorsed TIGHAR's project with his usual mix of graciousness and bravado. "I've done a number of searches. Unless I can get it inside a reasonable box, I pass," he said. "The *Titanic* was a 150 square mile box, the *Bismarck* was a 200 square mile box, the *Yorktown* was a 400 square mile box. Amelia Earhart's, when I looked at it, was thousands of square miles, and I just said, I pass." The enhanced photograph "just collapsed the box." But Ballard would have to wait seven years for the chance to search for Earhart's plane himself.

THE BEVINGTON OBJECT, AS THE TIGHAR folks took to calling it, wasn't the only piece of the puzzle to convince Ballard that the Nikumaroro theory was plausible. He'd also become intrigued by a notebook that had come into TIGHAR's possession.

In 1937, Betty Klenck was a 15-year-old girl living in St. Petersburg, Florida, where she spent long hours in front of her father's high-powered shortwave radio. While listening to music, she'd fill notebooks with sketches of fashionable women and lyrics from the latest popular songs like the Gershwin tune "They Can't Take That Away from Me." An antenna wire stretched from the house to a pole in a lot behind their yard, allowing Klenck to tune in stations from all over the world. Often, she'd cruise the dials, writing down snippets of what she heard.

One afternoon, likely early in July, as she was idly wandering across the airwaves, she picked up the voice of a woman saying, "This is Amelia Earhart. This is Amelia Earhart." Klenck was "so floored," she later told Gillespie, that she didn't write down what the woman was saying at first. The woman spoke quickly so Klenck could only collect fragments: "waters high ... help ... help us quick." There was a man with her, and Klenck got the impression that he'd been injured. The man and woman both kept saying "New York, New York, New York," which made no sense to the teenager.

When Klenck's father arrived home from work, he listened with her and became so alarmed that he hurried to the local Coast Guard station with the news. The servicemen brushed him off. Ships were already searching in the vicinity of Howland Island, they told him. They knew all they needed to know. Convinced she'd heard Earhart, Klenck kept the notebook for decades, until a friend reached out to TIGHAR in 2000 on her behalf.

Klenck's notebook added weight to an idea that had already been bouncing around TIGHAR: that Earhart and Noonan had landed on the reef; that they'd attempted to transmit radio messages when the tide was low and the engine would start; that the plane became a furnace during the day, so they could only transmit at night; and that, eventually, the tide lifted the plane and floated it off the reef.

To Gillespie, the clincher was the repetition of New York. New York City sounded like *Norwich City* to him. New York City. *Norwich City*. The place-names could easily be confused. Earhart and Noonan must have been in sight of the wrecked ship, he reasoned, and were trying to give their location to potential rescuers with its name. They hardly expected that the only person to hear their pleas would be more than 10,000 miles away.

The timing of what Klenck heard made sense to Gillespie as well. He and a colleague were able to compare the tides on Nikumaroro with their appraisal of the time when Klenck heard the call—as well as when others reported snippets of messages from Earhart. The tide was low then: Earhart would have been able to run the engines to power the radio. And it was evening. The sun was down, making the temperature inside the plane bearable.

Klenck's notebook wasn't proof. But it shored up TIGHAR's hypothesis and further convinced Ballard that the deep waters off Nikumaroro were worth a look.

BALLARD BELIEVES THAT THE NEXT GREAT age of exploration is happening now. "We will go farther than Lewis and Clark and learn the secrets of territories beyond even Jefferson's wildest imagination," he vowed in an article in *National Geographic*. But unlike Lewis and Clark's great land voyage, this new era of exploration would be underwater. In 1982, the United Nations Convention on the Law of the Sea allowed countries to claim sovereign rights from their territorial waters (12 nautical miles from shore) to their exclusive economic zone (an additional 200 nautical miles) and beyond, if the continental shelf extended farther and met certain conditions. With a proclamation from Ronald Reagan in 1983, the United States—with its extended coastlines and island holdings in the Pacific and Caribbean—roughly doubled in size, even though it hasn't joined the convention.

When Thomas Jefferson dramatically expanded the country's territory with the Louisiana Purchase in 1803, he sent Meriwether Lewis and William Clark to explore the country's new acquisition. This time around, the U.S. government sent Ballard—and that's what brought him near Nikumaroro in 2019. Since 2013, his ship, the E/V *Nautilus*—along with the National Oceanic Atmospheric Administration vessel *Okeanos Explorer*—had been mapping American waters, from Puerto Rico to California to Hawaii. In August, it had just finished charting the waters off American Samoa and was scheduled to transit up to Howland Island, part of what is now called the Pacific Islands Heritage Marine National Monument. Nikumaroro was on the way, and Ballard could not resist the detour.

He intended to find Amelia Earhart's plane. For an explorer with his track record of uncovering historical secrets hidden beneath the waves, "Amelia was the biggest thing out there," he said.

BALLARD DIDN'T PLAN TO APPROACH NIKUMARORO directly in the *Nautilus*. Instead, he charted a sweeping path that allowed the sonar to map the underwater terrain. The ship was equipped with a multibeam sonar on the hull, two ROVs with high-definition cameras, an autonomous surface vehicle (ASV), and multiple drones—plus Ballard's years of experience finding treasures under the sea. With each discovery, he's developed a greater understanding of the pattern debris makes as it falls from the surface through the water; he knows what to look for. But he couldn't get too close to the island, because the reef made Captain Pavel Chubar, a Ukrainian who'd been with Ballard for eight years, extremely nervous.

I was nervous, too, not least because the Pacific's enormous swells made me dramatically seasick and my berth shared a bathroom with Ballard's stateroom. The *Nautilus* was a sprightlier vessel than the cruise ship from the 2017 TIGHAR/Betchart expedition, and the people on board—the ship's crew, Ballard's scientific team, an eight-person National Geographic documentary crew, and me—weren't on vacation. We were there to do a job, and I needed to hold it together.

With the Electra, Ballard expected most of the plane's aluminum parts to be smashed to bits by the roiling surf against the reef. But the two Pratt & Whitney Wasp engines—each weighing nearly 1,000 pounds—would probably have tumbled down the cliff face. Ballard hoped they'd come to rest on a shelf along the slopes of the underwater mountain that formed Nikumaroro's base; that would make the engines easier to locate and retrieve. But even if they'd settled on the ocean floor—some 13,000 feet down—he thought his high-tech tools would spot them. In anticipation, he'd loaded materials on board to construct containers large enough to preserve the engines.

Once the *Nautilus* arrived at the island on August 9, 2019, a routine quickly developed: Send out the ASV (a robot boat, essentially) to map the terrain near the surf. When it returned, analyze the data to see what, as Ballard put it, "comes out of the soup." He and his colleagues were looking for targets—anomalies in the data—though a lack of them didn't mean there wasn't anything interesting below the waves.

Ballard put great stock in laying eyes on his quarry. "Everything I ever found was found visually," he said.

That's where the ROVs came in. Usually launched at night, together they can go as deep as 13,000 feet. *Hercules,* a bright yellow box with a metal base, offers a first-person view, while the smaller *Argus* keeps a camera pointed at *Hercules*.

The ROV pilots operated on four-hour shifts, day and night, from the control room of the *Nautilus,* where it was cold and dark and hushed. Banks of 20 or more monitors provided the only light. Moving around was treacherous: Wires hung along the walls, and the space between workstations was narrow. Despite the heat outside, crew members wore fleece to fend off the frigid air. Their voices were barely audible as they spoke softly to each other through headsets.

The screens mounted on the black-painted walls provided a vision of another world. One showed an ROV floating in shadowy blue light, dwarfed by what looked to be a massive cliff face. Another screen provided a closer view: bedrock and coral rubble occasionally obscured by a flurry of marine snow.

"We're looking for colors that aren't natural to the background," said Ballard, as he stared intently at the screens from his perch in the back row.

On the first night, they found wreckage: items that looked like a propeller, a boiler, a crankshaft, and much more. But all were from the *Norwich City*.

It wasn't what Ballard was looking for, but it answered an important question: How deep could the plane go? The *Norwich City* debris clustered at depths between 100 to 300 meters. "Anything of similar mass—part of a plane or part of a ship—would have been sliding downslope in that zone," explained expedition leader Allison Fundis, a former teacher whose superhuman ability to maintain her equanimity made her the perfect counterpoint to Ballard's relentlessness. "We're really focusing on that zone with the ROV dives."

When the pilots did spot something, their reactions tended to be muted. During one watch, a tube-shaped metallic object hove into view. The *Hercules* pilot murmured, "It looks anthropogenic. Should I pick it up?"

The answer was yes. After a moment of hesitation, *Hercules* stretched out its arm, very slowly closed its pincers around the tube, and delicately placed the item into a white storage container on its side.

What was it? The answer would have to wait until the ROVs were recovered and the box could be opened, which wouldn't be until the next day.

It wasn't part of Earhart's plane. Instead, it appeared to be a piece of oceanographic equipment—a sign that other explorers had been here before Ballard.

Ballard shrugged off false alarms, especially early in the search. "We did this for nine days with the *Titanic,*" he said.

Over the course of the expedition, which lasted 12 days, Ballard sent the ship five times around Nikumaroro to map with multibeam sonar. He sent the ASV around the island twice to map the shallower areas close to the reef. He sent drones flying over the island to peer into the water where the surf breaks over the reef. He sent *Argus* into deeper water to do side-scan sonar. And he sent both *Argus* and *Hercules* around the island to search for airplane wreckage with their cameras. "We did the whole enchilada," says Ballard. "That's total coverage."

What he learned is that Nikumaroro is a tiny island at the peak of a massive seamount. It drops to the ocean floor in a series of steep cliffs and ramps—most dramatically in the primary search zone. And as with a mountain's streams, chutes funnel debris down the slopes. Those chutes collect wreckage.

Hercules and *Argus* combed the chutes from top to bottom. Below the *Norwich City,* the ROVs illuminated propellers, boilers, and other bits of ship for the watching science team. "I've learned a tremendous amount from the *Norwich City*" about how objects drain off the reef, Ballard said.

It was a different story in the primary search zone: the site of the supposed landing gear in the photo. "If the plane was up there, pieces would be moving downslope," said Ballard. But the ROVs and the watching scientists found nothing.

Early in the morning of August 22, the expedition's last day, the crew pulled *Hercules* out of the ocean. As the ROV streamed water onto the deck, Ballard went to check the last samples it had brought up. The *Nautilus* was scheduled to leave Nikumaroro for Samoa in an hour.

Donning black plastic gloves, Ballard slid a container out of the ROV. Inside the seawater-filled bin was a laptop-size silver sheet and a crumbling black fragment that came from something that appeared to be a barrel.

Ballard examined the items in the ship's lab. The black fragment wasn't aluminum, so it couldn't have come from Earhart's Lockheed Electra 10-E. The silver sheet was more promising, especially since it appeared to have rivet holes. "It sure looked like aluminum underwater," said Mae Lubetkin, a member of the science crew.

Ballard picked up the piece. "It's not her plane," he said. "It bends too much."

This was a fitting end to what in many respects was a successful expedition. Something intriguing was recovered from the ocean floor with technology beyond any that had ever been used in the search for Amelia Earhart. Yet it wasn't what Ballard and his team were looking for.

"We visually examined 100 percent of the island down to 750 meters and did not see evidence of the plane," said Ballard. "We did 100 percent of the primary zone visually down to 900 meters."

No plane.

Ballard was not disappointed in this result. "This has been fun," he said. "It called upon everything we've got." And he didn't consider the search to be over. Indeed, he planned to perform an extended search of the waters around Howland sometime in the next few years. But he doesn't plan on returning to Nikumaroro unless definitive evidence is discovered that Earhart and Noonan perished on land.

That evidence, it turns out, may have ended up in Tarawa, the capital of Kiribati.

CHAPTER FOURTEEN

1928–32: "AIR-MINDED"

Amelia was getting dressed for dinner one July night in 1928, when George Putnam came rushing up the stairs and pounded on her door. His friend George Bye was on the phone, he said, and he needed an answer now.

She'd only been back in the United States for a few weeks after her flight in the *Friendship,* and it had been a whirlwind. She'd been greeted by a ticker-tape parade in New York, another parade in Boston, and yet another in Chicago. She'd given remarks as she received awards that she insisted over and over she did not deserve, deferring fruitlessly to Wilmer Stultz and Slim Gordon. But they didn't help her case; issuing short, embarrassed statements left plenty of room for the crowds to adore her easy charm.

Now she was ensconced in the airy stone and stucco home in Rye, New York, where Putnam lived with his wife, Dorothy, and their two sons, 15-year-old David and seven-year-old George Jr.; Putnam had insisted she'd be able to concentrate on writing there. After all, she owed him a book, and he expected her to finish it quickly. He also wanted her close for moments like this, when there was a deal to be made.

Bye had offered Amelia $1,000—more than $18,000 in today's dollars—to endorse Lucky Strike cigarettes. She'd refused because she didn't smoke. But he'd come back with another offer—$1,500 and she wouldn't have to say she smoked, just that Lucky Strike was the *Friendship* crew's preferred brand, which was true.

Putnam shouted the revised offer through the door of the guest room and waited for an answer—not patiently, because that was the one thing he was never able to do, but silently. After a few moments, she responded. "All right. If they'll be absolutely sure to say the cigarettes were used by the *crew,*" she said. Her voice was muffled at first—she was pulling a dress over her head, he thought—but then she was crystal clear. "I don't really want to do it, but I want the fifteen hundred bucks to give to Dick." She was referring to the explorer Richard Byrd, who had outfitted the *Friendship*'s flight and was raising money for an expedition to the South Pole. Amelia wanted to help him because he'd been so good to her.

The advertisement—featuring a serious-looking Amelia in a flight helmet brooding above her signature, her literal endorsement—ran shortly thereafter. "Lucky Strikes were the cigarettes carried on the *'Friendship'* when she crossed the Atlantic," Amelia is quoted as saying. "They were smoked continuously from Trepassey to Wales. I think nothing else helped so much to lessen the strain for all of us." The public could be forgiven for assuming their new airborne heroine was smoking continuously over the Atlantic.

Despite Byrd's public statement that Amelia had donated her endorsement money to him in "an act of astonishing generosity," the backlash to the ad was swift. Letters poured into the house at Rye, according to Putnam: "Sarcastic letters. ... Angry letters. ... Blue-nose letters. More-in-sorrow-than-in-anger letters. Tsk-tsk-tsk letters." One bereft member of the public ripped a later version of the ad out of a magazine and sent it to Amelia. Scrawled across the top were the pained questions, "Is this the face of a Lady? What Price Glory?"—with the latter underlined twice for emphasis. Amelia had sold herself out, and done so cheaply. Nice women didn't smoke, these scolds declared, and they certainly didn't recommend cigarettes to others.

Worse was yet to come. Amelia had nearly finalized a deal to be the aviation editor for *McCall's* magazine, where she'd have a platform from which to extol on her favorite subject—the wonders, convenience, and practicality of flying as well as the sheer opportunities it offered to women. She was thrilled, though apprehensive, at this new role. But *McCall's* wouldn't permit any member of its staff—especially a high-profile one—to be sullied by a whiff of cigarette smoke. After all, this magazine went into good, middle-class homes across the country. The offer was rescinded before she could begin.

The *Friendship* flight granted Amelia the freedom to pursue a career in aviation, but it came with a cost. Her life wasn't her own anymore; the public had claimed her. And to live as a flier, she needed them to like her, to want to read about her exploits, and to listen to her speak about her derring-do.

Luckily, she had George Palmer Putnam on her side. He would ensure she was the female aviator whose name every member of the paying public knew.

WHEN AMELIA RETURNED FROM ENGLAND, SHE'D thought she would return to social work once, as her sister put it, "the hullabaloo died down." But, thanks to Putnam, the hullabaloo never let up. She was now his project, and they would both profit from it.

First, there was the book. Written in several harried weeks, *20 Hrs., 40 Min., Our Flight in the* Friendship (subtitled "The American Girl, First Across the Atlantic by Air, Tells Her Story") breezily recounts Amelia's beginnings in aviation, the industry's history and women's role in it, and the flight of the *Friendship.* She turned in the manuscript on August 25, and it was in bookstores by September 10, with a dedication to George Putnam's wife, Dorothy Binney Putnam, "under whose rooftree this book was written." (Although Dorothy liked Amelia, she wondered in her diary whether the dedication was "a sop to me because she monopolized George all summer?"). Although the book never reached the sales heights of Charles Lindbergh's memoir, *We,* which Putnam had published the previous year, it provided her with an opportunity to capitalize on her newfound fame. And Amelia, whose financial situation had always been precarious, seized it—both for her own sake and for her family's. Still, she was determined to eventually earn the acclaim that so far, she believed, was undeserved.

Putnam soon wrangled a new position for her as *Cosmopolitan* magazine's first aviation editor, which she took, although *McCall's* had reversed itself and reoffered her the job. She was obliged to submit eight articles a year; the fourth of the month was her deadline day. As engaging as she was as a writer, she found it daunting. "Writing on a schedule frightened her," said her sister. "She would rather fly than write."

Her first article appeared in the November issue with the cover line "AMELIA EARHART Will Tell You All You Want to Know About FLYING." Inside was a photo spread in which she was depicted as fashionably dressed for any occasion an elegant young lady might encounter: horseback riding, flying, tennis, and, of course, a ball. In subsequent issues, she answered reader questions about flight, argued for how safe it was, explained what pilot training entailed, and tried to persuade parents to let their daughters learn to fly. They'll try it anyway, she contended, so why not ensure they do it with a parent-approved pilot and plane?

Although her return to social work was looking increasingly unlikely, she moved into Greenwich House, a settlement house in Lower Manhattan, which "gave her a balance of mental comfort," wrote Putnam later. She was shielded from the fame-starved public but introduced to those who were actually hungry—and to the leading social thinkers who were trying to do something about it. "It was *her* kind of place, perhaps the one type of place on the ground in which she could feel, just then, truly at home," Putnam wrote in *Soaring Wings,* the biography he published two years after her disappearance.*

While Amelia was at Greenwich House, she realized she wanted to devote herself to aviation. "I had entered the scene when the industry was boiling with new enterprises," she remembered in *The Fun of It,* her second book, and felt she couldn't turn away. For her, the profession was a form of social work: a way to change society and improve the lot of women, as well as to have adventures and make a better living than she'd ever experienced. There was money to be made from flying, but no one knew quite how. What did the public want from commercial flight? The public wasn't really sure.

In 1929, Amelia made her first foray into business for a luxurious airline called Transcontinental Air Transport (TAT). It wasn't an auspicious year or an auspicious business, though it certainly had star power. Amelia was on board to see to women's comfort; Charles Lindbergh plotted the airline's routes.

TAT combined plane and train travel to convey passengers between New York City and Los Angeles in 48 hours. The speed was astonishing at a time when it usually took at least three days to cross the country. Passengers would fly by day—two-hour hops between New York and Columbus, Ohio, one day, and Amarillo, Texas, and Los Angeles the next. By night, they'd travel in railroad sleeper cars.

---

* Authorship of *Soaring Wings* is disputed. Putnam hired journalist Janet Mabie to help with the biography then rejected her contributions, claiming he'd had to rewrite it all. In an August 4, 1939, letter to Amy Earhart, Mabie complained that, although she'd received no acknowledgment, the finished book "is, word for word, 85% (conservatively) mine." It's hard to know which version is true. Mabie wrote her own biography of Earhart, but her publisher rejected it and it was never released.

Although nearly 100,000 people showed up on July 9 to witness the airline's first flight from Los Angeles—the plane was christened by movie star Mary Pickford and piloted by Lindbergh—the company had trouble filling seats. For one thing, it was prohibitively expensive: A one-way fare ranged from $337 to $403 (more than $6,500 to $7,500 in today's dollars). And it didn't seem particularly safe. In addition to sundry ground loops and mishaps, two planes had crashed, killing all on board, within six months of the line's launch. By October 1930, TAT was out of business.

At TAT, Amelia met Gene Vidal and Paul Collins. Vidal was a former Olympian and West Point's first flying instructor, while Collins had been a pilot for the U.S. mail. As TAT began to lose altitude, the three of them banded together to run the New York, Philadelphia and Washington Airway Corporation (NYPWA). Founded by two wealthy Philadelphians, the new airline was nearly the opposite of TAT. Rather than going across the country, it would only fly between the three major East Coast cities of its name. And instead of offering a luxurious travel experience, it simply provided transport.

Dubbed the Ludington Line after its founders, the new airline was successful almost immediately. The line offered 10 hourly flights a day between the three cities. "It was the first really frequent service in the world," Amelia explained. "There were no frills about it." She worked in passenger relations, convincing people to fly and soothing those who ran into problems. That meant "endless letters to be answered, and many, many speeches to audiences of various kinds." She also flew the line every other day or so, claiming at one point she'd had to escort a canary who was traveling alone. Eventually, the workload grew to be too much, given her other obligations, so she narrowed her responsibilities to publicity: giving speeches, granting interviews, and writing articles.

Although the Ludington Line was notably efficient and profitable, it too collapsed after little more than a year. The U.S. Postmaster General had awarded the mail route to another airline, and NYPWA could not compete.

The Ludingtons sold it to Eastern Air Transport; Amelia, Collins, and Vidal took over Boston-Maine Airways from Pan American.

The lecture circuit was Amelia's main business. Putnam had told her, she "could easily earn several thousand dollars lecturing around the country." Later, he recounted that her speech income was "small at first, but later considerable." She gave as many as 30 a month. Her mother complained she had "no time even to talk to herself." Indeed, she wore herself out so completely that she was plagued by a sore throat and had to have her tonsils removed.

THE POINT OF ALL THIS ACTIVITY was to fly. The book, the jobs with various airlines, the lectures across the country—they all made it possible for Amelia to take to the air.

To that end, while she was in England, she had purchased an Avro Avian from Lady Mary Heath. The plane was tiny: With its folding wings, it fit in a garage. It was so light Amelia could move it around herself; to start the motor, she just had to pull down on the propeller with one hand. But the two-seater biplane was mightier than it looked. Heath had flown it solo from South Africa to England. Now it was Amelia's turn to take it on an adventure. Once she had finished the book and met with all the "editors, promoters, airline operators, and educators with propositions generous, preposterous, or inviting," she declared "it was time to get into the air again."

She'd wanted to fly across the country with her mother when they'd moved east from Los Angeles a few years previously but had to sell her little Airster. In 1928, she seized a chance to make the transcontinental flight. "I purchased a lovely assortment of air navigation maps and headed for California and the National Air Races there," she wrote. She called what she was doing vagabonding.

The trip didn't start off particularly well. On the first stop in Pittsburgh, with Putnam on board, she hit a ditch while landing and the plane "ground looped," making an uncontrolled rotation on the ground. The landing gear, propeller, and left wing were damaged. Putnam oversaw the repairs and Amelia's upended schedule. He arranged for another Avian to fly to Pittsburgh to sacrifice some of its parts and then, once the lengthy refitting was completed, for Amelia and the plane to reunite in Dayton, Ohio.

From there, she flew solo to Terre Haute, Indiana, St. Louis, Missouri, and Muskogee, Oklahoma. Finding her way proved to be more challenging than flying the plane. "Imagine trying to recognize a new town, the way flyers do," she wrote later, "a hundred-mile-an-hour look at a checker-board of streets and roofs, trees and fields, with highways and railroads radiating and crisscrossing and perhaps a river or two to complicate—or simplify—the geography lesson."

Towns had not yet become sufficiently "air-minded"—a favorite term of Amelia's—to create signage visible to pilots. Often fliers were forced to follow railroad tracks and hope they led to their destination.

Amelia pinned maps to her clothes so the wind wouldn't carry them away from the Avian's open cockpit. But that didn't always work. Flying west of Fort Worth, she hit severe turbulence. "In the strenuous moments over Texas, the pin was somehow loosened and the map blew away."

Rather than panicking, she stayed the course and looked for a road. Soon, she saw one to the north: "So many cars must be going somewhere, and I felt I would like to go there, too. In all the vast rolling country below, those automobiles were the only signs of life except an occasional ranch house or oil derrick at intervals of many miles."

But the road, soon devoid of cars, led only to a small cluster of houses. As evening approached, she landed on the hamlet's main street. The whole town—an oil-boom settlement only a few months old—came out to greet her. She ate dinner at the Owl Cafe, the sole restaurant in town, and a resident put her up for the night. When she took off the next day, a tire was punctured. Once it was repaired, she made it as far as Pecos, Texas, where she arrived in time to be invited to the Rotary Club luncheon. On her way to El Paso, she was forced down again, this time with motor trouble. Back to Pecos she went, towed along the road at 10 miles an hour. Others would have been frustrated by such a journey, but Amelia insisted "the fun of it is worth the price."

Despite one more incident—she flipped her plane near Long Beach, California—she managed to arrive at the National Air Races in Los Angeles in time to receive a standing ovation. Whether through her design or Putnam's, the casual hop across the country proved to be a publicity coup—and a reminder to the public that though she was a mere passenger on the *Friendship,* she was a daring pilot in her own right. It was the first solo trip by a woman from the Atlantic to the Pacific and back.

A year later, Amelia and 19 other women would participate in another historic first: a women's race in the National Air Races. The decision to include women in the event had nothing to do with feminism and everything to do with supporting the new airline industry. If women avoided plane travel—95 percent of airline passengers were men—the aviation business was doomed. On the other hand, the race's marketing director explained, "If the feminine is considered the weaker sex and this weaker sex accomplishes the art of flying, it is positive proof of the simplicity and universal practicality of individual flying."

Yet the race would be challenging and dangerous: nine days from Santa Monica to Cleveland. To ensure the participants' safety, the racing committee (all men) proposed shifting the starting point to somewhere east of the treacherous Rocky Mountains and requiring a male navigator to accompany each female pilot. Amelia and several other prominent pilots refused to enter the race under those "ridiculous" conditions, and the committee backed down. "No male person will be allowed to ride in this derby race," the committee decreed, though female mechanics were allowed as passengers. Participants were required to carry a three-day supply of food and one gallon of water per person.

To compete in the race, Amelia traded her Avro Avian for a powerful Lockheed Vega. Her first model was a demonstration plane Lindbergh had supposedly flown. But the plane turned out to be in such poor shape, according to Lockheed's own test pilot, that the company replaced it with an entirely new one. The Vega was a big step up from the Avian. Fast and capable of relatively long distances, the closed-cockpit monoplane could carry as many as five passengers.

The race was fraught from the beginning. Humorist Will Rogers dubbed it the Powder Puff Derby, while journalists nicknamed the pilots Ladybirds, Angels, Sweethearts of the Air, and other insulting diminutives. "We are still trying to get ourselves called just 'pilots,'" an exasperated Amelia wrote.

Some women alleged their planes had been sabotaged: Thea Rasche found sand in her gas tank, Bobbi Trout mysteriously ran out of fuel, and Claire Fahy discovered acid had eaten through wire braces. All three had been forced down but escaped injury.

Marvel Crosson, the first female licensed pilot in Alaska, wasn't so lucky. On the race's second day, her plane crashed—from engine failure went the speculation, or perhaps she fainted or succumbed to carbon monoxide poisoning in the cockpit. Her battered body was found in Arizona, entwined in a partially open parachute, about a hundred feet away from the plane's wreckage.

Yet the race would prove to have the highest percentage of finishers in any cross-country derby so far: an argument that "the weaker sex" could indeed accomplish the art of flying. Despite having the fastest plane, Amelia came in third and was satisfied with the result. It was a transformative experience.

The women had competed against each other fiercely, yet they'd also bonded. By the end of the grueling event, Amelia, Bobbi Trout, Louise

Thaden, Blanche Noyes, and Phoebe Omlie had decided to form an organization for women pilots. At a meeting called a few months later at Curtiss Field on Long Island, a fifth of the country's female licensed pilots showed up. There was widespread support for the organization and recognition of the need for it. But they struggled to come up with a name. Bird Women, Angels' Club, Sky Larks—those suggestions seemed no better than what the press had called the race participants.

Amelia had a better idea. Why not name it after the number of women who signed up to be charter members? The organizers sent letters to all 117 women who held pilot licenses in 1929, explaining that "the organization would be neither strictly frivolous nor entirely serious, that the social side should be emphasized but that problems which arise in connection with women in aviation should also be discussed and acted upon." Ninety-nine women signed up, and the Ninety-Nines—the first organization for women pilots—was born. Amelia was its first president.

Amelia's many commitments to the aviation business often prevented her from actually flying. Bobbi Trout had asked her if she'd join an attempt to break the world's endurance record, and Amelia was sorely tempted. Trout, although only 23, was already a respected pilot, and breaking the record of 400 hours would be a significant achievement. But it would take too much time in preparation and some two weeks in the air. Amelia regretfully said no (although later, she may have wished she'd learned how to refuel in midair when she had the chance). She did manage to squeeze in an attempt at the women's speed record, clocking 197 miles an hour in a Vega Executive that Lockheed loaned to her for that purpose.

But there was one thing Earhart couldn't resist: whatever was newest in aviation. In 1931, that was the autogiro, an aircraft with rotating blades that took off like a plane but hovered like a helicopter. Proponents argued that autogiros were a safe alternative to planes, because they landed by gently settling to the ground; Amelia thought they were more practical, because they didn't require a runway. "A smooth pasture or extra sized backyard should suffice for ordinary hopping up and down," she wrote later. Hunters might use it to travel to the wilderness; commuters could use it in cities.

The aircraft wasn't graceful—one passenger called it a "turkey buzzard," while reporters nicknamed it "the flying windmill"—but it was relatively easy for a pilot to master. Amelia soloed after her first 15-minute flight in one, although afterward she said, "I am at a loss now to say whether I flew it or it flew me." But she was soon confident enough to attempt an altitude record: "It was suggested that I take one upstairs and keep on going until it would go no further," she later recounted. She packed an oxygen bottle, which turned out not to be necessary, and ascended to 18,415 feet, setting a record that stood for several years.

Soon, the Beech-Nut Packing Company reached out to Amelia, offering her the use of their autogiro—splashed with the food company's logo, of course—if she'd make the first transcontinental flight in one of the odd vehicles. It was "a business venture which brought her pleasure, experience, and two new records," according to her sister, plus a "sizable fee."

It also brought inconvenience and bother. Because the aircraft was in the experimental stage, she had to travel cross-country with a mechanic and a hundred pounds of spare parts and tools. Its range was short—she had to stop every two hours to refuel—and it barely went faster than a car. Another pilot reached the West Coast before she did, but she was the first to make the transcontinental flight heading east.

Autogiros also seemed more vulnerable to the wind's vagaries. In Texas, a dust devil dropped the pressure under the rotor blades as Amelia attempted a takeoff, forcing the contraption down; she struggled to avoid hitting spectators and ended up landing in a parking lot, damaging several cars. In Detroit later that year, she crashed while landing, but the only person injured was George Putnam: As he raced to the smoking wreckage, his foot caught on a guy wire, flipping him over on his back and breaking three ribs. Amelia emerged unscathed.

PERHAPS THE CRASH IS AN APT metaphor for how Amelia's fame affected the people in her life—her family, her then fiancé, and her future husband. None of them walked away unscathed. And, eventually, neither did she.

At first, it must have been thrilling—especially for her family, who had watched her struggle and had shared her financial precarity. After the *Friendship* flight, Amelia was one of the most famous people in the world. She could finally devote her time to the activity she loved—and make a decent living doing it.

But fame warped her relationships almost immediately. Thrust into an onslaught of publicity they hadn't chosen, her family sometimes said too much. "Don't worry," she advised her mother, "but be careful about telling people whereabout I am." She told Amy not to mention her salary and business to her sister. "I don't want her to spread the news and always fear she will," she wrote in a letter. And if her family didn't know what to say to reporters, "please refer them to Mr. Putnam. Don't even say yes or no if you don't want to. Just say you can add nothing to their tales and to ask me or GPP. Tell 'em you know many of my plans but are not divulging." Amelia had quickly become an expert on media relations, but her family was clearly struggling to keep up.

Nevertheless, Amelia's first impulse was to share her financial bounty with them. "Please throw away rags and get things you need on my account at Filene's," Amelia instructed her mother. "I can do it now and the pleasure is mine." The same applied to Muriel (though not Muriel's future husband, Albert Morrissey, a skinflint Amelia disliked). "If you know something she wants, get it for her and I'll pay," she told her mother. "My treat, at last."

Though Amy worried about tapping her daughter's "hard-earned cash," Amelia set up a monthly payment of $100 for her, plus a yearly income from the earnings of stocks and bonds. She assured her mother she could afford it. She was living frugally: "I plan to work very hard this year and [do] little else but fly."

Amelia helped Muriel as well, but her disgust with her sister's husband limited what she would give. Albert left Muriel to run their household alone, though he gave her little money for it. Amelia perceived this as poor management on both their parts. When Amy slipped cash to Muriel, Amelia was outraged. "I am very much displeased at the use you have put what I hoped you would save," she scolded. "I am not working to help Albert, nor Pidge much as I care for her. If they had not had that money, perhaps they would have found means to economize before. I do not mean to be harsh, but I know the family failing about money."

Amelia did loan Muriel $2,500 for a second mortgage, but became annoyed with her sister for not sending proper documentation of the loan. "I suppose it is impossible to impress upon her the fact that [a] businesslike relationship between relatives is not an unfriendly act," she complained. Amelia wasn't sure she'd ever ask for the loan to be repaid. Still, she didn't want her largesse to be taken for granted.

For her father, who had remarried, Amelia paid his mortgage on a cabin in the hills outside Los Angeles. She would hold the title but his wife, Helen, who Muriel described as "mature and kindly," would have a life tenancy (Amelia also ended up paying their property taxes). Edwin was still sober—and happier, his daughters thought, than he'd been since they were small. He continued to work as a lawyer but rarely charged his clients, many of whom were his friends and neighbors. "I'm long on friends," he told Amelia, "but short on cash."

By 1930, he was ailing. "I'm afraid Dad may not enjoy his little cabin too long," Amelia wrote to Muriel. "He's done wonders in planting trees and vines on the hillside, but he looks thinner than I've ever seen him." Helen said he had no appetite and tired quickly.

He had cancer. Amelia flew out to visit him. Like Amy and Muriel, Edwin expected Amelia, the family's most competent member, to fix everything for him. "He ... waited for me to come and change doctors or get him to a sanitarium or change diet because he didn't want to go"—he didn't want to die. Amelia did what she could to please him, ordering x-rays he didn't need, pretending to read telegrams from Amy and Muriel that never arrived. "He hoped until he could not move his poor hands. He didn't miss [me] when I left as we gave morphine at the last so he wouldn't worry," Amelia wrote to her mother. He died on September 23, 1930, a few hours after her departure.

Two days later, Amelia crashed her plane in Norfolk, Virginia, injuring her scalp. She blamed a cabin door that came unlatched, but grief for her father undoubtedly played a role. She'd worshipped him as a child, disdained him as a teenager, and made peace with him as an adult. "He was an aristocrat as he went," she told her mother, "all the weaknesses gone with a little boy's brown puzzled eyes."

A month later, she agreed to marry George Putnam. She'd ended her engagement with Sam Chapman two years before in 1928, a few months after the *Friendship* flight. The cracks in their relationship that had appeared as Amelia embraced a career in social work only widened with her new fame. "Amelia's desire to continue at Denison House seemed unreasonable to Sam," Muriel explained many years later, "and the thought of living the life of a domestic robot was equally impossible for Amelia." Sam wanted a traditional life, with himself as the breadwinner and his wife at home; Amelia did not. His efforts to accommodate her didn't address this essential truth. "He should do whatever makes him happiest," she complained to Muriel. "I know what I want to do, and I expect to do it, married or single." George, as prickly and hard-charging as he was, understood that.

A photograph of George and Amelia taken before the *Friendship* flight, when they'd known each other only a few weeks, foretells what's to come. The expression on George's face is one of absolute wonderment, while Amelia looks calmly pleased. "She is an extraordinary girl," he told a reporter after the *Friendship* took off. "She has captivated all who met her."

George's wife, Dorothy, was jealous of the time he devoted to his protégée. She was also relieved, according to her granddaughter. A swimmer, pianist, and adventurous traveler, Dorothy was no more suited to domestic life than Amelia was. She'd been restless and bored for years as George's wife, until the marriage had become nearly unbearable. In 1927, the year before George met Amelia, she'd embarked on an affair with George Weymouth, a Yale student Putnam had hired to be their eldest son's tutor. She was "utterly indifferent" to her husband, Dorothy confessed in her diary. "Anyway he's far too occupied with affairs of business to give time to any emotional life."

Yet the gossip was spreading about George and Amelia, not Dorothy and her young lover. Reporters, noticing how often the publisher and aviator traveled together, began asking about a "Putnam divorce." As Amelia's business manager, George worried what the rumors would do to her reputation and tried to repair relations with Dorothy. "Life is topsy-turvy," Dorothy wrote in her diary, "and now G.P. is apparently breaking off all his dates with A.E. as a sop to me! Funny."

The wooing didn't last long, though the whispers continued. Dorothy's affair with Weymouth ended in August 1928; she soon took up with Frank Upton, a naval officer who'd received the Congressional Medal of Honor for a World War I rescue. On September 12, 1929, Dorothy and her younger son George Jr., then eight years old, boarded a train for Reno, Nevada, to get a divorce. George Jr. thought the trip was a grand adventure. But he never lived with his father again.

Despite desperate letters from George, who was devastated by the rupture of the divorce yet unable to alter his behavior toward Amelia or win Dorothy back, the split was finalized on December 19. The next day, newspapers across the country reported Amelia's denial that she was now engaged to George. Three weeks later, Dorothy married Upton.*

Amelia and George weren't in such a rush. She'd nicknamed George "Simpkin" after a cat in one of Beatrix Potter's stories who stored mice in teacups "against the danger of having time idle on one's hands." He conceded that the description was apt. "She early perceived that, important as the project of which she was the center became, it was really just then one of a group of enterprises in which I was engaged," he said. "One mouse at a time was not enough." No one knew him better.

For her part, Amelia realized that no one would pursue her career more aggressively than George did on her behalf. Although he tended to insert himself into photos with her, her glory was his mission. Unlike Sam—or his own assumptions about Dorothy—George did not expect her to retreat into the domestic sphere. Nevertheless, she was wary of marriage. She had watched her parents' relationship disintegrate and witnessed Muriel's unhappiness with a self-regarding spouse.

George was different, but still she resisted him, even as she cherished his company. "We lunched together, and dined together, took long horseback rides together," she told an interviewer in 1932, four years after they first met. "I don't quite know when it happened, when I could deceive myself no longer. I couldn't continue telling myself that what I felt for GP was only friendship." But eventually, "I knew I had found the one person who could put up with me."

Still, he had to propose several times over nearly a year before she agreed to marry him. And even then, she delayed. They applied for a marriage license in November 1930, but didn't wed until the following February.

---

* Upton was abusive, and Dorothy divorced him in 1934. She would marry twice more.

"To marry Miss Amelia Earhart would be swell," George told a nosy reporter, "but nothing in this vale of tears is certain."

Nevertheless, on February 7, 1931, they were married in the living room at George's mother's house in Noank, Connecticut. The witnesses were few: a judge and his son, George's uncle, his mother, and his mother's two black cats who twined around George's legs during the five-minute ceremony.

Amelia was ready to bolt until that morning, when she handed him a letter that spoke to her apprehensions.

Dear GPP,

There are some things which should be writ before we are married—things we have talked over before—most of them.

You must know again my reluctance to marry, my feeling that I shatter thereby chances in work which mean most to me. I feel the move just now as foolish as anything I could do. I know there may be compensations but have no heart to look ahead.

On our life together I want you to understand I shall not hold you to any medieval code of faithfulness to me nor shall I consider myself bound to you similarly. If we can be honest I think the difficulties which arise may best be avoided should you or I become interested deeply (or in passing) in anyone else.

Please let us not interfere with the other's work or play, nor let the world see our private joys or disagreements. In this connection I may have to keep some place where I can go to be myself, now and then, for I cannot guarantee to endure at all times the confinement of even an attractive cage.

I must exact a cruel promise, and that is you will let me go in a year if we find no happiness together.

I will try to do my best in every way and give you that part of me you know and seem to want.

AE

George's acceptance of her terms—and the tenderness with which he wrote about the letter after she disappeared—speaks to his love for and deep understanding of his new wife. He included it in his biography of her as a way to convey her "gallant inward spirit, for it is a document of striking integrity and independence," reflecting "a certain feminine viewpoint which seems to me of importance in itself." He called it "a sad little letter"—marriage seemed to frighten her more than any ocean flight—yet it was "brutal in its frankness ... beautiful in its honesty."

Once the deed was done, Amelia appeared to be all in. She wired Muriel, "OVER THE BROOMSTICK WITH GP TODAY STOP BREAK NEWS GENTLY TO MOTHER." Amy didn't approve of George: At 43 years old to Amelia's 33, he was too old for her daughter, she thought, and divorced. But when reporters came calling for her response, Amy was diplomatic.

Two weeks after the wedding, Amelia wrote, "I want you to know I appreciate more than I can say the interview you gave in Phila. about my marriage. I was so proud of you. I am much happier than I expected I could ever be in that state. I believe the whole thing was for the best."

Amelia's cruel promise was never enacted. One year later, she and George were still married and stayed so until the end of her life.

CHAPTER FIFTEEN

CASTAWAY: BONES

During the 2017 TIGHAR/Betchart expedition to Nikumaroro, you could often find Kaono Koura and Eria Tebaro smoking in the sun on the upper deck of the *Reef Endeavour*. Koura and Tebaro, stout men clad in shorts and flip-flops, were representatives of the Kiribati government; their presence was a key element of the agreement between the expedition and Nikumaroro's sovereign country.

Koura, the more outgoing of the two, represented the office of the Phoenix Islands Protected Area (PIPA). He was there to make sure the expedition didn't harm the flora and fauna of one of the largest marine sanctuaries in the world, though he didn't hesitate to pick up dinner plate–size coconut crabs by their shells to give us a closer look as their pincers waved impotently in the air. Tebaro was a customs agent. A conscientious man whose serious demeanor was transformed when he smiled, he ensured that all the passengers' paperwork was in order before we crossed into Kiribati waters.

As the expedition was winding down and returning to Fiji, Fred Hiebert, wearing his signature uniform of black jeans and oxford shirt in defiance of the oppressive heat, often joined Koura and Tebaro on the upper deck. With the foresight born of a lifetime of expeditions, the National Geographic archaeologist had packed multiple cartons of cigarettes. Kiribati, after all, has one of the highest rates of smoking in the world, with roughly half the male population lighting up. The rate in Fiji, where most of the ship's crew came from, is not quite so high, but still notable. As the expedition reached its end, Hiebert was one of the few people on board still with a supply—and the willingness to share it. Hiebert, Koura, and Tebaro became good friends.

The return voyage to Fiji was somber. What had started with such high hopes had ended with frustration. The forensic dogs had alerted where Tom King and other TIGHAR members thought Earhart had died a castaway, yet the archaeological team hadn't found any remains despite the enthusiastic assistance of passengers and crew. Instead of bones, they were returning home with bags of soil: a long shot for DNA recovery.

It isn't in Hiebert's nature to give up, though. Faced with a setback, his restless mind roves until it finds the next possibility, or two or three. He'd been the one to suggest collecting soil from under the ren tree, given recent advances in sequencing environmental DNA. A few months before the expedition launched, a team of scientists published a paper in *Science* announcing they'd extracted Neanderthal mitochondrial DNA from cave sediment in Belgium, Russia, and Spain. National Geographic aims to be on the leading edge of science and exploration. How perfect would it be, Hiebert argued, if one of the great historic mysteries was solved by this advanced technology?

In the meantime, he would pursue other paths. During one of many conversations on the return voyage about what to do next, King raised the issue of the bones discovered on the island in 1940. They'd been delivered to Fiji, where Dr. Hoodless examined them and declared they belonged to a man. But what happened to them afterward? TIGHAR had searched bone collections at the Fiji Museum and the Fiji School of Medicine in

Suva—even storage rooms in the basement of Government House, the colonial governors' residence and now the home of Fiji's president. Not a single bone matched Hoodless's measurements.

King wondered if they'd ended up on Tarawa, in Kiribati, when the country gained its independence from Britain in 1979. Most colonial records and materials were dispersed back to their countries of origin, he said. Hiebert remembered gossip he'd heard a few years previously: The then president of Kiribati had told one of National Geographic's top television executives at a dinner that Amelia Earhart's bones were rumored to be in a box at the Tarawa Post Office.

Hiebert wasted no time. He "moseyed"—his word—up to Tebaro and asked him what it would take to get forensic dogs into the main post office on Tarawa to sniff for bones.

"You mean for the box of bones in customs?" replied Tebaro.

Hiebert was stunned. The rumor appeared to be true.

Seeing Hiebert's astonishment, Tebaro turned bright red and said, "I shouldn't have said anything." But it was too late. Once he'd recovered from his shock, Hiebert began spinning plans for a detour to Tarawa.

On the afternoon of July 12, 2017, a day after disembarking from the *Reef Endeavour* in Nadi, Fiji, a small group arrived on Tarawa. From the airplane, we could see the atoll's triangular shape, its west side split by a wide channel leading into an enormous lagoon. A string of islands stretched to the north, while densely populated South Tarawa—narrow dashes of land connected by causeways—lay to the east. More than half of the country's population lives there, giving it the population density of iconic cities like Hong Kong or Tokyo (though without their glamour).

Bonriki International Airport lies at the conjunction of the atoll's two spurs. Two buildings—one for arrivals, the other for departures—stand along the only gap in the fence around the runway. Anthropologist Jaime Bach, who served in the Peace Corps on one of Kiribati's outer islands and now volunteers as a kind of cultural interpreter for TIGHAR, said the fence was to keep the pigs and children off the runway. Yet children clasped the chains in the fence, eyeing the passengers as we made our way across the tarmac toward customs.

There were seven of us: Hiebert, King, Bach, National Geographic videographer Corey Robinson, me, and Tebaro and Koura, who would act as guides (which meant postponing reunion with their own families). The forensic dogs hadn't come on the journey—permission to gain their entry would have taken months—but Hiebert thought they weren't needed. Tarawa only had one customs warehouse, and it wasn't very big. How hard could it be to locate a box of bones?

The team faced several problems, most of them self-inflicted. Hiebert and King had allotted less than 24 hours for the search. Flights were limited in and out of Kiribati, and family and work obligations demanded our return. I'd already missed my son's 13th birthday.

It was also the worst day of the year to do it. We'd arrived late in the afternoon on Independence Day, the country's biggest holiday. All government offices were closed, and government workers dispersed across the island.

Tebaro and Koura needed to track down the person with the key to the customs warehouse, and—most crucially—the person who would grant permission to enter it. In Kiribati, a phone call, an email, or a text wouldn't do. Business was conducted face-to-face. We loaded into a cramped station wagon belonging to PIPA and began to search for the person with the key.

Our first stop was the home of the postmaster, whom we surprised on his day off. A gaggle of children stared at us from the road as we got out of the two cars—one driven by Koura, the other by Tebaro—the additional one containing Tukabu Teroroko, the head of PIPA, crisply attired in a white dress shirt, and Tiiroa Roneti, PIPA's legal adviser, a quick intelligent man who wore sunglasses but no shoes. Bach spoke to the kids in Kiribati; their eyes widened briefly in wonder, then they laughed and ran away. They wouldn't have encountered many people like Bach: forceful yet friendly, a good deal taller than most of their parents, dressed all in black—and fluent in their language.

A man in a *lavalava,* or sarong, stepped out of the house and stopped when he saw the crowd of people in his yard, where a couple pigs roamed with ropes tethered to their ankles. When Roneti explained who we were and why we were there, the man immediately excused himself and retreated to the house. Within moments, he was back outside, now clad in a polo shirt and khakis. This was the postmaster.

He gestured us toward the *buia* next to his house—the thatch-covered platform that serves as the social center of Kiribati homes. We sat cross-legged in a circle as King and Bach tried to explain what they were looking for.

The postmaster hadn't gotten over his surprise at finding five Americans—one wielding a video camera—and various Kiribati officials at his home on a national holiday. King and Bach's tale about the bones—possibly the remains of a famous woman pilot discovered on Nikumaroro many years ago, sent to Fiji and lost, and now rumored to be in a briefcase somewhere in Tarawa—completely baffled him. He told Bach he hadn't heard of such a thing in his 27 years in the postal service. The news that the Kiribati president passed along the rumor to a National Geographic executive further astonished him.

He shook his head. "Sorry," he said in English, "I don't know."

And as quickly as we descended on him, we said our thank-yous and goodbyes, and piled back into the cars.

We were off to see the comptroller of customs. He wasn't at home. A member of his family told us he was at an official banquet; afterward, he'd attend the celebrations at the national stadium. We would have to track him down there.

It was getting toward dark now, but King and Hiebert decided to go to the warehouse anyway. Maybe someone there would let us in. The warehouse was on Betio, at the western tip of Tarawa, where a nightmarish battle took place during World War II in which U.S. marines struggled across the reef while Japanese soldiers mowed them down. We passed the ruins of Japanese gun emplacements, still pointing out to sea.

According to Bach, Betio was also the site of a notorious bar. When we arrived at the warehouse, the sun had set. Two men stepped out of the shadows, lurching like zombies. They were incoherent in their intoxication, yet determined to get close to us—especially to me and Bach, the only women in the group. Bach planted herself stolidly and spoke sharply. The men startled and staggered away. We were free to approach the customs office next to the warehouse, where we hoped to find the warehouse's former supervisor.

Tebaro went in first to prepare whomever was in the office for our arrival. He soon returned to guide us up a dark staircase to the customs office. There we met Anee Naunta, who wore a flower behind her ear and a shirt decorated with stars. Again, King explained—and Bach translated—that they were involved in a project to solve a mystery from 1937, and they trotted through the story of the lost aviator, the bones, the island, the missing box.

Naunta had seen them. Or at least she saw a brown briefcase, very dusty, back in 2007. Several people did, she said, when customs shifted its holdings to a new warehouse.

Hiebert and King could barely contain themselves.

"If possible to see, it would be ..." started Hiebert.

"Fantastic," interrupted King.

"It would be important for the United States, for Kiribati, for the world," finished Hiebert.

But Naunta didn't have the key and needed to call the person who could give it to her. While we waited, music from the Independence Day celebrations wafted in through the windows.

"Nobody's going to sleep tonight," said Bach.

"It's our lucky day," said Hiebert, ever the optimist.

"So far," said King, who'd been in this position of hopeful expectation many times before, only to be disappointed.

Naunta returned. We would not be gaining access to the warehouse that night. We needed to obtain permission from the comptroller, and we needed the key.

We headed to the stadium. It wasn't far, just off the main road near the president's house, but the streets were full of people. Koura inched the car through the masses near the food stands, where we were told the comptroller was manning a booth. Fireworks blasted overhead. Waves of people streamed past the car, too caught up in the festivities to pay much attention to us.

Standing amid this surging crowd, Hiebert and King were at a loss as to what to do next, until Bach registered the sound of a voice cutting through all the hubbub. "The only way to find him is to make an announcement during the event," she said. Koura hurried off to make that happen.

Within a few moments, the comptroller stood before us, a little worse for wear given the hours of merrymaking he'd already enjoyed. But he readily granted permission to search the warehouse the next morning. We bade him goodnight and retreated down the long road to the guesthouse where we were staying. We didn't have the warehouse key, but Koura assured us he would get it. After a dinner of bread and coconut water, I fell asleep under the watchful eye of a salamander on the ceiling of the room I shared with Bach.

Koura picked us up early in the morning. He and Tebaro had obtained the key to the warehouse around midnight and checked that it worked. Tebaro was waiting there for us.

Tarawa appeared newly washed. It had rained in the night, but now the sky was pure blue. Few people were on the streets, though I saw some swimming in the lagoon. It seemed a perfect morning for it, I thought, until Bach set me straight. They weren't swimming, she said. Tarawa—like many other Pacific islands—has an issue with open defecation, including in the waters. We zipped back to Betio down the empty causeway, while I looked with new eyes at the beautiful lagoon flashing by.

When we arrived at the warehouse, its doors were wide open. Tebaro and Naunta were there, along with five young men who had been recruited to sort through the boxes. A concrete block building with two big wooden doors, the metal-roofed warehouse was perhaps the size of a couple of suburban garages. It wasn't full. Embarrassingly, I'd been picturing a *Raiders of the Lost Ark* scene, with rows upon rows of shelves stretching into infinity. Instead, the space was a jumble of cardboard, some of it rotting, with mundane items spilling on the floor. Naunta sneezed at the dust.

Three motorcycles took up one corner. There was a Ping-Pong table, an overflowing box of Hello Kitty flip-flops, others with papers, binders, clothes—so many random things that didn't make it through customs and ended up in the netherworld of the warehouse where they appeared to be slowly disintegrating. More than 20 cases of Double Happiness cigarettes. Hundreds of cans of Tiger Beer from Vietnam. Jerseys from "Football Team Korea."

"It's mostly recent stuff, which gives me pause," said Hiebert. "What's interesting is that people who work at customs all know about [the briefcase containing bones] and all describe it in the same way."

Hiebert and Tebaro attempted to make the search systematic by moving through the warehouse in a circle, but Hiebert was afraid they missed something. He asked the men to go through the boxes one more time, especially those from a precarious stack in the far corner. Rats darted from the pile—startling Naunta into a laugh—but the men found nothing. "It's not here," said Koura. Tebaro last saw it in 2010.

The conversation turned to whether someone might have thrown it out.

"Someone who doesn't know its archaeological worth wouldn't know what to do with it," pointed out Roneti, who joined us mid-search with his boss, Teroroko. Teroroko wondered if someone would have taken the bones to use for magic.

Naunta, a little defensive, said she didn't know, but she assured us she'd have more custom officers look when they came back to work on Monday.

"At least we got them started," said Bach. "It's better than writing a letter."

Hiebert was right. The customs warehouse was small, and it didn't take more than a couple hours to search. Yet they didn't find the missing bones. And we had a plane to catch.

JUST AS THE TIGHAR TEAM COULDN'T quit Nikumaroro, Hiebert could not give up on the idea that the bones had ended up in Tarawa. In March 2019, as Bob Ballard was gearing up for his expedition to Nikumaroro, Hiebert and Bach returned to Tarawa. They wanted to revisit the warehouse to determine whether it would be worth the considerable trouble to bring the forensic dogs to sniff around. This time, they had three days.

Unfortunately, the warehouse proved to be a bust. It had been cleaned up in the two years since their last visit. The boxes were stacked and organized. The rats were gone, and the aura of mystery had been scrubbed away. "No one had seen a briefcase, suitcase, or box of human bones," said Hiebert.

No need to bring the dogs, then, but this elusive briefcase must have ended up *somewhere*. They debated what to do next. There were several post offices scattered across the atoll. Perhaps they had storage for unclaimed packages. And then there was the cultural center near PIPA's office, where they'd consulted their colleague Teroroko about permits. They'd passed it many times. Like everything else in Tarawa, it was just off the main road. Hiebert and Bach decided to stop by.

When they entered the Te Umwanibong museum and cultural center, a low-slung building with a steep-pitched roof, they encountered a cool tiled room filled with simple displays of coconut fiber armor and fearsome palm wood swords bristling with shark teeth. The staff were happy to show them around the one-room exhibit, and Hiebert and Bach expressed polite interest in the artifacts, peering at the textiles on the walls and jewelry presented in glass-topped cases.

Then they caught a glimpse of the back room. Behind a desk in a space clearly devoted to administrative work was a wall of human remains. They were on shelves, a jumble of skulls and other bones. Some were in plastic bags, while others were out in the open. Some were whitish, meaning they'd been exposed to the elements. Others were darker: They'd been buried.

Bach asked the museum staff members where the bones had come from, but they didn't know. Most employees had only recently been hired.

But they knew there were more bones. They opened the doors of cupboards in the office and pulled out cardboard box after cardboard box packed with bones.

"Holy shit," Hiebert said, "we don't need forensic dogs. We need a forensic anthropologist." He wanted to examine the remains but they hadn't brought gloves—they thought they were just in Tarawa on a scouting mission. He couldn't risk contaminating the bones with his own DNA.

Hiebert took a picture and texted it to Tom King back in the United States. "We might have found Amelia!" King, he said, responded coolly. He'd had his hopes dashed before.

There was one person, though, who might know about the bones' origins: a former staffer who was now a teacher. Hiebert and Bach said a hurried goodbye to the helpful staff at the cultural center—they couldn't do any more there—and hopped in the car.

When they arrived at the school, the teacher was in a staff meeting. Hiebert and Bach were so keyed up—and so conscious of the clock ticking away on their time in Tarawa—they pulled him out of the meeting. He didn't know anything about where the bones came from either. But he thought he knew who might: the museum's original curator.

The curator had recently retired to a new house in a quiet spot on the island's northern end. When Bach and Hiebert arrived, they found him asleep on a mat on his household's *buia,* the island's breezes wafting through the open walls. When he roused, they asked him the same question they'd asked the staff at the museum and the teacher at the school: Where did the many bones lining the office walls come from?

He didn't know. All he would say was that the bones had always been there.

They appeared to have reached a dead end. No one knew the provenance of the bones.

But then they had a fortuitous encounter with Anote Tong, who as president of Kiribati from 2003 to 2016 was instrumental in the creation of the Phoenix Islands Protected Area. More crucially, he'd been in the Ministry of Education, which oversees Kiribati's library and archives, when the country became independent. He told Bach and Hiebert that the colonial administration in Fiji had sent everything Kiribati-related back to the new country. Paperwork went to the archives. Everything else went to the museum—including, perhaps, the bones that were discovered on Nikumaroro and sent to Fiji for Hoodless to examine.

ERIN KIMMERLE'S LIGHT VOICE AND SUN-KISSED appearance belie the seriousness of her purpose. A veteran of United Nations war crimes investigations in Bosnia-Herzegovina, Croatia, and Kosovo, the forensic anthropologist came before the public eye when she led a University of South Florida team that discovered the unmarked graves of more than 50 children at the notorious Arthur G. Dozier School for Boys in Marianna, Florida.

But now she was examining bones at a table in the shaded interior of the Te Umwanibong museum and cultural center in Tarawa. A few months after Hiebert and Bach's scouting trip, Hiebert had managed to recruit Kimmerle into the Earhart project. Although she normally pursues the human rights component of anthropological investigations, this historical mystery intrigued her. Before she'd arrived on Tarawa, she'd reviewed Hoodless's measurements from 1940 and discovered they were flawed. He hadn't measured the femur, the best bone for estimating stature. Nor did the measurements on which he'd based his sex determination convince her. Indeed, nothing from his notes seemed to convincingly refute that the bones were Earhart's.

The bones at the museum had been reorganized since Hiebert and Bach were last there, with long bones sorted into one box and skulls into others—including one battered box containing three skulls submerged in foam peanuts. It made their job more difficult. Even so, Kimmerle quickly determined they were looking at the remains of eight individuals. And the variation between color and preservation made it easier to figure out which bones went together.

Kimmerle was looking for two characteristics very specific to Earhart. The flier had a diastema—a space between her front teeth—that should be obvious on her skull. And she'd had surgery to relieve the sinus pain that had plagued her since she became ill with influenza while living in Toronto. The operation would have left a hole in her skull to drain the sinuses. Together, those "would be great indicators that this could be her," said Kimmerle.

By the end of the first day, the team had managed to go through only four sets of remains—and they'd all belonged to men, judging by the thickness of their skulls. The dark color of their bones indicated that they'd also all been buried. They did not match the description of the bones found on Nikumaroro. Still, Kimmerle examined and measured each one. It was a painstaking process.

The next day was another national holiday—Youth Day on August 5—but Hiebert persuaded the museum staff to work overtime so Kimmerle could continue to work her way through their collection. By the end of her time at the museum, she had sifted through more than 600 bone fragments and seven skulls.

On the last day, in the last box, Kimmerle found what she'd been looking for—or nearly. She emptied a plastic bag full of fragments onto the table. They all came from a single skull and they were bleached white, indicating they'd been aboveground and exposed to the sun for a while. Wax on the fragments revealed that an unknown restorer had attempted to fit the pieces together. A rudimentary inventory suggested the skull had been excavated on another island in Kiribati, but Hiebert suspected that was incorrect. "The skull doesn't look like it was excavated," he said.

Kimmerle picked up a portion of the frontal bone. It was slight and didn't show the fusion an older adult's would, indicating it belonged to a female, middle-aged or younger. On another fragment she saw what she called "remodeling" in the nasal area. Something had been done—trauma? surgery?—to this area of the person's face. There weren't any teeth to reveal whether she'd had a gap in her smile.

Then Kimmerle found something better: two intact sections of the temporal bone that included the petrous portion, thick areas behind the ears that are rich sources for DNA. Perhaps they could be matched with the DNA of one of Earhart's living relatives.

Nothing about this skull so far eliminated the possibility that it belonged to Amelia Earhart. "We don't know if it's her or not but all lines of evidence point to the 1940 bones being in this museum," said Kimmerle. She packed each of the dozen or so fragments into a plastic bag and—with the Kiribati government's permission—brought the bones back to her lab in Florida.

ON A CRISP FALL DAY IN 2019, a crowd of people packed a windowless conference room at National Geographic headquarters in Washington, D.C. At the head of the table was molecular anthropologist Miguel Vilar, lead scientist for the National Geographic Society's Genographic Project, which aimed to trace historic migration patterns through genetics. Vilar was overseeing the DNA testing of the Tarawa skull.

In front of him, on his laptop, was the mitochondrial DNA genome of Amy Kleppner, Earhart's niece—Earhart's sister Muriel Morrissey's daughter. Next to him was a phone. Arrayed on the other side of the room were cameras, a television crew, and a few *National Geographic* journalists and staffers, all trying to be silent as we strained to follow the conversation between Vilar and Frankie West, the biological anthropologist who had extracted DNA from the Tarawa skull.

Also on the line were Hiebert and Kimmerle, calling in from her lab at the University of South Florida. Kimmerle had gone as far as she could with the skull. When she returned home from Tarawa, she'd carefully reassembled it. The lower portion of the left eye socket was missing, giving the skull a piratical air, but enough remained to allow her to revisit Hoodless's measurements.

According to Hoodless, he'd examined "a skull with the right zygoma and malar bones [cheekbones] broken off" as well as a "mandible [jaw] with only four teeth in position." Kimmerle did not have the teeth—and a good deal more of the skull's lower portion was missing from her sample—but luckily, she had enough to compare the Tarawa skull's measurements to Hoodless's. He'd measured the orbital width and height, as well as the skull's length and breadth.

Three out of four of those measurements matched the Tarawa skull. When Kimmerle put the matching measurements in Fordisc, the software program that classifies bones by ancestry and sex, the results indicated the skull belonged to a female with a European background. But when she added the fourth measurement—as well as a few others that align with modern forensic protocols—the skull matched much more strongly with local populations from the South Pacific. Still, the results weren't so definitive that she ruled out the skull as Earhart's.

Kimmerle had a few other tricks up her sleeve. Although the skull was missing the portions that would have contained Earhart's distinctive tooth gap and sinus surgery, the forensic anthropologist could compare the skull to the pilot's known facial structure through a process called superimposition. Kimmerle made a 3D scan of the skull, placing the remains on a thin metal shelf covered by a paper towel and propping it up with black sponges, while red lines from the laser traced its contours. When the scan was complete, she superimposed it on a photographic portrait of Earhart. The skull's brow, eye shape, and eye spacing corresponded to the flier's, but the nasal openings didn't. Again, the mismatch wasn't enough to completely exclude the skull. But the odds that it belonged to Earhart were greatly reduced.

Now it was West's turn. Kimmerle packed up the skull's right petrous bone and shipped it to West's lab at Western Carolina University.

West's first step when she received the bone was to decontaminate its surface with a bleach solution and ultraviolet lights. She wanted to ensure that whatever DNA she extracted came from the bone, rather than the unknown number of people who had handled it previously. She used a small dental bur tool to grind off 50 milligrams of bone powder. Through a series of chemical processes, she removed all other cellular material, leaving only the DNA itself.

Then she sequenced the DNA. Because the skull had apparently been exposed to the elements on a Pacific island and afterward kept in what West tactfully called "ambient storage conditions" at the museum, the DNA had probably degraded. So she decided to tackle the skull's mitochondrial DNA first. Stored in the hundreds of mitochondria in each cell and passed down from mother to child, mitochondrial DNA provides a less precise identification than nuclear DNA but is far more robust. If the skull sample matched Kleppner's, it would indicate Earhart's niece and the skull belonged to the same haplogroup. This shared ancestry might not actually be very close, but it would give West a reason to dive into the nuclear DNA. If it wasn't too degraded—only two copies are in the nucleus of each cell—West might be able to "individualize" the sample, to indicate who exactly this person was.

West had not examined Kleppner's genome. Vilar was similarly ignorant of West's results from the Tarawa skull. But today, they would compare notes—reading out locations on their respective genomes to see how well the sequences match.

They ran into a problem almost immediately. The sample, said West, is "very degraded and the DNA is fragmented." She had "very low coverage"—as she put it—on many of the segments Vilar wanted to compare.

"Frankie is looking at murky data," said Vilar, "and I'm looking at modern beautiful data."

They managed to identify 15 mutational points to compare. All would match if the samples came from a mother and child. For an aunt and a niece, Vilar expected a variation of only 2 percent. In this case, only two of the sequences matched.

"Two out of 15 does not suggest that we have found her," said Vilar. "But there's still a small possibility. And that's what keeps us going."

CHAPTER SIXTEEN

1932: "BECAUSE I WANTED TO"

The flight started smoothly enough. Amelia Earhart had taken off from Harbour Grace, Newfoundland, on May 20, 1932, soaring easily into the fair Friday sky. She was settled snugly in the cockpit of her cherry red Lockheed Vega, hands on the control stick, both feet poised over the rudder pedals. Arrayed before her were the instruments she'd rely on to fly through darkness and poor visibility: the climb indicator, turn and bank indicator, air speed indicator, compass, directional gyroscope, barograph, and altimeter. When she peered out of the cockpit's windows, she spotted two icebergs, then a small boat. Puffball clouds began to gather; a massive cloud bank loomed before her, as high and wide as she could see.

Preparing to dive below the storm, Amelia checked the altimeter. To her astonishment, the instrument's hands "swung around the dial uselessly." In all her 12 years of flying—which, as with any early pilot, were full of mechanical mishaps—she'd never had an altimeter fail.

It was dark now, around 11 p.m., and her troubles were just beginning. Soon she noticed "a small blue flame licking through a broken weld in the manifold ring." It wasn't causing engine problems yet, but the plane's vibrations would gradually make it worse.

She wondered whether she should turn back. An enormous storm was bearing down on her, she wasn't able to gauge her altitude above the sea, and the manifold might eventually splinter at the weakened weld, in which case there was no hope that the plane would ever reach land. But landing in the dark at the unlit Harbour Grace airfield, *if* she could navigate her way there, would be nearly impossible, and—given the heavy load of combustible fuel the plane was still carrying—potentially catastrophic.

She had more than a thousand miles left in her attempt to be the second person after Charles Lindbergh to fly solo across the Atlantic. She faced an agonizing choice.

EVER SINCE AMELIA LANDED IN ENGLAND in 1928—a "sack of potatoes" aboard the *Friendship*—she'd wanted to make the solo flight, to prove to herself and others that she deserved the fame that had burst upon her. She knew she wasn't ready at the time—she didn't have the hours in the air, the experience. But after four years of cross-country flying, of speed records and chaotic races, of experimental autogiros and state-of-the-art Lockheed Vegas, she was getting close.

She didn't talk about it much. "My own tendency was deliberately to keep away from the subject," admitted George. It terrified him. Still, "I must have known for four years really that she wanted to." And he knew whom he had married.

By the spring of 1931, it was clear that if Amelia was going to attempt the Atlantic, she would have to do it soon. No one had successfully made the solo flight since Lindbergh's triumphant landing in Paris in 1927, but others—men and women—had announced their intention to try. The most worrisome from Amelia's perspective was Ruth Nichols. A friend of Amelia's and fellow founder of the Ninety-Nines who lived nearby in Rye, New York, Ruth had spent the year breaking records, including the women's altitude record and Amelia's own speed record. In April, she announced her plan "to follow the Lindbergh trail." So confident was she that she sent publicist Hilton Railey ahead to France to smooth her arrival. If Nichols—attractive, wealthy, and charismatic—made it across the Atlantic, Amelia would be dethroned, perhaps permanently.

Harbour Grace in Newfoundland, the easternmost North American airfield, was to be Nichols's launching point. On her way there, she'd stop at St. John's to refuel, giving herself an easy flight before the long haul across the Atlantic. On June 22, 1931, she took off on the preliminary leg of her journey. She never made it as far as Harbour Grace. Hesitating too long on her touchdown in St. John's, Nichols hit the cliffs at the end of the runway, wrecking the plane and breaking five of her vertebrae. She planned to try again the following summer.

Elinor Smith, much younger than Nichols and Amelia, also announced that she would give the Atlantic a try that summer. She'd made her name as a teenage pilot by flying under all the bridges in New York City—earning herself a temporary license suspension in the process. Her plans were thwarted by an accident that damaged her landing gear; she couldn't get it repaired before the end of the Atlantic flying season. She also would try again.

Amelia watched the kerfuffle from afar, with an uncomfortable mixture of sympathy and relief. Few people knew as she did the anxiety of preparing for such a flight, the endless calculations, the dependence on the weather—the wait at Trepassey before the *Friendship* flight was one of the most difficult times of her life. She knew Nichols and Smith must have been devastated by the derailment of their plans. And yet, the Lindbergh trail remained open to her.

On a winter morning early in 1932, Amelia and George were in the dining room at Rye eating breakfast. In the companionable silence, she lowered her newspaper and looked over at him. "Would you *mind* if I flew the Atlantic?" she asked. His response was visceral: "the fusion of a clutch at the heart, and something akin to elation, in the presence of so adventurous a spirit." But he could not *mind* her flying the Atlantic "in the sense of putting out a proprietary hand to hold her back." What he could do—to dispel the clutch to his heart—was throw himself into the preparations.

AMELIA WAS JUST AS CASUAL WHEN she asked Bernt Balchen, whom she'd met in connection with the *Friendship* flight, to help her ready the plane. She'd invited him over for a leisurely weekend lunch with her and George. After they ate, the threesome drifted out back for a game of croquet. Midway through, when Amelia, according to George, was "for the middle wicket, on the way home," she laid down her mallet. "I want to tell you, Bernt—" The men lay down their mallets, too, and the three of them retreated to a nearby boulder to talk. She'd told no one else about her plans, but she wanted Balchen's honest assessment.

"Am I ready to do it? Is the ship ready? Will you help me?"

Balchen—"wise enough," said George, "to start an action in low gear"—paused a long minute.

"Yes. You can do it," Balchen responded at last. "The ship—when we are through with it—will be O.K. And—I'll help."

George was mightily relieved. "If it had to be, at least aiding AE as technical adviser would be altogether the best man we could get—a great pilot and technician, with the unique experience behind him of his polar and Atlantic flights with [Richard] Byrd."

Only two other people knew about the flight: mechanic Eddie Gorski and Lucy Challiss, her cousin "Toot" who lived with them. To protect herself from hordes of reporters descending on the airfield, from family and friends pleading with her not to go, from the opinions of the general public, Amelia would not announce her plans ahead of time. She wanted the freedom to change her mind, especially if it transpired she wasn't sufficiently prepared. She told Balchen to tell her straight if she or the plane weren't ready: She promised to listen and cancel the flight.

To maintain the secret, she chartered her Vega to Balchen. People would think the modifications he was adding to it were for Lincoln Ellsworth's upcoming Antarctic expedition, which Balchen was also planning. Amelia left the improvements in Balchen's hands, though she refused to allow him to add pontoons. She'd had enough of them in Trepassey. He reinforced the fuselage and installed a large fuel tank in the cabin and others in the wings, as well as a more powerful Wasp motor. He equipped the cockpit with a drift indicator and three compasses—an aperiodic, a magnetic, and a directional gyro. By the time he was through with it, the plane weighed 5,500 pounds and had a range of 3,200 miles.

Meanwhile, Amelia was spending "hour after hour, day after day, learning all she could about flying on instruments." Blind flying was relatively new; James Doolittle had become the first pilot to take off, fly a set course, and land solely on instruments when he flew with a hood over his open cockpit in 1929. The first manual on blind flying only came out in 1932.

Given the Atlantic's storminess, Amelia needed to be able "to handle the ship without looking outside of the cockpit." Within the cockpit, she had gauges to indicate how high she was, how much she was climbing, and how level the plane was. The compasses—especially the highly accurate directional gyro—told her whether she was heading in the right direction. As long as the indicators didn't fail and she avoided mountainous regions, all the information she needed was contained within the Vega's cockpit.

Amelia aimed to take off around May 20, the fifth anniversary of the start of Lindbergh's historic flight. One wonders if she and George considered postponing—perhaps to coincide instead with the fourth anniversary of the *Friendship* flight in June. For Lindbergh and his wife, Anne Morrow

Lindbergh, had become engulfed in tragedy. On March 1, their toddler son—also named Charles—had disappeared from his bedroom. After a series of misleading and cruel ransom notes, the child's body was discovered on May 12.

Ultimately, the weather would determine when Amelia flew. George was in charge of monitoring reports from James Kimball at the Weather Bureau, who had become the go-to weatherman for Atlantic fliers. Kimball wasn't told what Amelia's plans were, but he could easily guess. Reports came in from U.S. coastal stations, England, and ships at sea. Putting them together into a prediction for conditions some hours or even days in the future involved more guesswork than science. As the plane neared readiness, George spent "days and nights ... in nerve-stretching watchfulness of weather maps."

The reports did not sound promising for the period around May 20. On the morning of May 19—a Thursday—Amelia had no plans to leave. She drove down to Teterboro Airport in New Jersey, where Balchen kept the plane, with the intention of practicing blind flying in the afternoon. But around noon, she received a phone call. It was George, ringing from Doc Kimball's office. Visibility was good to Newfoundland, he said. "And by tomorrow the Atlantic looks as good as you're likely to get it for some time." She needed to leave soon.

Setting a departure time of 3 p.m., Amelia hopped back in her car and drove home—"as fast as I dared"—to change and collect her things. She wasn't bringing much: two cans of tomato juice, a thermos of soup, a toothbrush, and a comb. Any more would have been "extra weight and extra worry." She wore tan jodhpurs, a white silk blouse, a scarf, and a windbreaker. She had a flying suit stored under the pilot's seat. It took her just minutes to gather it all together and leave a note for her cousin, who was out to lunch with a friend. But she lingered "to drink in the beauty of a lovely treasured sight": "Beside and below our bedroom windows were dogwood trees, their blossoms in luxuriant full flower, unbelievable bouquets of white and pink flecked with the sunshine of spring. Those sweet blooms smiled at me a radiant farewell."

How hard it must have been to leave such a tranquil space for the uncertainty and risk of flying in the dark over the cold Atlantic. A few days earlier, Lou Reichers had attempted the same mission and ran out of gas miles short of land. He managed to ditch his plane near an ocean liner but was knocked unconscious during the water landing; miraculously, the ship's crew managed to rescue him. As Amelia inhaled the scent of the blossoms outside her window, she must have known how badly things could go.

She turned away from the cozy beauty, went down the stairs, and out the door, arriving at Teterboro at 2:55 p.m. George was waiting, slipping her $20 to cover telegrams when she arrived. They'd made no plans for him or any other publicist to meet her in Europe. Keeping the flight as low-key as possible, they'd adjust as needed. George could be counted on to act quickly if necessary.

At 3:15 p.m., Amelia's Lockheed Vega took off from the New Jersey airfield. Balchen was at the controls, with Eddie Gorski the mechanic sitting in the back, while Amelia stretched out and slept. She needed to rest before the all-night flight and had the enviable talent of being able to sleep anywhere, practically on command. They landed without trouble at St. John's, where they stayed the night.

The next morning—May 20, the Lindbergh anniversary—Balchen flew them to Harbour Grace, where the airport was ideally situated on a plateau. There, they checked weather reports. A storm loomed south of Amelia's intended route, which would take her to Ireland first, where she'd decide if she wanted to land or fly on to Paris. Nothing Amelia heard in those reports dissuaded her from taking off that evening. She headed off for a nap, while Balchen and Gorski went over the plane one last time. She preferred to fly through the night in order to land in daylight.

At dusk, she returned to the airfield. The press had caught on to her plans, though she wasn't surrounded by the scrum that had dogged her steps in

Trepassey. Instead, AP reporter Bill Parsons watched her with muted amazement. "There seemed to be an aura surrounding her," he wrote. "Even though everyone wanted to get as close to her as possible, to shake hands, to wish her well, to touch her, she was very patient, and showed no signs of anxiety or fear."

She read one last telegram from George and shook Balchen's hand. "O.K.," he said. "So long. Good luck." She clambered into the Vega's cockpit, swung the plane around, and took off. It was 7:12 p.m. "The plane gathered speed, and despite the heavy load rose easily," she wrote in an account of the flight. "A minute later I was headed out to sea."

The first stage was uneventful. "I flew along with nothing happening until 11:00," she said. Then everything happened all at once. "An enormous dark cloud loomed before me, stretching as far as I could see." Doc Kimball had predicted a storm to the south of her; this one was directly in her path. Amelia watched the moon disappear behind the blackness, which soared up some 20,000 feet, "entirely too high for me to climb over." She didn't have an oxygen apparatus, and the ascent would expend too much fuel. She'd have to fly straight through.

At that moment she saw "with awe rather than horror" the hands on the altimeter spinning wildly. A short time later she noticed the flames from the broken weld on the manifold: "It might take a long time to burn through. It might not. When it burned through, or the vibration splintered it completely, the ship was doomed."

Storm, instrument failure, and engine damage: Each was dangerous enough; together, they reduced her odds of surviving the flight considerably. But her odds weren't entirely diminished. With skill and luck, she might outfly her fate. The question drummed in her mind: Should she turn around? She thought about landing at Harbour Grace in the darkness. She wasn't sure she could retrace her course. The airfield wasn't lit at night; no one was expecting her. She couldn't trust the altimeter to tell her how high above the field she was. The extra fuel tanks in the Vega were full; if she misjudged and crashed, they would explode. She didn't appreciate those odds at all. "There was nothing to do about it," she said. "There was no use turning back."

She plunged into the storm.

She'd never encountered such rough air. "For about an hour I could not keep my course absolutely," she said. "I was tossed about to such an extent that accuracy was impossible." She was flying utterly blind. "I could not see out of my cockpit at all."

When she tried to climb out of the storm, slush began collecting on the windshield. "Ice began to coat my air speed indicator so that it refused to register accurately on the panel before me," she wrote in her second book, *The Fun of It.* To avoid the ice, she descended, but without the altimeter, "I could not tell whether I was 50 feet off the water or 150." When she saw whitecaps from the wind-whipped waves, she knew she was too close and climbed again. And again, the plane picked up ice so she had to descend, concluding "I must fly under the altitude, whatever it was, where I collected ice, and over the locality where I thought the water waited." At best, she was guessing.

At one point, the plane iced up and went into a spin. Her barograph, which measured changes in atmospheric pressure and therefore altitude, recorded an almost vertical drop of 3,000 feet. "How long we spun I do not know," she observed. She managed to pull out of the spin just above the water.

The storm lasted all night. "When daylight came, I could see on my wings traces of the ice which had gathered: droplets of water and very small frozen particles. Probably, if I had been able to see what was happening on the outside during the night, I would have had heart failure then and there; but, as I could not see, I carried on." She was close to losing her nerve as it was, until she remembered Lindbergh had also struggled with ice. It was "a hazard which all flyers dread."

When day broke, her eyes were dazzled by the reflection of the sun off the clouds. "I had dark glasses but it was too much for me even so," she wrote, "and I came down through the lower layer to fly in the shade, as it were."

While she was relieved to be out of the storm, the flight's last two hours were the hardest. The exhaust manifold vibrated ominously. When she opened the reserve gas tanks, the gauge started leaking fuel onto her shoulder. Everything seemed to be falling apart. Worse, she wasn't entirely sure where she was. The storm had been forecast south of her route so maybe she had somehow veered south too. She didn't think she could hold the plane together until France, so she steered east toward where she thought Ireland should be.

Eventually, much to her relief, she spotted a fishing boat too small to venture far from land. She circled it "that all might know I had got so far, anyway."

Not long afterward she made landfall. Assuming she was south of her course, she turned northward up the coast in search of train tracks to lead her toward a town with, she hoped, an airfield. She found tracks and eventually a town, but no airfield. Her only option was one of the pastures she saw dotting the countryside. Picking the one least crowded with cows and sheep, she set the Vega down. She'd made it. She was the second person—and first woman—to fly the Atlantic alone.

EARLY IN THE AFTERNOON ON May 21, 1932, the Gallagher family was sitting in the garden outside their house two miles away from Derry in Northern Ireland. It was a Saturday, "one of those lovely hot afternoons that you sometimes get in May," remembered Mrs. Gallagher. The children were home from school, and the family was enjoying the fine weather together.

Around two o'clock, they heard an engine. A great red airplane circled low over the house and landed in a field behind it. "The afternoon was hot, and I felt lazy so I'm afraid I didn't pay very much attention to it," admitted Mrs. Gallagher in an interview with the BBC three years later. "I was too comfortable where I was." But her young children were very excited and ran with her husband to see it, converging with farmhands and workers from the surrounding fields.

"My curiosity got the better of me after a minute or two, and I went up to the plane as well," said Mrs. Gallagher. "Standing beside it was a tousle-headed girl in trousers and leather coat. She didn't seem at all excited." All she wanted was a telephone. "She would not wait to talk but went off as fast as she could over the fields to the nearest house with a line. She explained as she went that the only thing she wanted was to get through to her husband and tell him she had arrived safely."

Mrs. Gallagher returned to her home, where she prepared a meal for her unexpected guest. Amelia Earhart would stay at her house that night.

GEORGE WAITED FOR NEWS at the Hotel Seymour in New York, prowling the room "wild like a bear," remembered his son David, who'd joined Amelia in the aviation business when he was just out of college. They'd had a false alarm early in the morning. Someone had called from the Press Association to say Amelia had crashed near Le Bourget, the airport near Paris where Lindbergh had landed. It wasn't true, not entirely. Someone had crashed, but it wasn't Amelia. But the news "remained uncorrected for 12 interminable minutes, and the memory of those minutes was not likely to dissolve for some time to come," said George.

When a reporter from the New York *Sunday Mail* called promising an update on Amelia, George was wary. But somehow the *Londonderry*

Sentinel, alerted by the local police, managed to get the news out by teleprinter before Amelia had made her call to George. When George realized the reporter had good news to share, he spluttered "tell her to telephone me wherever she is. All I want is to hear her voice and tell her she is the greatest woman in the world." His relief almost overwhelmed him. "I knew that if any woman could do this great feat she was the one; but I have been in deadly fear of the terrors of the Atlantic all night. For Heaven's sake tell her to telephone me at once. I shall not leave the phone."

By the time the couple did speak, George had regained his poise. They decided to wait 48 hours before he booked passage for Europe. By the next day, Amelia had changed her mind. The reception to her feat was overwhelming, and she needed George by her side.

Although she'd had a quiet night at the Gallaghers, sleeping in nightclothes provided by Mrs. Gallagher, crowds had converged on the farm the next day, including reporters and film crews. For their benefit, she motored around the field in the plane while cameras whirred as if she'd just landed. But she wouldn't take off; she wasn't willing to risk pushing her wounded bird any farther. Instead, the Vega would be dismantled and shipped to London. She'd fly in a plane chartered by Paramount, the movie studio where George was to be the chairman of the editorial board. She would stay with the American ambassador, and the plane would be displayed on the first floor of Selfridges, the spectacular department store in London.

Her second trip to London resembled her first—a whirlwind of accolades—but this time she felt better able to handle them. Cables flooded in: from the grieving Lindberghs, WE DO CONGRATULATE YOU STOP YOUR FLIGHT IS A SPLENDID SUCCESS; from Ruth Nichols, YOU BEAT ME TO IT FOR THE SECOND TIME BUT IT WAS A SPLENDID JOB; and from Phil Cooper, her dry cleaner in New York, KNEW YOU WOULD DO IT STOP I NEVER LOSE A CUSTOMER. She danced with Prince Edward—three times!—and met the acerbic playwright George Bernard Shaw. On June 3, she sailed from England on a friend's yacht for Cherbourg, France, where George Putnam was due to dock the next day.

Their reunion was subdued but full of feeling. She greeted him with a casual "hi!" he remembered. "It had a fine sound, that characteristic greeting. It took account of nothing—the strain and exactions of the flight, the chances that it would fail in mid-ocean—and it took account of everything. She was there, and there was nothing to be excited about."

She told him she'd used the $20 bill he'd given her to pay for telegrams, then bought it back with English money loaned to her by the Paramount crew. She signed it and gave it to George, who claimed, "It became one of my most treasured souvenirs."

The rest of their journey was headier. Amelia spoke at the French Senate, the first foreign woman to do so. They traveled to Italy to catch the tail end of an aviators' conference and met the dictator Benito Mussolini, whose philosophy was antithetical to Amelia's own. "But she was interested by what lay underneath," remarked George, "that, under the Fascist philosophy, woman's place was not merely in the home but, so far as possible, in the obstetrical ward." A casual outdoor lunch a few days later with the down-to-earth Belgian king and queen was much more to her liking.

Once home, they dined at the White House, where Amelia did her "valiant best to be entertaining at the right hand of the glum-faced president" Herbert Hoover, soon to be ousted in the midst of the Great Depression by George's friend Franklin Delano Roosevelt. Later that evening, Amelia received the National Geographic Society's Special Gold Medal at an event attended by Hoover, the chief justice of the United States, "enough Senators and Representatives to make a quorum in either House of Congress," high officers from all three branches of the military, and diplomats from 22 countries—and broadcast nationally over NBC Radio.

Despite the grandeur, Amelia insisted in her speech that "my flight has added nothing to aviation." Hundreds had already made the same ocean crossing by air, "if those who have gone in heavier-than-air and lighter-than-air craft are counted and those who have crossed the North and the South Atlantic," she said. "However, I hope that the flight has meant something to women in aviation. If it has, I shall feel it was justified; but I can't claim anything else."

Nor did she feel she needed to. As she wrote in the last chapter of *The Fun of It,* hastily published a few weeks after her solo flight, "I chose to fly the Atlantic because I wanted to. It was, in a measure, a self-justification—a proving to me, and to anyone else interested, that a woman with adequate experience could do it."

CHAPTER SEVENTEEN

SANK: THE LONGS' LONG QUEST

On November 28, 1971, Elgen Long set his sights on Howland Island. Like Amelia Earhart and Fred Noonan, he was making a world flight—one he hoped would set multiple records. And like those two lost aviators, Long aimed to locate the speck of an island with celestial navigation. The 44-year-old pilot would use the same tools too: a bubble octant, which measures celestial bodies' angle above the horizon, and a wet compass. He didn't land on Howland; the island's airstrip had long since been abandoned. He was just making a slight detour on his flight from Fiji to Wake Island to see if he could find the island Earhart and Noonan had missed. He had no idea he was launching himself on a decades-long quest.

Throughout his world flight, Long had relied on a system called the Carousel IV, which allowed him to automate navigation by plotting latitudinal and longitudinal waypoints—especially helpful when flying extended distances over water. But for this leg, he put a hood over the instrument so he wouldn't be tempted to cheat. As the plane flew north, Long used the octant to periodically take sights on the sun—measuring its angle above the horizon to calculate his line of position. He then estimated his location on the line by comparing it to where he thought he should be, given his speed and the weather conditions. From there, he could determine if he needed to adjust his compass course to Howland.

A sweep of thunderstorms forced Long to adjust his altitude and impacted his fuel supply. Later, it became so hot he flew shirtless. Nine hours into the 19-hour flight, he started his descent toward Howland.

At first he couldn't see it; there were too many clouds. But then the sun broke through and there it was, half a mile away and exactly where he'd thought it would be. His celestial navigation was spot-on. Lozenge-shaped and featureless, Howland barely rose above the waves. It wasn't much to look at, but if the two lost fliers had spotted the island, they might have lived to a hearty old age. "There was no reason that I could see why Noonan couldn't find it," said Long.

This wasn't Long's first sighting of Howland. As a radioman on Navy PBY Catalina and Coronado flying boats during World War II, he had flown patrols over the island just six years after Earhart and Noonan had disappeared. The Oregon native had signed on with the Navy on his 15th birthday, eight months after Pearl Harbor, even though 18 was the minimum age for enlistment. But his parents claimed that he was of age; they thought he'd be safer during the war if he went into the service with his older brother. The strategy didn't work: The boys didn't see each other again until the war had ended.

The young teenager thought he'd be getting out of school for good; instead, he spent the next year in training. But to his delight, he discovered he'd be learning all about aviation. Most people of that era remembered where they were when they heard Pearl Harbor had been attacked. Long was different: His memory was seared by the news on August 15, 1935, that the famous one-eyed pilot Wiley Post and the actor Will Rogers had fatally crashed on takeoff from a village in Alaska. As a kid, "airplanes stood out to me as individual things," he said.

The Navy first sent Long to radio school. From there, he went on to aerial gunnery school, radar school, and eventually, the war in the Pacific. For a time, he flew with PBY Squadron VP-34 out of Canton Island, 423 miles southeast of Howland, and also with VP-102. During downtime, when the crew got tired of playing pinochle, they would practice celestial observations, making a game of who came closest to their actual position. Long even flew over Howland, which had been abandoned after a Japanese attack killed two colonists. He and the other Navy fliers would peer at the rough landing strips below and wonder why Earhart and Noonan hadn't located it as easily as they had.

By the time the war ended, Long had flown more than 100 combat patrols, serving in Saipan and Okinawa, China and Japan. He was 18 when Japan surrendered. At 19, he was hired as a radio operator with the Flying Tiger Line, the first scheduled cargo airline in the United States. Later, he became a navigator with Alaska Airlines, where he participated in the Berlin airlift and Operation Magic Carpet, which relocated more than 40,000 Jews from Yemen to Israel. Returning to the Flying Tiger Line, he at last received the training he'd been aiming for. At 25, already a 10-year aviation veteran, he officially became a pilot.

In the 1950s, Long began thinking of making his own round-the-world flight. "I always had this urge to go places," he said. "I always wanted to do it." For some 20 years, he talked about it as he, his wife, Marie, and their two children settled into a comfortable life in the San Francisco Bay Area. But when he reached his forties, he realized he had to either commit or give up forever on the idea of that sort of adventure. The choice was clear: "Having the resources and abilities to do it," he said at the time, "I feel it is almost mandatory."

Marie agreed—"if you take out a big enough insurance policy on yourself," she told him. She would end up putting in more air miles than he did as she traveled the world arranging logistics.

Amelia Earhart had piloted the warm route around the world, sticking close to the Equator. Long planned to do something a good deal colder:

He would circumnavigate the globe at the poles. No one had made that flight alone before.

Long had flown plenty of polar flights for both Flying Tiger and Alaska Airlines, including to remote areas of Alaska, establishing radar sites for the Distant Early Warning Line detection system, designed to detect Soviet bombers or intercontinental ballistic missiles during the Cold War. He knew how to land on ice and how to navigate near the magnetic pole, where compasses were unreliable.

What he found difficult was raising the money to fund his attempt. He began reading up on Earhart to figure out how she'd paid for her record-breaking flights and quickly realized neither he nor his wife had the fund-raising capabilities or public relations brilliance of George Putnam. Still, Long managed to persuade a neighbor to lease him a plane: a two-engine Piper Navajo that had previously been used for mountain rescue work and was much smaller than Earhart's Lockheed Electra 10-E. All the seats, except the pilot's, were removed to make room for four extra fuel tanks. An inertial navigation system, which partially automated navigation, was installed by the company that had designed it for the Apollo missions. Flying Tiger supplied him with a polar compass, but he bought his own $2.98 alarm clock to keep himself awake.

The Longs ended up shelling out $50,000 of their life savings (nearly $400,000 in today's dollars) to fund the 28-day, 36,000-mile flight. He called the expedition "Operation Crossroads" because he'd be flying over the "crossroads of the geography of the world"—the North Pole, the South Pole, and the Equator at both the Greenwich meridian and the international date line—and landing on every continent. His 21-year-old son Harry, who was in charge of radio communication from their home in Woodside, California, wrote a theme song for it.

On November 5, 1971, Long took off from San Francisco, heading north to Anchorage. Unlike Earhart, he experienced few mechanical problems. Two days in, one of his two radios lost contact over the Arctic—"I should have known better in the first place than to put a new model in," he observed. He got it fixed in London. More painfully, the plane's heater failed over both poles because the air intake vents iced up. The temperature plummeted to 25 degrees Fahrenheit in the cockpit over the North Pole and to zero degrees over Antarctica. His only other mishap was a delayed takeoff on the homestretch from Hawaii to San Francisco: He'd overslept. "The heart was willing," he told reporters when he landed, "but the body was weak. I'm very, very glad it's over. I didn't realize how physically punishing it was going to be."

He would bring that knowledge to his understanding of Earhart's flight.

Elgen Long officially broke three records for his class of airplane with his world flight, including fastest around the world at both poles and speed between the poles. Unofficially, he set many others but couldn't afford the several-hundred-dollar fee to confirm those. The Fédération Aéronautique Internationale awarded him the Gold Air Medal—an honor he shared with his childhood hero, Wiley Post.

After the ceremony in Paris, in which he met French president Georges Pompidou, he and Marie discussed what they would do next. He was still piloting for Flying Tiger, but the couple needed another project. Aviation had been so good to them that they decided they'd do something to give back: They'd solve one of its greatest mysteries. They'd figure out what happened to Amelia Earhart.

LONG WAS UNIQUELY QUALIFIED TO CONDUCT this search: He'd been a radioman, a navigator, and a pilot. He'd flown in the Pacific just a few years after Earhart disappeared. He'd trained in accident investigation at the University of Southern California, the first major research university with an aircraft safety program, and had served as an aircraft crash investigator for the Air Line Pilots Association. And he was one of the very few people who had flown solo around the world. Marie would bring her formidable organizational and research abilities. As with the world flight, they'd conduct this search as a team.

They decided to approach the mystery of Amelia Earhart as if it were any other investigation: They'd interview witnesses and examine the data. But Long knew they were up against some seemingly insurmountable hurdles. There was no black box, of course—U.S. planes weren't required to carry flight recorders until 1965. More significant, they didn't have the plane—no wreckage to painstakingly piece together for signs of structural failure, no smashed instruments to decipher for clues as to what was going on in the cockpit, no crash site to sift through for evidence of what went wrong. The plane had disappeared. If it ditched in the ocean, it would be far out of reach.

What they did have were witnesses: the people who knew Earhart and how she piloted a plane; those who knew Noonan and how he navigated; the many technicians who helped prepare the Lockheed Electra 10-E and its equipment for the world flight; the mechanics who serviced the plane as it circled the globe; and most crucially, the people in Lae who prepared the plane and watched it take off, and the crew of the *Itasca* waiting at Howland Island to guide it in.

But all of this had happened so long ago that many of the key players had died, including Commander Warner K. Thompson, the captain of the *Itasca* (in 1939, suddenly, in Alaska); Amelia's husband, George Palmer Putnam (1950, of kidney failure); and Earhart's technical adviser Paul Mantz (1965, plane crash). Others were quite elderly. The Longs knew they had a limited window before the chance to interview these crucial witnesses was lost forever.

Their approach was methodical. They started by interviewing witnesses close to their California home: William Galten, an *Itasca* radioman; Lawrence Ames, a director at Lockheed; and Henry Anthony, a Coast Guard communications officer who discussed the radio schedule with Earhart before her first attempt at the world flight (and whose opinion of her was blisteringly negative and sexist). They spent a Hawaiian vacation meeting with the former colonists who had prepared Howland for Earhart's arrival, including Yau Fai Lum, Ah Kin Leong, Paul Yat Lum, and Joseph Anakalea. They spoke with Arnold True, who had provided the weather forecasts, and William Swanston, the *Itasca* navigator who surveyed Howland and the other Line Islands. They talked to Noonan's former colleagues at Pan Am and Vernon Moore, who built Earhart's radio direction finder. They tracked down Bo McKneely, Amelia's personal mechanic, and the widows of Noonan, Mantz, and Putnam, who'd remarried twice after losing Earhart.

Eventually, thanks to the practically free travel that was a perk of Elgen's job, they flew as far as Australia to interview Stanley Rose, who had changed the fuse on the Electra's radio receiver in Darwin, Australia; Robert Iredale, who'd filled the plane's fuel tanks at Lae; and James Collopy, the district superintendent who'd been in charge of civil aviation at Lae. They made it to Lae to speak with several people who had encountered Earhart and Noonan at the hotel where they stayed before their last flight. They interviewed Earhart's sister, Putnam's sons, and Neta Snook, the woman who taught Earhart how to fly. Slowly, they filled in the picture.

They got to Leo Bellarts, the chief radio operator on the *Itasca,* in 1973, a year before he died. He gave them a sense of the frustration on board the ship: "She apparently didn't listen for us at all." He sounds angry in the interview recording. "That's what really disturbed us, and no little bit. She'd call or she'd come on and just say well, the weather's overcast this, that, and the other thing and hang it up. Not 'go ahead.' She never tried to establish contact until the last quart of gas she had."

Thomas O'Hare, another *Itasca* radio operator, confirmed the confusion. Elgen Long caught up with O'Hare in 1975 at a bar in Fort Lauderdale, Florida. O'Hare was on a bender.

"I won't be on it all the time. You just happened to hit me at it," he said with the careful diction of someone who has had quite a lot to drink. Long, methodical as usual, recorded it all. "Twice a year it happens. Maybe three times. I've noticed it's been coming more frequently."

"Better watch that," said Long.

"Ordinarily I can sit in a bar all day and not drink," added O'Hare.

But when Long, patient and genial, pressed O'Hare on the details of what happened in the ship's radio room 38 years earlier, the former radioman was more lucid. As it had with Bellarts, Earhart's disappearance had evidently weighed on him for the past four decades. "Why couldn't she hear me on [the frequency] 3105?" asked O'Hare. "I don't care how stupid she was, and I'm putting out a hell of a lot more than she is. Why couldn't she hear me?"

Earhart had never responded to his messages on the frequency she said she'd be listening to, and O'Hare still didn't understand why; the transmitter he was broadcasting on was powerful. She should have been able to hear him hundreds of miles out.

"I often wonder, Was there something wrong with her fucking transmitter or was it all her fault?" he said.

Long didn't answer him then. He waited until he could spend a long, sober day with O'Hare at his home nearby, going over the radioman's logs and that of the ship, walking him through the events of July 2, 1937, moment by moment.

The Longs sifted through reams of documents: plane diagrams, inspection and repair reports, receipts for gas and oil. They went over Earhart's notes and Noonan's charts from the early legs of the world flight, which had been sent home from Australia. Long especially scoured the *Itasca*'s radio logs, as well as the ship's official report describing the catastrophe and Pan Am's account of what its Pacific radio stations heard of Earhart's transmissions. Two decades into their research, they discovered a lost memo that proved crucial to their understanding of what happened.

It took the Longs more than 25 years to publish their conclusion: After a cascade of errors, the Lockheed Electra 10-E ran out of fuel and crashed into the ocean near Howland. In their accounting, nearly everyone involved in the flight made mistakes or had the wrong information. None of these errors were insurmountable individually. Compounded, the Longs argued, they almost inevitably doomed Amelia Earhart and Fred Noonan.

Earhart and Noonan never knew about their first mistake. Indeed, it wasn't a mistake, just a matter of bad timing. When Earhart radioed the *Itasca* at 7:42 a.m. on July 2, 1937, to say, "We must be on you but cannot see you," she was going by what their charts and Noonan's dead reckoning was telling her. And she was right to rely on Noonan, who had pioneered Pan American's commercial routes across the Pacific; few navigators were more experienced than he was in that region of the world. Yet the island wasn't where he thought it would be.

The *Itasca* had been traveling down to the Line Islands—Howland, Baker 42 miles south, and Jarvis more than 1,000 miles to the east—since 1935, as part of the bid to establish them as U.S. territories. On one trip south from Hawaii, the ship's navigator surveyed the islands and discovered existing maps put Howland nearly six miles east of where it actually was. (The island had last been charted by the U.S.S. *Narragansett* in 1872.) The *Itasca* sent the updated coordinates to Coast Guard headquarters, but an updated chart wasn't published until June 1937—too late for Noonan to be apprised of the island's real location.

Compounding the error, Noonan made what Long considered a baffling mistake: He assumed his compass presented the actual magnetic heading, without any deviation. Long examined the charts Noonan sent home, which included his calculations. "Whenever it came to deviation, he wrote zero," said Long. But most compasses on most planes deviate, reacting magnetically to metal objects and electrical currents on board. "There's no such thing in my navigational experience (and I've had a lifetime of it) in those days as a perfect compass," he explained. He estimated Noonan's compass was actually off the mark by nearly four degrees—not a big deal for short flights (the Federal Aviation Administration now allows for deviations of up to 10 degrees) but potentially catastrophic in a long flight like theirs. This error may have put the Electra short by another six miles. Add that to the six miles from the incorrect map and Earhart's "must be on you" was actually 12 miles west of Howland.

Meanwhile, a wind blowing at exactly the wrong speed put them even farther off course: The *Itasca* had reported an easterly wind at four to eight miles an hour. Too weak to create whitecaps on the waves, thought Long, such a breeze would have been invisible to Earhart and Noonan. Noonan would have had no other way to measure wind speed as he had left his drift bomb behind in Lae. This light little wind pushed the Electra another six or so miles west. Now they were some 18 miles west of Howland, beyond visual range in the early morning sunlight.

But all wasn't lost. Unpredictable conditions are a predictable element of any long journey, and Earhart had prepared for them. She knew finding Howland would be one of the trickiest parts of the world flight, and that the smallest error could put them off their course to the island. That's why she'd established a radio communication plan with the Coast Guard—through their cutter, the *Itasca*—so they could talk her in if need be. That's why she'd had a cutting-edge radio direction finder installed on her plane, and why the *Itasca* was waiting at Howland with its own pair of radio direction finders: a powerful low-frequency model on the ship and a portable high-frequency counterpart on the island. With these backup systems in place, she and Noonan would be able to make a slight course correction and within minutes see the rough runways on Howland Island.

Unfortunately, according to the Longs, every one of those backup systems failed.

The trouble began early on. Earhart had informed the *Itasca* she would transmit 15 minutes before and after the hour and listen for their messages on the hour and half hour. The radiomen misunderstood; they were used to keeping to schedules, which to them meant making an appointment with another radio operator to be on the same frequency at a set time. They thought that's what Earhart would be doing and assumed they'd be able to communicate back and forth.

But Earhart meant what she said. She'd flip on her transmitter to send messages at set times and turn on her receiver to listen for messages at others. She didn't have time to hang out on a frequency waiting to chat. The *Itasca* had four radio operators whose sole responsibility was managing communications for the ship. The Electra only had Earhart. The discrepancy didn't register with O'Hare, Bellarts, and their colleagues. When O'Hare demanded to know why Earhart didn't keep monitoring her receiver, Long responded with uncharacteristic heat: "She's flying an airplane. She's got to keep track of her fuel. She's marking the engines. She's navigating. She's watching her autopilot. She's doing everything."

"Has she got the cans on her ears?" asked O'Hare. The headphones, he meant.

"For 20 hours?" Long replied, his voice rising. "Her ears would fall off, for Christ's sake."

To Long, who'd flown solo around the world, it was clear: Earhart had to keep to the schedule she described so she could take care of everything else.

And there was another big problem with the communication plan—one the Longs called "the simplest of booby traps": the time zones. Earhart was operating on Greenwich Mean Time (now Coordinated Universal Time or UTC) while the *Itasca* crew was on Greenwich time plus 11:30 (one hour behind Hawaiian Standard Time). In other words, the Longs wrote, "Earhart's 'on the hour' was their 'on the half hour.'" They weren't transmitting when she was listening for them, and they were when she wasn't. She never heard them, except once right toward the end.

"The half-hour difference? Never gave it a thought," said O'Hare. In Long's recording of their interview, the former radio operator's breath sounds short, as if the wind had been knocked out of him.

The one time Earhart did hear them, the *Itasca* was sending a message on 7500 kilocycles in Morse code. And therein lies another big error, according to Long: Neither Noonan nor Earhart knew code, but the radiomen on board the ship assumed they did. In their world, everyone who operated a radio knew code. But because she didn't, she would have turned the switch to off on her receiver for CW—continuous wave Morse code signals. When they transmitted code, all she would have heard was an undecipherable whoosh.

But despite the misunderstandings between the Electra and the *Itasca,* Earhart and Noonan might have landed safely on Howland Island if the cutting-edge technology they were all relying on as the ultimate backup had worked. And in this case, according to the Longs, the failure was not that of the Coast Guard crew—at least not completely—but of Earhart herself.

Earhart had originally planned on having a dedicated radio operator on board for the first few legs. But Harry Manning, a ship's captain as well as an accomplished pilot, navigator, and radio operator who knew Morse code, backed out after Earhart crashed on her first attempt around the world. When the radio direction finder was installed on the plane, Manning had been the one to learn how it worked.

When Manning returned to his ship, Earhart received a brief tutorial. But she was too busy to practice using the device, which was so new that it didn't even come with a manual. Not realizing that low frequencies were crucial to direction finding, she removed the trailing wire that would have made receiving them possible. She never figured out why she couldn't get the direction finder to work throughout the world flight.

The problems with direction finding didn't end there. If the Electra couldn't receive signals on 500 kilocycles, it also couldn't transmit them. The *Itasca* direction finder was powerful, but only worked at low frequencies; it would not be able to guide the plane in.

There was still the high-frequency direction finder loaned to the *Itasca* for this mission. None of the crew members knew how to operate it. A young radio operator was temporarily transferred from another ship. But he didn't know how to operate it either. Later, he would claim the batteries had run out, and that's why he never homed in on Earhart. But when he finally returned to the ship with the direction finder, the wires were "twisted up like a bunch of rats' tails," as if the loop had been turned too hard. It was inoperable.

And there was one last miscalculation, according to the Longs—one that didn't prevent Earhart and Noonan from finding the island but did stop them from searching a little longer. The Electra had less fuel than Earhart realized. The tanks had been filled the day before they left Lae; tropical heat had affected the fuel's density, effectively reducing the gallons on board from 1,100 to 1,092.

"She was in the middle of her last radio message when they went in," said Long. "I can tie that down pretty good."

Long also thought he had a pretty good idea where the plane went down. Or at least where it didn't.

He calculated that the Electra couldn't have crashed anywhere within visual range of Howland Island—so nowhere within 20 nautical miles to the north, south, or east. To the west, the visual range shrank to 15 nautical miles because the aviators were flying toward the sun's glare, which reduced visibility.

Knowing what Noonan didn't know about the charts, his compass, and the wind, and making the standard assumption that dead reckoning is 90 percent accurate, Long calculated that at 8:43 in the morning on July 2, the plane crashed somewhere within a rectangle 62 miles north and south of Howland, 29 miles to the east, and 41 miles to the west. "If this approximately 2,000-square-nautical-mile area is searched, there is a 90 percent probability that the Electra will be found within it," he wrote.

The Longs were convinced they'd figured out what had happened to Earhart. Now they just needed to find the plane.

CHAPTER EIGHTEEN

1932–37: "CLEAR THINKING, ENERGY, AND VISION!"

On the evening of September 26, 1934, some 3,000 people, mostly women, gathered at the Waldorf Astoria Hotel on Park Avenue for the *New York Herald Tribune*'s fourth annual Conference on Current Problems. The day had been warm, and the three-year-old hotel—the largest in the world—did not have air-conditioning. Yet the 2,450 seats arranged on the floor of the Grand Ballroom and its two tiers of balconies were full. "The accommodations of the hotel have been extended to the utmost," the *Herald Tribune* reported. To handle the overflow, hotel staff set up 1,000 additional seats in adjoining rooms with "amplifying devices."

Marie Mattingly Meloney, editor of the *Herald Tribune*'s Sunday magazine and chairperson of the conference, had assembled a formidable line-up—"the best minds we could enlist"—to address the country's looming problems, which included the Great Depression, now five years on, and the rising threat of fascism in Europe. First Lady Eleanor Roosevelt opened the conference earlier in the day by urging labor and business leaders to improve their ethics, while New York mayor Fiorello La Guardia argued for changing the U.S. Constitution to match modern times. Secretary of Labor Frances Perkins, the first woman appointed to the Cabinet, advocated the establishment of unemployment insurance to help the 22 percent of the population struggling to find work.

Amelia Earhart spoke, too, seemingly undaunted by the notables who had preceded her over the course of the day. "I have been instructed to direct my brief talk to youth," she began, "but it is with trepidation I do so." The modern world, she said, had its elders—her 37-year-old self included—on the run. "Under the circumstances, I hope whatever words of encouragement I may fling back over my shoulder as I gallop by may not sound hollow or insincere," she continued. She was convinced that "today there are opportunities for a satisfying life unparalleled in the history of the world."

For Amelia, talk of opportunities and a satisfying life naturally segued into talk of aviation. "There is need for every kind of talent to advance the business of flying," a business that would only increase, even with the troubled economy, she argued. "What opportunities lie here for clear thinking, energy, and vision!"

But those opportunities must include women, whose progress she said was being blocked by two capital *T*'s: "One is Training—or lack of it. The other, Tradition. It is a fact that women, because they are women, are denied certain types of training in a number of institutions of learning." She pointed out that New York University, then the largest university in the country, prevented women from taking aeronautical engineering courses. "One graduate student battled her way in," Amelia claimed, "but no undergraduates have." It followed, then, that men outnumbered women in aviation by 40 to 1. "I am inclined to think from such examples as this that the tradition of women's inability in certain lines is based almost entirely on their lack of opportunity to try, which is in turn opportunity to learn," she proclaimed.

After she was finished speaking, Meloney turned to the crowd and said, "I wish that all the youth of the land might feel the personal inspiration of contact with Amelia Earhart."

At least one person in the audience keenly agreed: Edward Elliott, president of Purdue University. A severe-looking man with a face composed of sharp angles, Elliott was known as one of the most progressive educators in the country. Under his direction, Purdue had opened its first residence hall for women and built a new hangar for its airfield: the first to be operated by a university. Despite the Depression, the school had managed to place more than 90 percent of its graduates in jobs, most of which were in the fields they'd studied.

During his keynote address for the session "New Frontiers for Youth," he declared, "American youth, ladies and gentlemen, is not made up of those who falter, even in the present stumbling times." And it was a good thing, too, because "today the new frontiers have come to the pioneers. There are no sanctuaries left for those without strength and the spirit of adventure." It was an energetic perspective Amelia shared.

The next day—the last of the conference—Elliott managed to sit next to Amelia at a luncheon for the presenters. "I learned that she had an abiding interest in the problem of the education of women," he told a biographer. "Our ideas as to the nature of this problem and its solution fitted." They arranged to meet for dinner at the Coffee House Club, "the most civilized and homely clubroom in America," according to George, who joined them.

After dinner, George and Amelia sat on a couch—"AE with her feet tucked up under her like a little girl," remembered George—and Elliott, lean and intent, faced them from a chair. He had a proposal to make.

"We want you at Purdue," he told her.

AMELIA HAD BEEN BUSY SINCE SHE'D made her solo flight across the Atlantic in 1932. On June 20, she'd returned from Europe. Three weeks later, on July 10, she'd launched an attempt from Los Angeles at a transcontinental speed record. After 19 hours and 14 minutes—and one unplanned stop in Columbus, Ohio, due to a problem with the fuel feed—she made it to Newark, breaking Ruth Nichols's women's record by nearly 10 hours. But she was disappointed: She'd missed the men's record by an hour and 36 minutes.

On August 24, she tried again. This time, she made it without any stops—the first woman to do so—and broke Nichols's 2,000-mile-long distance record. The winds hadn't been in her favor, though, so the speed record remained out of reach. Even so, she was satisfied. Few pilots had accomplished what she had, and she wanted to capitalize on her success.

Flying was her great love, but it was also how she made a living. George, despite appearances, was not wealthy; a family dispute over the Putnam publishing house, with the additional blow of the 1929 market crash, had made sure of that. Both George and Amelia needed to earn their keep.

"Flying with me is a business," she explained at one point. "Of course I make money. I have to or I couldn't fly. I've got to be self-supporting or I couldn't stay in business."

Although her first brush with endorsements—the Lucky Strike cigarettes advertisement after the *Friendship* flight—had led to controversy, Amelia continued to bestow her blessing on a range of products. Some of them made sense for her line of work: Pratt & Whitney Wasp engines, Stanavo engine oil, Longines watches, Chrysler cars, Eastman Kodak movie cameras and film. Others were more of a stretch: Time Saver stationery and "a mail order kitchen firm." George reportedly arranged the latter in exchange for a set of cabinets to install in their home.

For a time, she had her own clothing line, which introduced tiny propellers as buttons and parachute silk as the material for shirts. Designed for "women who lead active lives," the clothes were sold in department stores such as Macy's and Marshall Field's. She was the star of the advertising campaigns: "I tried to put the freedom that is in flying into the clothes. And the efficiency too." She was deeply involved in their design, swamping the

New York apartment she and George kept with swaths of fabric and dress-making tools. And the fashion line was featured favorably in women's magazines. But it was all too much work, especially as she hadn't let up on anything else to make room for this new career. By 1934, she'd shut it down.

Her foray into luggage was much less taxing: She advised the Orenstein Trunk Company on how to design bags suitable for air travel and allowed them to be branded with her name; in return, she received royalties. The result was Amelia Earhart Luggage, "the first truly practical and genuine airplane luggage." The bags were dubbed "air-light" because, at Amelia's suggestion, they were constructed from aircraft veneer wood. A huge success, the luggage was manufactured into the 1990s.

Meanwhile, she remained deeply involved in the aviation industry, which she found satisfying though less immediately lucrative. After the Ludington Line failed, she and her partners took over Boston-Maine Airways from Pan Am, renaming it National Airways. She was in charge of publicity and sales, convincing cautious New Englanders that it was safe to fly, even in winter.

Amelia advocated for aviation in general too. In March 1934, she appeared before the U.S. Senate Post Office Committee to testify in favor of allowing private companies to fly airmail routes, rather than limit it to the U.S. Army. She held strong views on what the government's role should be in aviation. It should provide "essential aids," she said, "like radio beams, night flying beacons, emergency airports, weather reporting and broadcasting." Safety tools were, in her eyes, "no more of a subsidy [for the aviation industry] than is the provision of a lighthouse thought to be a subsidy to shipping."

But the most lucrative—and exhausting—aspect of her flying business was lecturing. "It's routine now," she said. "I make a record and then I lecture on it." In a November 1935 letter to her friend Gene Vidal, she wrote, "I spoke twenty-nine times in October alone, usually driving at night and sleeping during the day." She hadn't even had time to renew her pilot's license. As Vidal was the director of the Bureau of Air Commerce (a precursor to the Federal Aviation Administration), she hoped he would help her out.

George planned the lecture tours, cramming in nearly more than she could bear. She had lectures based on her solo Atlanta flight scheduled until February 1933, nine months after the actual event. "They were much more intensive than I had planned because the management [G.P.] kept trying to squeeze in more," she wrote to her mother. But she didn't dare say no. "In these times I thought I might as well do as much and get as much as I could." Her rate per speech topped out at $250. Two years later, she made $300 an appearance, earning $40,000 in a year when most Americans didn't pull in $1,000.

But to make those lectures worth the price to her audience, she had to keep breaking records.

ONE DAY IN SEPTEMBER 1934, GEORGE hurried in the front door of their home in Rye, New York, with his arms full of evening newspapers and his briefcase. He intended to head straight for his study to drop off his burdens and perhaps a care or two.

Amelia was idling by the fire in golden crepe pajamas, a detail he never forgot. When she heard him come in, she looked up "in the way of a person thinking out loud," he recalled, and declared, "I want to fly the Pacific soon."

No one had made the solo flight before. Seven pilots had died in the attempt with three more soon to come.

His forward momentum halted, George leaned against the archway between the entryway and the living room.

"You mean from San Francisco to Honolulu?" he asked.

"No; the other way; it's easier to hit a continent than an island," she replied.

"When do you want to do it?" he asked.

"Oh, fairly soon. But only when I'm ready—and the ship."

Within weeks, they'd closed up the house in Rye and rented a place in Hollywood—very fitting, as Paul Mantz, who would be her technical adviser for the Pacific flight, flew stunts for the movies. His company, United Air Services, provided planes and pilots to the studios, while his charter service, nicknamed the Honeymoon Express, discreetly flew stars wherever they wanted to go. Mantz knew everyone in aviation on the West Coast and was up on the latest technology. Most crucially, he had a reputation for meticulously planning every daredevil stunt to ensure that pilot and plane came through safely.

By Christmas, George and Amelia and Mantz and his wife, Myrtle, were aboard an ocean liner sailing to Hawaii, with the Vega strapped to the deck. This wasn't the same plane that took Amelia across the Atlantic; she had sold that one to the Franklin Institute in Philadelphia for $7,500. However, she kept the Wasp engine, which she had installed in a Vega Hi-speed Special. And for the first time, she'd be flying with a two-way radio, the first to be installed in a civilian plane for a long-distance flight and only to be used, according to the Federal Communications Commission, "for communication with ships and coastal stations when in flight over the sea."

When reporters found out about the radio, they suspected that a Pacific flight was in the works, though Amelia had made no announcement. The backlash was surprising and swift. Earlier in December, noted Australian navigator Charles Ulm had taken off from Oakland for Honolulu with a two-person crew on the first leg of a flight to Australia; they never arrived in Hawaii. The U.S. Coast Guard and Navy searched for the fliers for 27 days, eventually giving the three men up for lost. This brought the death toll for Pacific attempts to 10.

Why risk such an outcome again, newspaper editorials demanded, when the Pacific had already been flown successfully several times by crewed planes, including six U.S. Navy planes that accomplished it on January 11,

1934. "If Amelia Earhart Putnam intends to fly solo from Hawaii to the mainland responsible authorities should stop her from doing it," wrote John Williams on the front page of the *Honolulu Star-Bulletin* in an article picked up across the country. "Even if she was successful in making the flight, nothing beyond what is already known would be learned. If she failed in the attempt, the ghastly Ulm search would be repeated, probably with even more intensity, which in the air means greater risks and possible loss of life."

The public outcry increased in volume when news broke that the flight was sponsored by "Hawaiian sugar men," as newspaper headlines called them. Amelia, through George, had already been paid $5,000 of a $10,000 contract, according to the *Riverside Daily Press,* "part of a huge plan of the Hawaiian Sugar Planters' association to defeat the Jones-Costigan sugar act," which imposed tariffs on non-mainland sugar production. George denied the deal at the time, but later admitted she'd been paid.

But there was absolutely nothing wrong with it, he argued. She made the flight because she wanted to do it. "Record flying was expensive business," he wrote. "In news-attention, Hawaii received its money's worth. I am sure it never got, or asked for, any service connected with sugar legislation. About that sweet subject AE knew nothing and did nothing." Yet after the flight, she managed to slip generous praise of the islands into many interviews.

Although Amelia wasn't used to such negative publicity, the Hawaiian businessmen crumbled before she did. With four days to go until her scheduled takeoff, they asked her to cancel. She refused. At a meeting at the Royal Hawaiian Hotel, she was withering: "Gentlemen, there is an aroma of cowardice in this air ... Whether you live in fear or defend your integrity is your decision. I have made mine. I intend to fly to California within this next week, with or without your support."

They bowed to her wishes. Laden with 520 gallons of fuel, she took off from a muddy runway at 4:45 p.m. on January 11, 1935, with Mantz yelling as he watched, "Get that tail up! *Get that tail up!*" She did, but the experience of watching and waiting so exhausted George that he said he'd rather have a baby than go through that again. Reporters assumed he meant he'd rather Amelia stayed home and got pregnant, but he was referring only to himself.

Meanwhile, Amelia was enjoying her adventure. Unlike on the Atlantic flight, she didn't experience any alarming equipment failures or encounter any storms. "It was a night of stars," she later wrote. "Stars hung outside my cockpit window near enough to touch." And she wasn't entirely alone. For the first time, she was flying with a two-way radio, a 50-watt Western Electric she could operate from a black box next to her seat in the cockpit. She broadcast messages at a quarter to and a quarter after the hour, which involved unspooling a trailing wire antenna through a hole in the fuselage, "another thing for a pilot to think about." She also tuned in commercial radio stations, such as Honolulu's KGU, though she kept the volume low.

A few hours in, she heard, "We are interrupting our musical program so that Mr. Putnam may try to communicate with his wife."

She heard him as if he were in the next room, chastising her. "A.E.," he said, "the noise of your motor interferes with your messages. Please speak a little louder." Hearing his voice was a high point of the flight.

She landed at the Oakland airport some 18 hours after takeoff to be met by a crowd of as many as 10,000 people. Many more had been following along via their radio sets, breathing a collective sigh of relief when she arrived safely. For a flight so marred by criticism, it proved to be a great success. "You have scored again," exulted President Roosevelt in a letter, showing "even the 'doubting Thomases' that aviation is a science which cannot be limited to men only."

Four months later, Amelia pulled off two more stunning aviation feats, flying from Burbank, California, to Mexico City, and from Mexico City to Newark, New Jersey—the return flight notching yet another first for Earhart. Again, she faced controversy over how the journeys were funded. The Mexican government had suggested the trip as a goodwill gesture and came up with a creative scheme for covering the costs: Mexico would overprint limited-issue airmail stamps with the words "Amelia Earhart, *Vuelo de buena voluntad* Mexico 1935"—"Amelia Earhart, good will flight Mexico 1935." She'd carry 200 or so with her to Newark to sell to collectors. Gimbels, the New York department store, advertised them at $175 a stamp, which raised the ire of many observers. According to historian Susan Ware, "This episode blatantly revealed to the public what was usually a behind-the-scenes process of paying for and profiting from record-breaking flights."

George claimed they never profited from a flight—the stamps and the sugar barons barely covered the flights' expenses. But the flights made lucrative lecture tours possible—funding the activities she found meaningful, however little they added to the coffers.

WITHIN THREE WEEKS OF MEETING PURDUE president Edward Elliott, Amelia was on the university's campus giving a speech on "College and Careers." But when Elliott told Amelia he wanted her at Purdue, he hadn't meant for the occasional talk. Despite her peripatetic education and lack of a college degree, let alone an advanced one, he wanted her on staff as a visiting professor and adviser on aeronautics. And he wanted her especially to work with the female students.

"We've a feeling the girls aren't keeping abreast of the inspirational opportunities of the day nearly as well as might be," he explained. "I think you could supply some spark which would help to take up the lag between the swift eddying of the world around modern women and the tardier echoes of the schoolroom."

Amelia was immediately on board. "I'd like that if it can be arranged," she told him.

Elliott was an expert arranger. By the time she completed her epic flight from Mexico City, he'd set in motion a new department at Purdue for the study of women's careers. He proposed Amelia as its first appointee, spending two weeks of each semester on campus counseling and lecturing women students. When the appointment was officially announced on June 2, 1935, Elliott declared, "Miss Earhart represents better than any other young woman of this generation the spirit and the courageous skill of what may be called the new pioneering." She'd start during the fall semester of 1935.

In the meantime, Amelia had been pushing for women's rights in other arenas. She refused to give money to Denison House unless she could be certain her donation would be used "for *girls* in some way." She'd begun researching how menstruation affected women's abilities in other physically taxing fields. Men seemed to feel it was exceedingly dangerous for all women to fly during menses. Women themselves knew better: A few women were truly laid low by menstruation, but most women weren't. "It has been my experience that any such periodic handicap in a girl comes from a structural cause and that such a girl would naturally not enter a career of dancing," the ballet mistress at Radio City Music Hall told Amelia. "I would think the same thing would apply to a woman who wanted to be a professional pilot. The girl with any important deficiency wouldn't attempt to be a pilot." In other words, individual women were capable of making that determination themselves.

Amelia also took up the cause of Helen Richey, hired by Central Airlines as the first woman copilot for a scheduled airline. A publicity coup for Central, Richey's appointment quickly turned into a disaster. The Air Line Pilots Association refused her membership application and complained to the Department of Commerce that women weren't strong enough to fly in bad weather. It was too dangerous for the public, they argued—but their real concern was the perceived danger to themselves. "If the practice of hiring women to pilot airliners continued," they asked, "where would that leave the men?" They threatened to strike.

To placate the pilots without inciting a public uproar, Central Airlines loaded Richey's schedule with luncheon speeches, photo ops, and airport tours—leaving her little time to fly. Eventually, with little fanfare, she resigned.

Amelia, as a friend of Richey's as well as an advocate for women, was apoplectic. Yet she managed to contain her anger long enough to devise a sly way for getting the word out. In a letter to a group of women raising funds for a marker commemorating her Hawaii flight, she advised them that any excess donations they raised should go to "break down the barriers and help woman to gain her proper place in aviation." The reasons such a fund was necessary, she explained, was because Helen Richey, the "one girl [who] did succeed in landing a job recently as copilot," was blackballed—not due to "lack of ability (all her co-workers admitted she was OK as to flying) but because she was a female. The result of this action was that the department of commerce refused to let her fly passengers in bad weather, so the poor girl could not do her part at all, and had to resign."

As Amelia—savvy in the ways of publicity—had calculated, someone leaked the letter to the press. The news broke on November 7, 1935. The president of Central Airlines spluttered that as far as he knew, Richey had resigned due to poor health. When reached for comment at a friend's house, Richey confirmed her resignation but refused to say more: "Miss Earhart has told the story better than I could."

Amelia started at Purdue the same day her letter hit front pages across the country—underscoring, in case anyone doubted it, her total commitment to breaking down barriers for women. She stayed for nearly three weeks. Living in the new Women's Residence Hall, she ate companionably in the dining hall, where the young women watched her every move. She drank buttermilk, so they did too. She arrived at meals in her flying togs and propped her elbows on the table when she was engrossed in conversation. They wanted to be casual, too, but the official response, according to one student, was "As soon as you fly the Atlantic, you may!"

Although Amelia ended up spending only two extended periods on campus, she took her responsibility seriously. One of the first things she did was issue a questionnaire to the female students; she was gratified to learn that some 92 percent of them wanted careers. But the women were limited by what she saw as the arbitrary division between home economics and engineering. "It is almost as if the subjects themselves had sex, so firm is the line drawn between what girls and boys study," she said in one lecture. Women who tried to cross that line by enrolling in engineering classes were hounded out by male professors and students who felt Amelia was undermining them by encouraging women to pursue careers after graduation. "It's hard enough to get the girls to marry us as it is," a group of senior men complained to Amelia.

She was undaunted. "It is my kind of school," she told George, "a technical school where all instruction has practicality, and where a progressive program for women is being started too." In a way, it was a revival of her time at Denison House: helping people with the practical matters of life, but this time through aviation as well. "The work has been very interesting," she wrote to her mother, "and has served to crystallize some of my ideas which were rather formless before."

She looked forward to all she'd accomplish there. Then Purdue offered her a plane.

CHAPTER NINETEEN

SANK: "WHERE THE ELECTRA WILL NOT BE FOUND"

When Elgen Long met Dave Jourdan at his Maryland office in 1997, he took to him right away. Like Long, Jourdan was courteous and soft-spoken—and like Long, his mild manners masked relentlessness and deep expertise. Long knew the air, while Jourdan excelled at exploring the deep sea. Here, thought Long, was a man who got things done. Here was a man who could help him find Amelia Earhart's plane.

When Elgen and Marie Long launched their research into Earhart's fate 25 years earlier, they'd been aiming to unravel the historical mystery: to figure out the area where the Electra went down and why. Although conducting an ocean search felt beyond their scope, they couldn't resist imagining what it would be like to find the plane. They'd finally know for certain whether they were right—and be able to bring some peace to the lost aviators they'd come to know so intimately after more than two decades of research.

Trouble was, Elgen and Marie had neither the cash nor the expertise to organize an expedition. But they did have a story, which Elgen told at the slightest opportunity. Eventually their tale reached the ears of Steve Lyons, a producer at WGBH, the Boston public television station responsible for the science program *NOVA*. Lyons suggested that Long present his theory to Jourdan.

A graduate of the U.S. Naval Academy, Jourdan had served as a submarine officer, then worked as a physicist in the ocean engineering program at Johns Hopkins Applied Physics Laboratory. In 1986, he and two colleagues founded Meridian Sciences to provide technical support to Navy underwater operations. The company soon ventured into ocean exploration, making news in 1995 by locating Japan's "golden submarine," the long-lost *I-52*, which U.S. forces had sunk in 1944 as it sailed to Nazi-occupied France with two tons of gold bullion and three tons of opium.

Before Long made his appearance at the headquarters of Meridian Sciences (soon renamed Nauticos), Jourdan was skeptical. This wasn't the first pitch Jourdan had entertained from Amelia Earhart researchers. Ric Gillespie with TIGHAR, the group behind the Nikumaroro hypothesis, had approached him the previous year to present his case—and Jourdan had not been convinced. If Earhart had truly flown down the line of position to the Phoenix Islands, he wondered, why didn't she radio the *Itasca* while she was doing it? The rest of TIGHAR's evidence—the post-loss radio transmissions, the aluminum airplane skin, the navigator's bookcase, the shoe heel—he dismissed as "folklore."

But Long's case interested him from the beginning. In addition to Lyons, Long was accompanied by Fred Culick, a Caltech professor with an expertise in combustion who'd been commissioned by *NOVA* to analyze the Electra's fuel consumption. Culick estimated that the plane couldn't travel longer than 20 hours and 38 minutes, which was only 25 minutes longer than Earhart had been flying at her last transmission. It fit with Long's theory. "By the time the first meeting ended, we realized we could find the Electra," Jourdan later wrote. "Elgen's ideas, research, and analysis were serious, professional, and quantifiable"—which is exactly how Jourdan liked to work. It also played to his company's strengths: deep-sea exploration and an ability to reconstruct nautical events through an analytical process they called Renav or renavigation.

Jourdan was confident the search field could be narrowed into something manageable. Since radio communication appeared to be the crux of Earhart's problem, he reached out to contacts at Rockwell Collins (now Collins Aerospace), which provides communications technology to the space program. They'd be able to figure out what went wrong with the radio—and what that meant about where the Electra went into the ocean.

In an effort to raise funding, the team went public with their plan, emphasizing that, unlike previous searches on Saipan and Nikumaroro, their approach was a rational one. "We're out to solve a mystery," Lyons told the *Baltimore Sun*. "It's a great mystery, but one we think can be solved by science."

Meanwhile, Jourdan was daydreaming about what to do with the plane once they found it. A traveling exhibit, he thought, and then a judicious donation to the Smithsonian.

He hadn't reckoned with the irrationality of luck and human behavior.

ELGEN LONG HAD IDENTIFIED A SEARCH area for the Electra that accounted for every possible deviation from its flight plan—and spread some 6,000 square miles across the Pacific, where ocean depths can be greater than 18,000 feet. "That was clearly impractical," Jourdan told me. It couldn't all be searched. "Our objective was to try to come up with less than 1,000 square miles out of that, that we felt would be the prime search area." Nauticos tended to find what it was looking for, he said. He was "quite confident that our chances were really good."

As a trained engineer, Jourdan took a methodical approach. The first step was what he called the decision tree. After absorbing all the information

Long presented to him, Jourdan developed scenarios of what might have happened at each known point of the flight. For instance, in the last message the *Itasca* received from Earhart, she said they were running north and south on the line of position 157-337. That gave Jourdan two obvious scenarios: The Electra was either flying north during the last transmission, or the Electra was flying south. "You can analyze each one of these scenarios and come up with a different search area," says Jourdan. "And all those areas combine for a larger area that should contain the plane, given that you haven't missed any scenarios or that your assumptions are correct."

Once he had a list of scenarios, he brought them to his team to collectively determine each one's likelihood, what the probable next event might have been, and ultimately creating a map—a decision tree—based on these if-then statements. If Earhart had been flying north when she sent the last message, for instance, then she would have run out of fuel somewhere in this range of the ocean. "If you can train your team to get in that mindset, it becomes actually kind of fun," says Jourdan.

Next, he used the Monte Carlo approach, a statistical analytical tool named after the famous gambling spot that predicts the possible outcomes of an event based on known information. He plugged what he did know about the flight—the speed the Electra was capable of, for instance, and the distance it had to travel—into the program. "If you set up the problem right and let the computer 'roll the dice,' which is where the name comes from, then you can generate millions of possible scenarios and analyze them all," he explains.

For the last approach, Jourdan says, "we just looked at the basic statistics of the problem." If, for instance, Noonan had managed to get a line of position at sunrise, the plane would have had to have been within a certain range, just as it would've had to have been in a certain range if they were approaching Howland from the west. Those ranges might overlap. "You blend all those together without making any assumptions about the trajectory and that comes up with an area," he says. "We did that, and we were satisfied that we were getting consistent results."

In March 2002, after five years of statistical analysis, logistical exercises, and fundraising challenges, Jourdan thought he knew where they needed to go to find the plane—and he had a plan to go after it. Nauticos chartered the 175-foot-long R.V. *Davidson* to take a team out to a lonely patch of the Pacific near Howland Island. Among those on board were Elgen Long himself, then an active 74 years old, and members of the Collins Amateur Radio Club (CARC), professional radio engineers at Rockwell Collins who messed around with ham radios as a hobby.

The plan was to search some 600 square nautical miles of ocean floor. For comparison, when Robert Ballard went hunting for the *Titanic,* he and his colleagues outlined a search area of 100 square miles at depths of some 13,000 feet—a much more manageable endeavor. Searching at greater depths, the Nauticos team was looking for a far smaller object: The Electra was 39 feet long with a 55-foot wingspan, while the *Titanic* stretched 883 by 92 feet and towered 175 feet high. In contrast, the Electra was a pinprick.

Still, Jourdan was confident in the logic of his system. He and his team had narrowed the search area and reduced uncertainties as much as seemed mathematically reasonable. They had a state-of-the-art sonar system called NOMAD (Nauticos Ocean Mapping and Analysis Device), which could operate as deep as 20,000 feet. If the plane was there, they would find it.

The expedition started out well enough. As they sailed the 1,700 nautical miles from Hawaii, they practiced deploying NOMAD, which looks like a sled. Its operation is far trickier, however. To avoid any interference with the sonar, NOMAD doesn't have a power source; instead, the one-ton device is towed by a six-mile-long, 13-ton cable. Lowering it to the ocean floor takes about four hours. If the ship travels too slowly, the sled and cable pull it backward; too fast, and NOMAD floats high above the ocean floor where its sonar is ineffective.

Jourdan and his team had divided the search area into 39 rows, each one mile wide and more than 30 miles long. When they reached the end of a line, the ship would take three to four hours to make the turn to the next one, to avoid whiplike motions that could destabilize both NOMAD and the ship. It was an agonizing process, but by the end of the first week, the team had searched 100 square miles. By the third week, they'd covered nearly two-thirds of the planned search area. They felt confident and optimistic.

Then the expedition took a turn for the worse. It'd been difficult for them to calculate ahead of time how quickly the ship would burn through fuel as it pulled NOMAD behind it. Now they had their answer: so quickly that they were in danger of running out before the expedition concluded. After some desperate calls, Jourdan determined they'd have to take a break from the search to sail the two and a half days to Tarawa to refuel. While they lost six days of searching in the process, they avoided being stranded at sea—until they nearly were for an entirely different reason.

The evening the *Davidson* returned to the search area, they lowered NOMAD back on its search path. It had only been descending underwater for moments when monitors warned of a catastrophic leak. The watch team hauled the device back on deck and discovered that a single piece of plastic tubing had popped off. After securing it and filling the empty oil reservoir, they sent NOMAD back down. Catastrophe averted.

The next evening, the Pacific sun had set when the crew began preparing for the long slow turn that marked the end of a search line. Three people were on watch in the ship's control room, including the person in charge of the winch that raised and lowered NOMAD. As they were about to make the turn, he calmly noted that the joystick controlling the winch wasn't responding. When one of the operations technicians hurried to the aft deck to investigate, he saw something horrifying. The cable on the winch's reel was unspooling, faster and faster, shrieking as it accelerated. The 13-ton cable was attached to the one-ton NOMAD; if it completely unspooled, it might yank the ship backward with deadly results.

Someone shouted for the ship to stop. NOMAD settled on the ocean bottom. The reel kept spinning, becoming thinner and thinner. The technician grabbed a hand wrench to set the manual brake. He was next to the winch; if he failed to engage the brake, he'd be the first casualty of the disaster that was surely coming. The machinery shrieked as he cranked and cranked, racing with the unraveling spool until the brake finally engaged. NOMAD was on the seafloor and the *Davidson* was anchored to it, stranded in the Pacific far from any help. "I realized at that point," Jourdan wrote later, "there was almost no chance of continuing the mission."

Of the winch's two motors, one was destroyed and the other heavily damaged; they'd brought only one spare. Jourdan and his team discussed cutting the cable and leaving their treasured exploration device underwater, to be recovered someday. But first they'd try to repair the damaged motor. Though the ship's engineer gave them a 10 percent chance of success, a Collins radio engineer and a navigation analyst managed to put the motor back together. By midmorning the next day, over the course of four tense hours rewinding the cable, the team pulled NOMAD back on deck.

They'd retrieved Nauticos's million-dollar vehicle without anyone being killed or even injured. But Jourdan couldn't risk another incident. He called off the search for the Electra, and the R.V. *Davidson* steered north for Hawaii.

In 2006, Nauticos tried again. This time, they were funded by Ted Waitt, the billionaire co-founder of Gateway Inc. and a National Geographic Society board member. In addition to a side-scan sonar system called Ocean Explorer, they had a nimbler ROV named *Magellan,* operating off a much larger ship called the R.V. *Mt. Mitchell.* If the sonar revealed a promising object, *Magellan,* armed with a camera, would be able to see what it actually was.

Yet somehow, despite Jourdan's careful preparations, they ran into even more difficulties during this second expedition. The plan was to reexamine four blips on the screen from the 2002 expedition—all roughly the same dimensions as the Electra—and then complete the survey of the original search area. But a mere three hours into the search, in an eerie replay of the incident that ended the last expedition, the winch lost hydraulic power.

This time, the brake held. Ocean Explorer didn't hit ocean bottom, and a temporary repair allowed them to bring the device back up to the ship. But the repair wouldn't hold, and again, they didn't have the spare part to fix it. Waitt was nearby on his yacht. He promised to sail back to Tarawa to obtain the part. It took him six days.

The winch was repaired, but their problems continued. One of the ship's two generators failed. These provided the internal power for the ship, including search operations. The *Mt. Mitchell* could operate with just one generator—and didn't require them for propulsion—but it was yet another thing to put the mission at risk.

Then the expedition took a bizarre turn. Hours after Waitt agreed to fund it for a few more days to make up for the winch mishap, two crew members—identical twins—went into convulsions. Shirley Mira worked in the galley, and her sister Sherry Hubler was a steward; everyone adored them. Their seizures were unrelenting, and the doctor on board was baffled. Jourdan again had to make the difficult decision to cancel the mission; the ship aimed for the nearest location where a medevac flight could reach them, which—again—turned out to be Tarawa. The sisters made it safely to Hawaii, but Jourdan never learned what afflicted them.

Nauticos didn't mount another expedition until 2017—just a few months before TIGHAR brought the dogs to Nikumaroro and Les Kinney announced that he'd found a photo proving Earhart and Noonan had been captured by the Japanese. This time, they had no mechanical problems, but they also didn't find the plane. "We know with near certainty where the Electra will not be found," according to the final expedition report. "This leaves other area[s] where the Electra will eventually be found"—areas they hoped could be narrowed down by radio tests on the other side of the world.

BEFORE DAWN ON A CLEAR DAY in the autumn of 2020, Tom Vinson and fellow members of the Collins Amateur Radio Club boarded the *Nellie Crockett* at Cape Charles, Virginia. The historic vessel—an oyster buy boat once used to transport shellfish to market—was preparing to leave the calm Chesapeake Bay for the Atlantic's rough waters. The 95-year-old ship wasn't built for the open sea—it has a wide beam ideal for shallower depths—but owner Ted Parish had volunteered it for an experiment. Today, the vessel would play the role of the *Itasca,* the Coast Guard cutter that awaited Amelia Earhart and Fred Noonan at Howland Island. Some 30 miles to the north at Accomack County Airport, a restored Beechcraft Model 18 plane was being prepared for takeoff in a few hours. It would serve as a stand-in for Earhart's Lockheed Electra 10-E.

The Collins crew believed that if they re-created the circumstances of radio communication between the *Itasca* and the Electra during Earhart's last flight "electrically and radio frequency wise," as Vinson put it, they could figure out what went wrong and how far the plane was from the ship when it went down. They'd spent years hunting for, and then restoring, the same models of radios and transmitters used on the *Itasca* and the Electra. It had taken nearly a year to arrange the use of the *Nellie Crockett* and the Beechcraft 18. Now the day had finally come for the experiment. Or rather, two experiments. Vinson called them the 7500 test and the 3105 test.

On the morning she disappeared, Earhart tried repeatedly to reach the *Itasca* on 3105 kilohertz (kHz). (Modern radio experts use kilohertz for frequencies; in 1937, the same unit was called kilocycles.) The *Itasca* radiomen heard her and recorded signal strengths at the highest level. For the modern radio engineers, the 3105 test would determine how close the plane must have been to send such strong signals.

Earhart never heard the *Itasca*'s replies on 3105 kHz. At 7:58 a.m. local time, she asked the radiomen to transmit on 7500 kHz so she could take a bearing with her direction finder. This time she heard their signal—a series of *A*'s in Morse code—but could not get a minimum, the drop in volume indicating where the signal was coming from. CARC's 7500 test would use modern technology to see if they could visually identify the minimum.

Down in the *Nellie Crockett*'s cramped hold, a rack of 1930s-era radio equipment took up the narrow floor space between the bunks and fixed table. Vinson and his colleagues Rod Blocksome and Bryan McCoy had collected an RCA high-frequency CGR receiver like the one the Coast Guard radiomen used as well as a Western Electric 13C transmitter—"the only one that anybody has ever heard of or saw," according to Blocksome. Loaded next to the historic equipment was the modern technology set up to monitor it all—software-defined radio receivers to measure signal strength and GPS receivers to make time and distance measurements. The *Nellie Crockett*'s mast had been extended to accommodate an antenna matching the height of the one on the *Itasca;* towing behind it was a small boat carrying another antenna, calibrated to serve as a point of comparison.

Just after dawn, the *Nellie Crockett* motored out of Cape Charles at six knots an hour. A few hours later, the Beechcraft 18 plane took off. Blocksome and McCoy were on board with Sue Morris, a veteran of several deepwater searches for the Electra. She would perform the role of Amelia Earhart.

First produced in 1937, the Beechcraft 18 was a worthy replacement for the Electra. Its two big engines generated about the same amount of noise and interference in the cockpit as the Electra had. Its size and shape were similar too—and the CARC team would know. They'd clambered around an Electra 10-E at the Pima Air & Space Museum in Tucson, Arizona, measuring its dimensions. They'd even temporarily installed an antenna on the museum's plane to determine its impedance, or effect the aircraft would have on the antenna's electrical flow.

Now the plane, dubbed the *Amelia* by its owners at Dynamic Aviation in Bridgewater, Virginia, was equipped with historic radio equipment. A

Bendix direction-finding loop antenna had been mounted on its fuselage, along with a V-shaped high-frequency antenna with a lead wire matching the measurements of the one on the Electra. Inside the cockpit, a Bendix aircraft radio receiver like the one Amelia had struggled to use was installed on a rack behind the pilot's seat.

They'd been lucky to secure a boat and a plane that would both serve as suitable substitutes for the *Itasca* and Electra—and with owners willing to donate their services. But their location in the Chesapeake Bay region added complications. The airspace around the southern Chesapeake is dominated by the military, limiting where they could go in the air and on the ocean. East of Norfolk, Virginia, at the southernmost tip of the bay, the plane was only permitted to follow one air route. They also needed to warn any military listeners that the messages they were about to send did not reflect a real emergency.

A further wrinkle was that, as amateur radio operators, they didn't have access to the same frequencies Earhart used. Instead of 7500 kHz, they had to use 7299 kHz, the closest frequency they were licensed for. The military already claimed 3105 kHz, so CARC had to settle for 3096 kHz. But these radio experts believed the substitute frequencies were close enough to the originals for their purpose.

The Beechcraft 18 would fly 200 miles out from shore, while the ship would stay three miles from land. Once they were both in position, the 7500 test, which was aimed at understanding what Earhart and Noonan heard in the Electra, could begin. From the ship's hold, Vinson tapped out a series of *A*'s in Morse code, transmitting them on 7299 kHz. Blocksome and his colleagues had the Bendix RA-1 receiver tuned up and ready to go. But even though they knew the message was coming and roughly in what direction it was coming from, they could barely hear the minimum they knew was there. They'd re-created Earhart's situation all too well.

"She's been flying in this aircraft for 20 hours," said Vinson, with "these two big engines on either side. It's not insulated. It's not a pressurized cabin or anything. And it's just deafening." Even with headphones on, "it is very difficult to get a minimum on that setup."

Blocksome and his colleagues on the Beechcraft 18 had an advantage over Earhart: They could *see* the minimum when it was transmitted. The modern transmitters they'd hooked up to the 1930s equipment visually showed the dip in volume. "If you're watching it, you can hear where the minimum is," says Vinson. "But if you don't have that visual aid, just hearing it aurally was very tough." They repeated the test every five miles, until the plane was so far out of range the modern receivers on board could no longer identify the minimum.

Some of their questions were answered: The conditions within the plane made it nearly impossible for Earhart to use her direction finder, the one piece of equipment she was relying on to locate Howland. They also knew how close she had to have been to hear the signal sent on 7500 kHz. They have "a good idea of how far away she was at eight o'clock in the morning," said Vinson.

But the test didn't solve one mystery: Why did she opt to use 7500 as the frequency in the first place? "It's just not optimal for doing that kind of work," said Vinson. "You're supposed to be down around 500 to 1500 kHz." He wondered if she misread instructions from her former radio operator Harry Manning, whose handwriting used a Europeanized "1" that could easily be mistaken for a 7.

The 3105 test promised to answer another burning question: How close was Earhart when the radiomen recorded her transmissions at signal strength five, the highest possible? To determine that, Sue Morris on the Beechcraft 18 read from a transcript of the transmissions the *Itasca* logged from Earhart, while the modern receivers on the *Nellie Crockett* measured their strength. Although the Western Electric transmitter started smoking, and they had to make a quick trip back to the airport for a part, the 3105 test worked smoothly. "Her voice gets loud and clear with a beautiful signal," said Vinson. "It was beautiful."

Even more beautiful to this crew—engineers to the core—were the results. "We have data now for signal strength versus distance for each HF [high frequency] transmission at 1,000 feet, flying toward and away from the ship," Vinson explained.

What that means now is that they're pretty sure they know how far away Earhart was at 8 a.m., which yields a radius of a certain length around the *Itasca*. And they've narrowed down where on the circle the Electra was. They'll use that information to plot their next expedition.

CHAPTER TWENTY

SANK: A DISCOVERY?

On January 27, 2024, a South Carolina company named Deep Sea Vision announced on Instagram that it had found "what appears to be Earhart's Lockheed 10-E Electra." Three grainy images appeared with the post, all showing an oblong shape with what looked to be two swept-back wings and an off-kilter tail. These pointillist pictures were collected some 16,000 feet below the surface of the Pacific.

Deep Sea Vision's search area was delineated in part by Liz Smith, a woman who never intended to get involved with the hunt for Amelia Earhart at all. An astronomer and filmmaker by training, Smith had spent several years working in communications for NASA. But in 2008, she took a job at the Waitt Institute, an ocean research group spearheaded by the same Ted Waitt who had sponsored Dave Jourdan's 2006 expedition. "When I got there the first day," Smith said, "they had me sign an NDA [nondisclosure agreement] and said, 'Hey, we're actually looking for Amelia Earhart.'" After the disappointment of the earlier attempt, Waitt was mounting his own search, and they needed Smith on board to film the second seven-week leg. It would be her first time at sea.

A few things about Earhart's disappearance stood out to Smith. "I got hung up on the 'We must be on you, but cannot see you' radio call," she said, referencing the message Earhart sent to the *Itasca* at 7:42 on the morning of July 2. To her, it indicated that Earhart and Noonan thought they'd reached the correct spot on the map. "Why did they think they were there and they weren't?" Smith wondered.

She also noticed the discrepancy between radio calls. At 6:15 a.m., Earhart radioed that they were about 200 miles out from Howland. At 6:45 a.m., she reported they were 100 miles away. The Electra couldn't travel 100 miles in 30 minutes. Something must have happened to affect their estimation.

The international date line marked on the maps in the Longs' book jumped out at her. If the Electra was truly 200 miles out, as Earhart said, they hadn't crossed the date line yet; by the 100-mile report, they would have.

Time is crucial for celestial navigation: It pinpoints where a celestial body will be in the sky at a given moment. Earhart delayed the takeoff from Lae to ensure that Noonan's chronometer was accurate down to the second. Smith, who is familiar with celestial navigation from her astronomy studies, pointed out that "the date is also part of the time." Was it possible Noonan focused too much on small details and forgot about that large one? When he was navigating, did he fail to account for the international date line?

Such an error seems inexplicable—Noonan made 18 Pacific crossings as a navigator for Pan Am—but becomes less so as one considers the specific timing of the Lae to Howland flight. The Electra had taken off from Lae at 10 a.m. on July 2, and was in the air when the calendar flipped to July 3. Then, just before dawn, the plane crossed the international date line, which shifted the fliers back to July 2. The question Smith raises is whether Noonan, after advancing his charts to July 3 at midnight local time, forgot to change them back to July 2 when the plane crossed the date line. By then, they'd been flying for some 2,300 miles and 18 or so hours. He was probably exhausted and definitely busy, according to Smith: "The sun would be rising shortly after they crossed the date line. Just before they crossed it, he may have been attempting to get his last star fixes as the morning twilight was drowning them out—and just after they crossed the date line, he may have been preparing to take a fix on the rising sun."

If, in the flurry of activity, Noonan missed that one small step of turning back the pages of his almanac, he would have calculated their longitude to be one degree farther east than it was, which translates to 60 nautical miles closer to Howland Island than they actually were. When Earhart radioed the *Itasca* to say "we must be on you," she would have been fatally wrong.

Smith brought her research to Waitt and the rest of the expedition team. Ultimately, they determined—and she agreed—that the highest area of probability for their search lay closer to Howland than her theory indicated. They didn't find any signs of Earhart, Noonan, or the Electra.

After the expedition, Smith wrote up her theory and built a website around it, in case anyone was interested. "I put it out there as sort of a hey, if not these places, there's also this next place," she said. To her, it had just been a fun intellectual exercise. She moved on, eventually becoming Bob Ballard's director of communications for several years and ultimately a freelance filmmaker.

Then, one day in 2022, she got an email from Tony Romeo.

TONY ROMEO HAD SPENT MUCH OF his career as a real estate investor. But in 2021, he read an article in the *Wall Street Journal* about magnet fishing that changed his life. Devotees toss hand-size magnets into waterways and haul out bicycles, safes, shopping carts, and other odds and ends. People have recovered weapons and unexploded ordnance; they've found evidence of crimes. Boosters tout it as part treasure hunt, part environmental cleanup. To Romeo, it sounded like a fun activity to share with his six-year-old son.

They both loved it. Father and son pulled up fishing hooks, scissors, coins—small items with high value for a kid. "A battery on the side of the road is nothing," Romeo said, "but a battery pulled up from the lake? Suddenly, it's like, wow, how did this get here?" He kept a box of their treasured finds.

"It got me thinking about well, golly, if we can pull stuff up with the magnet, what else is out there? Soon my mind went back to Amelia," he remembered. "The ocean swallowed up Amelia. There's a story there that's never been told."

His ideas, at first, were far-fetched. He approached his brother Lloyd, who had grown up with him on Earhart stories told by their father, a Pan Am pilot for four decades. "What if we string a row of magnets that are a mile long," he asked, "and just drop it into the water and drag it along the bottom?" Could they find Amelia Earhart's Electra?

Lloyd, an engineer, patiently explained that advanced technology for searching the ocean already existed. A sonar system would work much better than magnets. Tony let go of his magnetic dreams and began making calls.

He thought he could afford a sonar system. A former Air Force intelligence officer and licensed pilot, he'd developed a real estate app called Kwkly, which he sold in 2011 for over a million dollars. Afterward, he went to law school and built a lucrative career in real estate. But when he called the Norwegian technology company Kongsberg, he learned that leasing one of its HUGINs, a state-of-the-art autonomous underwater vehicle, would cost $25,000 to $30,000 a day.

"That's a bit expensive," Romeo recalled telling the sales representative. But as he was about to hang up, the rep tried one last pitch: "He says, you know, you could buy one of these for about $7 or $8 million and turn it into a business. There's only a few of these in the world. And there's a whole backlog of work out there in the Pacific."

Romeo already knew he was ready for a big life change: The magnet fishing and Earhart obsession were early signs. High interest rates and high inflation had made it harder to work in real estate. "I couldn't make any good buying decisions anymore," he says.

So he sold his real estate holdings and for $9 million bought a HUGIN 6000, which came equipped with synthetic aperture sonar (HISAS), a multibeam echo sounder, and a high-resolution camera: everything Tony and Lloyd would need to search for the Electra. In 2022, one year after he'd first dipped a magnet in the water, he founded Deep Sea Vision, a company offering clients the ability to survey underwater pipelines, locate deep-sea mineral deposits, map seabeds, and hunt for wrecks.

He had to clear one major hurdle: The Norwegian government was reluctant to approve the sale, as they feared he was acting as a middleman for the Chinese. Romeo admitted he looked suspicious: Individuals don't usually buy devices like the HUGIN, and his company barely existed. Even his email address (a personal Microsoft account) and LinkedIn page, which made no mention of ocean exploration, came under scrutiny. Eventually the U.S. Department of Defense and the FBI weighed in, attesting to his military service and previous top secret clearance. "I'm not really sure exactly what happened in the background," Romeo said. "They released it, but they said you can't use it in these 15 countries in these parts of the world. Which is fine. I mean, I'm not planning on doing any jobs for North Korea or China anytime soon."

Once they had the HUGIN, Deep Sea Vision was ready to start booking clients. But Romeo already knew what the company's first expedition would be: a search for Amelia Earhart's plane. They would set the autonomous underwater vehicle, or AUV, to roam, in part, over the area outlined by Smith's date line theory.

Smith had estimated that Earhart and Noonan would have been aiming for a point 65.9 nautical miles west of Howland. Assuming they conducted a search pattern to find the island until they ran out of gas, Smith believed the Electra may have crashed and sunk into the ocean somewhere within a 3,200-square-mile swath centered on that point.

And that's roughly where Deep Sea Vision searched. Setting sail from Tarawa on September 7, 2023, on the *Offshore Surveyor,* a 110-foot research vessel, the crew sent the HUGIN down some three miles below the ocean's surface for 30 hours at a time where it was "mowing the lawn" 50 meters above the seafloor. They'd recover the AUV, swap out its battery and hard drive, analyze the data it had collected, and launch the device on its next dive.

The HUGIN revealed underwater calderas and seamounts, massive geological formations no other humans had ever seen. Occasionally it would unveil promising targets—objects seemingly man-made, marked by straight edges—but those inevitably ended up being shipping containers or pipes, detritus from ocean commerce.

Some glitches arose. The camera broke early on, which would make confirming the plane more challenging if they ever found it. Another occurred on day 32, when they couldn't access the data from the hard drive. Some crew members suffered from seasickness; all of them missed eating fruits and vegetables. Otherwise, it was a smooth first voyage.

In late November 2023, after nearly two months at sea, they still hadn't found the plane, and the company's first paying job awaited them in American Samoa. Disappointed, Romeo called off the search and directed the *Offshore Surveyor* toward the U.S. territory. A few evenings later, he sat with his crew eating dinner while Craig Wallace, the company's head of operations and a former Kongsberg engineer, organized data on the hard drives up on the bridge.

"Guys," Wallace suddenly called out, "you need to take a look at this."

Convinced something was seriously wrong, Romeo rushed to the bridge. Wallace calmly sat at his computer, fingers poised to click play on a clip from the corrupted drive. Against the black of the seafloor, bright gold dots indicating the side-scan sonar's pings gradually coalesced on the screen. "That's when we realized, holy smokes, that's definitely something we missed," Romeo said.

A golden image had emerged from the data. It appeared to be a plane.

At first Romeo wanted to celebrate. What else could it be but Earhart's Electra? Someone proposed toasting the find with the 1937 whiskey they'd brought. Eventually they realized the limitations of what they had.

Wallace had managed to retrieve data from the side-scan sonar, but not from anything else—not the synthetic aperture sonar, which has much higher resolution, or the magnetometer, which detects metals. Plus, the camera on the HUGIN wasn't working on day 32, when the sonar collected the image, and it wasn't working now. Without the ability to photograph what they found, they couldn't confirm whether it was the Electra. The malfunctioning equipment wasn't the only hurdle: They didn't have time to return to the site. It would be a three-day sail there and another three days back, and they were due in American Samoa for their next gig.

Even so, Romeo decided to release the sonar images. In late January 2024, the news ricocheted across the media—and so did the names Deep Sea Vision and Tony Romeo. Romeo attended the famed Explorers Club annual gala in New York City; Deep Sea Vision was booked through most of the year.

Other Earhart theorists expressed varying degrees of skepticism. TIGHAR's Ric Gillespie scornfully dubbed the object "Tony's anchor," while Dave Jourdan was politely, if profoundly, skeptical that what they'd found was the plane. He didn't buy the date line theory, and he knew how misleading sonar images could be.

Smith, who isn't overly invested in her own theory, awaited confirmation. "I've done a lot of other underwater archaeology work," she said. "That target, it looks like a plane but I've seen rocks that look like that." Still, the consensus seemed to be that the images sure looked like *a* plane. Whether it was *the* plane remained to be seen.

Deep Sea Vision returned to the site on November 1, 2024, with a documentary crew poised to record their find. This time, the hard drive wasn't corrupted, the camera worked, and they managed to collect high-resolution sonar images. Alone in the ship's control room, Romeo and Wallace piloted the HUGIN directly over the target, watching as the high-resolution image populated their screen.

"We knew right away," said Romeo. It was "the cruelest trick of nature."

The target wasn't the Electra. It wasn't a plane. Smith was right. It was a rock formation.

"It was a bummer moment, but at the same time there was a little bit of excitement," he said. "When you've eliminated 95 percent of the area that we think was high probability, and there's only 5 percent left, there is some excitement to knowing, well, she's gotta be in this last 5 percent, right?"

But she wasn't—and, again, they had to head back to American Samoa for a paying job. "That was the biggest bummer moment," said Romeo. "We didn't find her. We didn't get her."

But like Jourdan before him, Romeo is certain he knows where she isn't. "She's not on line 157-337, you can take that to the bank," he says. "You want to go 50 miles [from Howland] in any direction, I can tell you she's not there either."

CHAPTER TWENTY-ONE

1937: WORLD FLIGHT

Before dawn on March 20, 1937, reporters and other spectators began gathering at Luke Field in Honolulu. A rope barrier separated them from the hulk of a plane barely visible in the darkness. Sentries lined the field's concrete runway, wet from rain earlier in the night.

The beam of a flashlight danced across the plane. Paul Mantz, Amelia Earhart's technical adviser, was conducting a preflight inspection, casting light over landing gear struts and tires, confirming that external access panels and covers were secured, and probing for leaks. The right propeller was stuck at 1,600 revolutions per minute on the flight from Oakland and the generator had failed. He wasn't taking any chances. He climbed into the cockpit and ran the engines: a startling sound in the early Hawaii morning.

Amelia stepped out of the hangar and took Mantz's place in the cockpit. Navigators Harry Manning and Fred Noonan followed shortly afterward, boarding through the rear cabin door. Neither took the copilot's seat in the cockpit lest there be any confusion about who was flying the plane—a precaution urged by Amelia's publicist husband, George.

As the sky brightened, Amelia taxied the plane to the northeast end of the runway and swung it around to face southwest. At 5:45 a.m., she released the brakes and pushed the throttles forward. The plane accelerated down the runway, smoothly building up speed. All seemed well except for a slight drift to the right side of the runway. Then a mechanic who'd stationed himself halfway down the runway heard the right engine surge. The officer in charge of the field's operations saw the wings waver. The plane twisted sharply left. The right wing tipped toward the ground. The landing gear collapsed on the right, then the left. In a shower of sparks, the plane slid on its belly in the direction it had started from. Gasoline poured from the plane's ruptured undercarriage.

A fire truck rushed to the scene, but by the time it reached the plane, Amelia had emerged from the hatch in the cockpit. Shaken but uninjured, she'd managed to power down everything before the fuel ignited. "Something must have gone wrong," she told Mantz as he put a steadying arm around her.

Amelia Earhart's bid to fly around the world had ended almost before it started.

PLANNING FOR THE TRIP BEGAN MORE than a year earlier—and it began with Purdue and a plane. Early in Amelia's time at the university, its president Edward Elliott asked George what her ambitions were, beyond her mentorship to women at Purdue and all that she'd accomplished so far in aviation. "I told him she was hankering for a bigger and better plane," said George, "not only one in which she could go to far places farther and faster and more safely, but to use as a laboratory for research in aviation education and for technical experimentation."

Elliott saw an opportunity, as George suspected he would, to boost Purdue's reputation in aviation research and gain some welcome publicity as well. Elliott arranged a dinner in the fall of 1935 for Amelia, George, and donors to the Purdue Research Foundation, where Amelia pitched an idea that had been "burbling" in her mind since her solo Pacific flight earlier in the year. "Not only did I want to make a longer flight than any I had attempted before, but I wanted to test some human reactions to flying. Of myself, and others as I found them, I planned to make human guinea pigs." For that she needed a new plane—a "flying laboratory," she called it. "The aviation industry has been so busy with mechanical and economic problems that the effects of flying on personnel have not always been given the attention they deserve."

By the dinner's end, two wealthy alumni, David Ross and J. K. Lilly, had pledged $20,000 each. Aviation-adjacent corporations such as Bendix, Western Electric, Goodrich, and Goodyear would later give a total of $33,000. In April 1936, Elliott announced that the money and any further gifts would go toward the newly created Amelia Earhart Fund for Aeronautical Research, which would "provide ways and means for pure and applied aeronautical research backgrounded on the facilities already established at Purdue." In reality, it would provide Amelia with a plane.

She chose the Electra 10-E, a dual-engine, all-metal monoplane with a top speed of roughly 200 miles an hour. She'd sworn to herself as she flew over the Gulf from Mexico to Newark in 1935 that "any further over-ocean flying would be attempted in a plane with more than one motor, capable of keeping aloft with a single engine. Just in case."

The Electra's twin Pratt & Whitney Wasp engines fulfilled that promise. Removing the seats in the fuselage to make room for six fuel tanks further equipped the plane for long-distance, over-ocean flights. Already, Amelia was planning to fly it around the world. Although she had emphasized the scientific possibilities of the flying laboratory to the Purdue donors, she knew that if she was going to make a round-the-world flight—the last major aviation feat left for her to accomplish—she'd better do it before someone else did.

In truth, others had already claimed the title of first and fastest to fly around the world. In 1924, U.S. Army Air Service pilots took off from Seattle in four open-cockpit, single-engine seaplanes. Only two of these managed to finish their course around the globe in what was, by all reports, an absolutely miserable 175-day slog through the northern latitudes. Wiley Post, the famous one-eyed pilot, and navigator Harold Gatty cut the record down to eight days, 15 hours, and 51 minutes in 1931. In 1933, Post—flying solo—made it in seven days, 18 hours, and 49 minutes.

So Amelia would not be the first. But however grueling their flights, these men had merely circled the northern tip of the globe. Amelia proposed circumnavigating the world at the Equator—"as near its waistline as could be"—a journey almost twice the length of Post's 15,596-mile, record-breaking flight. And she would be the first woman ever to circle the planet at any latitude.

The round-the-world flight was a monumental task to plan, far beyond any of her previous exploits. "Each country has its rules and regulations governing aircraft licensing, landing rights, overflying rights, passports, visas, vaccinations, insurance, airports, charts and maps, weather, fuel, maintenance, communications, hotels, and last but not least, money," explained Elgen Long, who'd circumnavigated the globe at the poles in 1971. "In those days it could take three months just to exchange letters of inquiry with a distant country. Multiply that by twenty or thirty different jurisdictions and the magnitude of the task becomes apparent."

The first puzzle to solve was the route. It was fine for Amelia to say she wanted to follow the Equator, but she needed to stop at suitable aviation facilities along the way. For guidance, she turned to two friends she'd made after her solo Atlantic flight: Violette Selfridge and her aristocratic husband, Vicomte Jacques de Sibour. When Amelia arrived in London with only a toothbrush and the clothes on her back in 1932, Violette's family had opened the doors of Selfridges, their famous department store, to her in exchange for displaying her Vega on the ground floor. Now, Amelia needed another favor. De Sibour's role at Standard Oil Aviation Products, a company with ties across the British colonies, made him a vital resource. He ended up coordinating some 30 caches of fuel and supplies to await her at stops around the world.

But de Sibour couldn't solve the knottiest problem: how and where to cross the Pacific. For that, Amelia and George required the U.S. government's assistance. Gene Vidal, head of the Bureau of Air Commerce, was invaluable, though Amelia would ultimately reach all the way up to President Roosevelt to obtain the arrangements she wanted. Vidal and Amelia had worked on three airlines together, and one biographer has suggested they'd had an affair. They were certainly close friends. Vidal assigned J. Carroll Cone, who handled regulations, to coordinate the required permits for each country with the Department of State, and William Miller, in charge of special projects, to work with the U.S. Navy and Coast Guard on the Pacific leg.

The Pacific was too vast for the Electra, even with its 4,000-mile range, to cross in one go. Tokyo was 3,900 miles from Honolulu, which left no room for error, while Manila was an impossible 5,800 miles away. Pan Am had established airports at Wake, Guam, and Midway Islands, but those just serviced seaplanes. The only solution appeared, at first, to be refueling from Navy planes in midair—a daunting task that would require Amelia to manage the refueling equipment while holding the plane at a steady altitude and speed in the midst of an estimated 26-hour flight to Tokyo. When an admiral was slow to respond to this risky proposal, Amelia wrote to President Roosevelt asking him "to help me secure Navy cooperation." The president did and the Navy agreed, with the caveat that "considerable special training will be required to assure the success of the undertaking"—and that the training, as well as the "actual tangible costs such as that for gasoline and oil to be used in her own plane, and for the expenses of personnel engaged in this work ... should be borne by Miss Earhart."

Luckily, Vidal came up with what appeared to be the perfect solution.

In 1935, he'd assigned Miller another "special project": the colonization of Jarvis, Baker, and Howland Islands, ideal spots for airfields to connect the United States with Australia and New Zealand—and to serve as a string of outposts against Japan's expansion in the Pacific. To prove the American claim to the Line Islands, so called because they bordered the Equator, young men recruited from the Kamehameha Schools in Hawaii were shipped out to live for months at a time on their barren shores. But no airfield had been built until Amelia began planning her flight. Once she'd dislodged a Works Progress Administration appropriation with a well-timed telegram to the president early in 1937, construction of a rough airstrip on Howland began.

Even with the new airfield, Howland was, in Amelia's words, "a fantastically tiny target." She'd need help to find it. For the first time, she explored inviting a navigator to join her. Among the candidates she and George considered was Bradford Washburn, a photographer, cartographer, and Arctic explorer as well as the director of Boston's Museum of Science. Washburn spent a pleasant evening with the Putnams sprawled on their floor discussing maps and itineraries. But he refused the assignment before they could ask. "My navigation experience was not adequate to handle that kind of a job," he explained later. "Very frankly I knew all about how to get it done, but I couldn't do it."

Amelia asked Harry Manning instead. Manning was captain of the S.S. *President Roosevelt,* the ship that brought Amelia home from her "sack of potatoes" flight across the Atlantic in 1928. During the crossing, he "gave her the practical instruction in navigation which she never had." They promised each other they'd fly together someday. In the ensuing years, Manning, though still a ship's captain, had obtained his pilot's license. He'd never undergone a long-distance flight like this, but Amelia trusted him.

George and Mantz weren't so sure. Manning hadn't navigated at the speed the Electra would be traveling. During a practice cross-country flight, Manning identified their location as southern Kansas when they were actually over northern Oklahoma. In reality, he was off by only a few miles but George, who wasn't a pilot or a navigator, viewed it as a monumental error. Mantz suggested testing Manning over the ocean, flying from Burbank to San Francisco, and then using celestial navigation to plot a course back to Southern California. Again, Manning was off target—this time by more than 20 miles, a miss that's possible "without having made any unreasonable error," Elgen Long pointed out. "That was the reality of aerial celestial navigation." George and Mantz were not reassured.

When George found out Fred Noonan had left Pan Am, he jumped at the chance to hire him for the flight. Noonan, who'd charted Pan Am's routes across the Pacific, had the experience that both Manning and Washburn lacked. However, there was a catch: The navigator known to be the best in the business was also rumored to have a serious drinking problem. Word was it didn't affect his work.

Amelia still needed Manning. He was a skilled radio operator who'd spent far more time than she had understanding the complicated workings of the plane's radio setup and direction finder. Indeed, only Manning had been shown how to use the Bendix receiver and direction finder. The first time Amelia tried it herself was during the flight to Honolulu. Manning also knew Morse code, the most common form of communication between ships and an international language for radio operators. With Noonan on board, Manning could focus on communications, while Amelia piloted the plane.

They took off from Oakland for Honolulu on March 17, 1937. Noonan wore a shamrock to commemorate St. Patrick's Day. Mantz was on board too—for romantic reasons, Amelia claimed. His fiancée, Terry Minor, was on a ship bound for Hawaii; he wanted to meet her there. (He'd recently gone through an ugly divorce in which Amelia was named as a co-respondent, a situation she described to her mother as "silly accusations.") Mantz told a different story later. George, he said, had been worried that Amelia was exhausted from all the planning and asked Mantz to join her on this leg so she wouldn't have to fly the 16-hour route on her own.

They encountered a few surmountable problems during the flight: The generator burned out a fuse (from Manning's excessive use of the radio, said Mantz) and the right propeller got stuck at one speed. As they were nearing their destination early the following morning, Amelia was so fatigued, Mantz claimed, that she asked him to land the plane, which he did with a little too much Hollywood showmanship. Banking steeply over the waiting crowd, he brought the plane down with a hard jolt, which may have weakened the landing gear. It was a foolish thing to do with a partially disabled propeller.

Amelia planned to leave for Howland later that day or early the following morning. But repairing the propeller, which hadn't been lubricated properly in Oakland, delayed their departure until March 20. In the meantime, they stayed at the lush Waikiki home of Christian Holmes, heir to the Fleischmann's Yeast fortune and Mantz's good friend. Mantz planned to stay behind in Honolulu. Noonan would hop off at Howland and sail home aboard the Coast Guard cutter *Shoshone*. After the flight from Lae to Port Darwin, Australia—the last Pacific leg—Manning would disembark, leaving Amelia to fly the rest of the way on her own.

They never got off the ground in Hawaii. The plane, overloaded with fuel for the long haul to Howland, ground-looped, leaving the Electra "helpless on the concrete runway, a poor battered bird with broken wings," wrote Amelia in the aftermath. The next few hours were a whirl of activity. After assessing the damage to the plane, Amelia whipped out an article for the *Herald Tribune* on the crash, filing it just after 8 a.m. Back in California, George was already on the phone drumming up pledges to cover the repairs. He'd cabled Amelia immediately upon hearing the news: "SO LONG AS YOU AND THE BOYS ARE OK THE REST DOESN'T MATTER AFTER ALL ITS JUST ONE OF THOSE THINGS. WHETHER YOU WANT TO CALL IT A DAY OR KEEP GOING LATER IS EQUALLY JAKE TO ME." By noon—a mere six hours after the crack-up—Amelia, Noonan, Manning, Mantz, and Minor had boarded a ship back to California, leaving the Electra to be packed up and shipped later.

Amelia did not want to call it a day. Before "the slithering slide along the concrete ended," the thought flashed through her mind: "If we don't burn up, I want to try again." Only the complete wreckage of the plane would have stopped her. "I knew we'd not be able to get another."

George, of course, was amenable, despite the near-unbearable stress he experienced while she was flying. "I think my husband has always found a sort of grim satisfaction—a species of modern martyrdom—in being, for once, the male left behind while the female fares forth adventure-bound," Amelia wrote in *Last Flight,* her posthumously published account. Although she wrote this lightheartedly, George suffered during her exploits. He learned of the Hawaii crash when a reporter called him to say the plane was in flames. He immediately handed the phone to Miller and strode "out into the cold morning trying to walk steadily." In a few agonizingly long minutes, someone ran after him calling "No fire ... no fire at all. False report! No one hurt!" In 1932, during Amelia's Atlantic solo, he'd received a similar false alarm. Now, "the black wings brushed close again."

The Electra required a new right wing, propeller blades, and replacements for the antennae that had run under the fuselage: repairs that Lockheed accomplished by May 18 for $12,500. Transporting the plane back to the mainland cost $4,100; other expenses included paying for the travel of an engineer who'd been hired to meet Amelia in Karachi to overhaul the engines that now had to be recalled. "Those days in April and May were full of horrid realizations like the costly Karachi excursion, forcibly driving home the sad truth that the stress and strains of an airplane accident and its aftermaths are just as severe financially as they are mechanically," Amelia wrote. George managed to wheedle $20,000 out of Vincent Bendix and $10,000 from Floyd Odlum. "OUR SECOND ATTEMPT IS ASSURED," she wired Elliott. "WE ARE SOLVENT. FUTURE IS MORTGAGED, BUT WHAT ELSE ARE FUTURES FOR?"

She and George expected to recoup all their expenses. George had already booked Amelia for a series of lectures at $500 each, in addition to the exclusive contract he'd arranged with the *Herald Tribune* for firsthand reports from her journey. And, as with the Mexico flight, she'd be carrying souvenir covers presold through Gimbels department stores. She also had a contract for a book, five chapters of which she wrote while the plane was being repaired, the rest she sent to George in dispatches from the flight. The Putnams were gambling on the success of the world flight to put them back in the black and then some.

As they were sorting out the financial issues, they also "set to studying again the weather maps of the world and consulting with meteorologists who know the habits of fogs and rains and temperatures around the long equator." The delay put them dangerously close to the stormy seasons in the Caribbean, Africa, and Asia—unless they covered that ground first. The obvious choice was to reverse the world flight's direction, which would give Amelia the added benefit of a shakedown flight from California to Miami, where Pan Am's mechanics could fix any problems that arose. De Sibour organized moving the fuel and spare parts from the original stops to the new ones, while George badgered the Navy and Coast Guard to ensure that ships would be standing by along the Pacific route. They wouldn't have Bill Miller's help this time: Vidal had been forced out of the Bureau of Air Commerce, and the new management made it clear they didn't want Amelia to attempt the trip again, although they didn't withdraw their permission.

During this period, "I was seemingly busier even than before," Amelia reported. She spent hours at the Lockheed plant, consulted with Mantz on "refinements of technique in the installation of fuel lines, tanks, dump valves, instruments and the rest of it," and reconfigured charts with Noonan, who was joining her for the whole trip. She spent only one short session with engineer Joseph Gurr going over the radio operations Manning had known so well. When Gurr asked her to tune in a local radio station, she turned the knob so slowly he realized she wasn't yet proficient in the device. She left on the world flight a few days later.

THE SECOND TAKEOFF WAS A SECRET, even from Mantz. On May 20, he and Amelia flew up to Oakland to retrieve the souvenir covers from the post office—updated with a "Second Take Off" overprinting—and stowed them in the plane's nose. Lockheed had delivered the repaired Electra just the day before, so Mantz assumed she'd spend a few more days airing it out. That evening, he left for an aerobatic competition in St. Louis. Meanwhile, Amelia had counted the flight from Oakland to Burbank as the first leg of her eastern-bound world flight.

The next day, Amelia, George, Noonan, and mechanic Bo McKneely took off on a leisurely cross-country jaunt to Miami. They'd planned the "sneak takeoff" weeks earlier; if something went wrong, they'd claim it was a shakedown flight to avoid tarnishing Amelia with a second failure.

Their first stop was in Tucson to refuel. When the left engine backfired and burst into flames, it seemed like it would be their last. But Amelia responded quickly, as she had at Luke Field, pulling the handle that discharged a fire extinguisher into the engine and put out the flames. A few rubber fittings were damaged, but those were easily replaced. They stayed overnight anyway.

On May 23, they arrived in Miami, where they planned to stay a week. Amelia's favorite reporter, the *New York Herald Tribune*'s Carl Allen, was in on the secret, accompanying her as she worked with Pan Am mechanics to service the plane. Many of them knew Noonan, who'd once been stationed in the Caribbean; they pitied him for undertaking a flight they viewed as a pure stunt, with a mere woman as the pilot. They changed their minds when they saw that Amelia "knew her stuff," Allen wrote.

"There was an almost audible clatter of chips falling off skeptical masculine shoulders."

The radio transmitter caused the mechanics the most problems. Gurr had removed the trailing antenna wire that allowed for transmissions on 500 kilocycles, the optimal frequency for Morse code, believing that lengthening the fixed antenna would make code transmissions possible if needed. The Pan Am technicians didn't think it worked and shortened the antenna Gurr had lengthened. Calling the radio that operated at 500 kilocycles "dead weight," Amelia explained to Allen that "both Fred Noonan and I know Morse code but we're amateurs and probably never would be able to send and receive more than 10 words a minute." Given the amount of fuel the Electra would have to carry for the long ocean hops, every ounce mattered.

At 5:56 a.m. on June 1, the Electra took off from Miami. George had said goodbye to Amelia in the privacy of the hangar. "There in the dim chill we perched briefly on cold concrete steps, and the feel of her hands in mine told more than the words we did not speak," remembered George. When she'd settled into the cockpit, he clambered onto the wing in his suit and dress shoes, his hair slicked back as usual despite the heat and early hour, and said one last farewell. Then she was gone.

Amelia and Noonan were bound for Puerto Rico, a nearly eight-hour flight. They stayed the night with Clara Livingston, where they established the routine they would follow for the rest of the journey, going to bed early and awakening long before sunrise. "We wanted quiet and sleep," wrote Amelia. "When politely possible, it was helpful to avoid functions and people—even the pleasantest people, for meeting and talking to them adds immeasurably to the fatigue factor, nervous and physical."

The next day, they flew south. Only four "reasonably satisfactory" airports had been built between San Juan and Natal, Brazil, the jumping-off point for flights across the southern Atlantic to Africa. Amelia and Noonan stopped at all of them, from Caripito, Venezuela—where the "splendid airfield" was managed by Pan Am and Standard Oil—to Paramaribo, Dutch

Guiana (now Suriname), "one of the best natural landing areas I have ever seen." There, a bonfire burned to show the wind direction and a man waved a white flag to guide them in. On the way to Fortaleza, Brazil, they crossed the Amazon River's lower delta, "from aloft a crazy-quilt of variously colored currents, each flowing its chosen course, each retaining its own particular hue of yellow or brown muddiness, and all bearing seaward, like matches, countless thousands of giant trees wrenched up at the roots." In her dispatches, Amelia touched on a theme that would recur throughout the world flight: a wish to retrace her steps "next time really seeing the lands I've only skimmed now—all of them entirely new to me—and visiting their peoples in a decently leisurely and civilized manner."

In Natal, Air France crews advised them that the worst weather across the Atlantic would be in the first 800 miles; better to leave early in the morning to make their way through it in daylight. Amelia and Noonan took the advice, though she was amused by the givers. "Frenchmen all rotund," she noted in her log. "Berets. Champagne bottles along walk."

At 3:15 a.m. June 7, the Electra set course for Dakar, Senegal, a French colony. "The blackness of the night outside made all the more cheering the subdued lights of my cockpit, glowing on the instruments which showed the way through space as we headed east over the ocean," Amelia wrote. She flew most of the way using the Sperry autopilot, which kept the plane on course while she took notes. Noonan sat at the navigator's station behind the fuel tanks in the cabin. As they neared the coast of Africa, he passed a note to her telling her to change the compass heading to 36 degrees to reach Dakar. She scrawled back on the paper, "What put us north?" Although she had no known reason to doubt his navigation—and many documented reasons to trust it—she'd thought they were south of Dakar.

Noonan was correct, of course, but following Amelia's hunch they ended up in St. Louis, Senegal, 163 miles north. "The fault was mine," admitted Amelia. "A 'left turn' seemed to me in order" when they reached the coast; instead, it delayed them by a day—a day she needed to take in this new place.

She found her first encounter with Africa overwhelming. Flying, she wrote, gives travelers "no period of preparation, of becoming acclimatized, socially and geographically, as must happen on slow steamer voyages with recurrent stops." Fascinated though she was, she struggled to process "the riot of human color" and "strong human tang of people." For all her travel and work at Denison House, she had little experience being a minority among people of other races. She'd noticed in Venezuela that "we had chosen a route which lay in lands of exclusively brown-eyed people"; her first observations of Africans in Senegal were crude and reductive.

The next day they flew to Dakar, where Air France mechanics fixed the fuel meter, which had failed during the Atlantic flight. They stayed with the governor-general. The French "have a genius for colonization," Amelia noted approvingly. "Certainly they seemed miraculously at home in this particular far corner of the world." A French Air Force captain provided them with maps and weather information, telling them what they already knew: The weather was extremely hot. In the interior, tornadoes loomed to the south and sandstorms to the north. "I must try to squeeze between," she wrote.

On June 10, they left for Gao in French Sudan, now Mali, where they found "my usual calling cards," wrote Amelia, "fifty gallon drums of gasoline, each with my name printed large upon it in white or red lettering"—all thanks to de Sibour. From there, they flew to Fort-Lamy (now N'Djamena, Chad). Fred wrote to his wife that he found navigating over this land more difficult than water: "The maps of the country are very inaccurate and consequently extremely misleading." Still, he did not get lost. "In all the distance I don't think we wandered off the course for half an hour, although there were times when I couldn't have bet a nickel on the accuracy of our assumed position." They saw birds "in great numbers" and hippos but, disappointingly, no elephants or crocodiles.

From Fort-Lamy, they flew to El Fasher in French Equatorial Africa (now Sudan), where the airport was surrounded by an "eight foot thorn hedge" to keep out the animals. They stayed with the governor and his wife, who lived in what had once been a sultan's palace—another colonial stopover. Of all the countries they visited on the world flight, only three (Venezuela, Brazil, and Siam, now Thailand) weren't colonies—and each of those were heavily influenced by foreign business interests such as Standard Oil and Pan Am.

Onward they flew to Khartoum in Anglo-Egyptian Sudan across "a cartographical blank space as large as an outstretched hand with not a contour line on it or a river." They lingered only briefly to refuel though, Amelia wrote, "seeing this cradle-land of history for the first time and having come so far one could weep to pass so briefly." The night of June 13, they slept in Italian Army headquarters in Massawa, Eritrea. From there, they traveled to Assab, the "sweltering outpost of Italian authority on the Red Sea."

Assab was their jumping-off point to Karachi on the far shore of the Arabian Sea. They'd be the first to fly the route nonstop but were forced to take a curving path. "We were not to fly over Arabia itself but along the edge of the sea," wrote Amelia. "Flying by foreigners over Arabia is not welcomed." Should they be forced down, she carried a letter in Arabic explaining that they were on a mission for the British crown, as well as full canteens, concentrated foods, a land compass, and very heavy walking shoes. But the only serious problem they ran into during the flight was a miscommunication that led George and de Sibour to anxiously expect them a day earlier.

When Amelia and Noonan landed in Karachi, de Sibour was waiting for them. Amelia had a phone call from George. "As casual as that!" exclaimed Amelia. "And we almost exactly on the other side of the world." He asked her if she was having a good time. "You betja!" she replied. "We'll do it again, together, some time." She told him she'd see him in Oakland.

They stayed two nights in Karachi. Amelia rode a camel and went to the post office to get stamps for the souvenir covers she carried. Their travels left such little time for sightseeing: "the geography of our journey likely will remain most clearly memorized in terms of landing-field environments; of odors of baking metal, gasoline, and perspiring ground crews; of the roar of warming motors and the clatter of metal-working tools."

On June 17, they took off for Calcutta, where their flight was nearly ended when black eagles surrounded the plane at 5,000 feet. "They soared about us lazily," recounted Amelia, "oblivious of the Electra and giving its pilot some very bad moments."

In Calcutta, the weather turned against them. Monsoons during the night soaked the runway, making the takeoff "as risky as any we had," wrote Amelia. "The plane clung for what seemed like ages to the heavy sticky soil before the wheels finally lifted, and we cleared with nothing at all to spare the fringe of trees at the airdrome's edge." They made it to Akyab, Burma (now Sittwe, Myanmar), where they planned to refuel and continue on to Rangoon (now Yangon, Myanmar). However, once they were in the air, "the heavens unloosed an almost unbroken wall of water." They had to turn back, Amelia reported. "By uncanny powers, Fred Noonan managed to navigate us back to the airport, without being able to see anything but the waves beneath our plane."

The next day gave them their first sight of Rangoon, "the sun touching the Shwe Dagon Pagoda ... its covering of pure gold a burnished beacon for wayfarers of the air." Having seen the Buddhist monument from the air, Amelia determined to "examine it from the ground" while they waited for the next bout of rain to pass. "For the first time on the trip Fred Noonan failed me," complained Amelia. "He would not take off his shoes and socks and go inside with me." She found all she saw of Rangoon enchanting. The streets were "colorful," the people "slim," and their garments "graceful." She took note of the streetcars with compartments reserved for women and commented approvingly that "women in general here seem to have more freedom and education than in most places we have been. Many are in business and they have had a vote for many years."

On June 20, they flew to Bangkok, stopping only to refuel before they headed on to Singapore, where the $9 million airport, "an aviation miracle of the east," had opened the week before. From there, it was on to Bandung on the island of Java, where Dutch mechanics with the airline KLM attempted to fix the fuel analyzer, flow meter, and generator motor. Their stay lasted six days; they attempted to leave on June 24, but instrument troubles forced them to return to "the admirable Dutch technicians and equipment." A traditional 21-course meal called *rijsttafel*—and the stomach trouble it caused—also slowed them down. Amelia told George in another phone call that she thought she'd be home before the Fourth of July.

Finally, on June 27, they flew from Bandung to Kupang on the island of Timor, where the airfield was surrounded by "a stout stone fence to keep out roaming wild pigs." From there, it was a relatively short hop to Darwin, on the northern edge of Australia. When they arrived, a communications officer named Stanley Rose asked why Amelia hadn't contacted the Darwin direction finding unit, as was mandatory in the country. She admitted she hadn't been able to use the direction finder since leaving the United States—and apparently hadn't missed it. Rose got it to work by replacing a fuse. But Amelia's familiarity with the device she'd be relying on to cross the Pacific hadn't improved since her brief training with Joe Gurr more than a month earlier in California.

The fliers left their parachutes behind in Darwin. "A parachute," Amelia wrote, "would not help over the Pacific."

On June 29, after flying 22,000 miles for more than a month, they landed in Lae, on the island of New Guinea, 7,000 miles from home. Their next stop would be Howland Island. "My Electra now rests on the shores of the Pacific," wrote Amelia. "Somewhere beyond the horizon lies California."

The next three days were a period of "restlessness and disappointment." Lae was a hub for gold mining on New Guinea but of precious little else. Communication with the *Itasca,* the U.S. Coast Guard cutter waiting at Howland, required transmitting messages through Samoa; responses could be delayed by as much as a day. Messages to San Francisco had to be relayed via territorial headquarters in Rabaul, on the island of New Britain, and Sydney. On Lae, they had no phone service at all; Amelia would not be able to speak with George before this most dangerous leg.

Each morning they hoped to leave, but Noonan couldn't set his chronometers; the radio in Lae encountered too much interference for a clear time check. They couldn't leave without it: "Any lack of knowledge of their fastness and slowness would defeat the accuracy of celestial navigation," Amelia reported. If the clocks were off by as little as four seconds, they'd miss their target by a nautical mile.

On July 1, at 10:30 p.m., Noonan finally received his time check. His chronometers were three seconds slow. They could leave. "The whole width of the world has passed behind us—except this broad ocean," wrote Amelia. "I shall be glad when we have the hazards of its navigation behind us."

They took off at 10:00 the next morning.

CHAPTER TWENTY-TWO

SURVIVORS

In the summer of 2019, a few weeks before I joined Bob Ballard on his expedition to Nikumaroro, I traveled with a National Geographic podcast team to Atchison, Kansas. One sultry morning, we met up with a group of Amelia Earhart's descendants at the Amelia Earhart Birthplace Museum. Amelia's niece, Amy Kleppner, a vigorous 87 years old, insisted on making the long, steep climb from the downtown hotel where we were all staying to Earhart's childhood home. Amy's sons Bram and Caleb and their wives and children gamely followed in her wake. Not all of the kids had visited the place where their famous ancestor had been born.

The children were appropriately impressed by the Victorian-era decor, the dormer window where Amelia had looked out over the bluff to the Missouri River, the room where she'd slept, the library where she'd whiled away many hours. They paused over memorabilia such as a photograph of her as a young nurse in Toronto and the cigarette advertisement that caused her so much trouble after the *Friendship* flight.

But what really interested them was the basement.

"I'll get a flashlight," said our tour guide Ann Shaneyfelt, an exuberant woman whose eyes sparkled nearly as much as her bedazzled Amelia Earhart

T-shirt. "Make it feel like even more of an event." A pilot herself, Shaneyfelt is a member of the Ninety-Nines, the women's aviation group that Earhart founded and that operates the museum.

We followed her outside to the back of the house, where she unlocked a door leading down a steep staircase to blackness below. Stepping cautiously, Shaneyfelt swept the flashlight across the wall, located a switch, and flicked on the light. We descended behind her into a low room. Two chest-high mounds, each stretching the length of a tall man, filled the space.

Some people believe these mounds are where Amelia Earhart and Fred Noonan are buried.

"Mysterious big cement things in the basement of the Birthplace Museum," said Amy's son Bram. "What else could it be?"

As the theory goes, Earhart defected to the Japanese, planning and leading the attack on Pearl Harbor. She returned via submarine to Tokyo, where she lived in the Imperial Palace and served as air marshal and chief of staff of the Japanese Air Force. After the war, she and Noonan returned to the United States, where they lived under assumed names, necessitating a secret burial site. Naturally, she chose the cellar of her childhood home, where she remains to this day, according to Barry Bower, whose posthumously published book *The Amelia Earhart Saga: Plausible Suppositions* ends with photographs of the basement lumps.

Another theorist paid to have the site x-rayed, said Shaneyfelt. She waited a beat. "He said it was inconclusive." Everyone laughed.

"So it is, like, the best outcome you could have hoped for," said Bram.

Shaneyfelt doesn't know what the lumps are—they were added to the basement before her time at the museum—but she shrugged off any idea that they contain the remains of Amelia and Fred. Amelia's family hadn't lived in the home since her grandparents died in 1912; the Ninety-Nines didn't acquire it until 1984. She assumed the mounds were the result of renovations or repairs conducted by one of three families who occupied the house during the intervening years.

"There are lots of people who have lots of theories about what happened to Amelia and some are more coherent than others," explained Bram, a gregarious man who often serves as the family spokesman. "But you know people inclined towards conspiracy thrive on uncertainty and the fact that no one can say why these two big lumps of cement are here feeds perfectly into what they're inclined to believe anyway."

To me, Amelia's birthplace felt like an all-too-apt metaphor for her place in our culture now—a celebration of a legend's life and legacy resting uneasily atop an unhinged obsession with her death. On my first trip to Nikumaroro, I'd understood Earhart only in terms of these opposing forces. But in Atchison, at her birthplace, as I listened to the beautifully ordinary banter of her descendants, she also began to take shape as an actual person, with a place and a family.

The annual Amelia Earhart Festival, which is what had brought Amy, Bram, and the rest of the crew to Atchison, presented a similarly strange juxtaposition of adulation and fixation, with the ghost of the real woman flitting in the background. In some ways, the festival is typical small-town Americana: a fun run, carnival rides, a craft fair, a car show, and fried food. At least one Amelia reenactor performs, and visitors enjoy cake in celebration of Earhart's July 24 birthday. The organizers bestow a Pioneering Achievement Award each year to someone who exemplifies Amelia's spirit: Amy accepted it on behalf of her mother, Earhart's sister, Muriel, who died in 1998. Some 30,000 to 50,000 people attend, many drawn by the spectacular air show and fireworks, which *USA Today* named as among the top 10 in the country.

But far away from the cotton candy and carnival crowds, the Earhart diehards gather. At the Speaker Symposium, held in a cavernous auditorium at Atchison's Benedictine College in front of a sparse but enthusiastic crowd, Nicole McElhinney and Bronagh Sharkey took the stage. The two Irish women wore matching red dresses with red polka-dotted scarves, in honor, they said, of Amelia's red Vega—"the little red bus," she called it—

which landed near their hometown of Derry in Northern Ireland after she crossed the Atlantic in 1932. Founding members of the Amelia Earhart Legacy Association of Derry, they gave a giddy talk about why the American pilot meant so much to them. "Women didn't drive [in Northern Ireland], yet Amelia landed in a plane," said McElhinney. "Women didn't wear trousers. She was in a flying suit."

"I'm not a feminist," added Sharkey. "I love men." Even so, she said, "I get quite emotional about Amelia sometimes. I don't know why."

Sharing the stage with them was Grace McGuire, who also was being awarded a Pioneering Achievement Award. As a young pilot, she was told she looked like Amelia Earhart, a resemblance she cultivated. In 1984, McGuire acquired a Lockheed Electra 10-E, aiming to restore it with contemporary parts so she could follow Earhart's flight path around the world. "I was going to do that flight and everything would be identical except the outcome," she said.

But a debilitating bout with Lyme disease scotched McGuire's plan. After more than three decades of meticulous work, she sold the plane to the new Amelia Earhart Hangar Museum, which made the Electra its centerpiece when it opened in 2023. McGuire kept her comments short at the symposium. But later, during a looping conversation, she hinted that she was related to Amelia in ways she couldn't divulge. She also claimed she'd figured out that Earhart and Noonan had the wrong coordinates for Howland, but that she didn't get credit for her discovery because she fell ill. There was more to the story, she said, but "I just can't share any of that right now."

In the symposium audience was Alex Mandel, a mustached, suspender-wearing Ukrainian who described himself as "an admirer of Amelia Earhart." He'd been one ever since he first encountered the pilot on a summer afternoon while reading his father's old magazines in the backyard of his childhood home in Odesa. "It was just a brief biography of her and a story of how she disappeared," he said. That was enough.

Through what he called the "Amelia community," he met a fellow admirer and soulmate, Michelle Cervone, who moved to Atchison from New Jersey after she retired to be near Earhart's birthplace. With Cervone, Mandel made a pilgrimage to all the important sites in Earhart's life. In 2005, he contributed a carefully argued rebuttal to the small but impassioned discourse around the theory that Amelia Earhart assumed the identity of Irene Bolam after World War II. For years, Mandel planned vacations around the festival, even after Cervone died in 2016. When asked why the aviator has held his attention for so long, his answer was simple: "She was an inspiration."

Such devotion may seem odd, if not borderline obsessive, but consider this: Amazon lists more than 1,000 books about Amelia Earhart; the top sellers are aimed at children, some as young as infants. Parents are hoping to impart Earhart's spirit of fearlessness and accomplishment to their children, especially their daughters. She's been made into a Lego mini-figure *and* a Barbie.

Of course, Earhart's story—and the retelling of it—resonates for adults as well. Distinguished actresses Amy Adams, Diane Keaton, and Hilary Swank have all portrayed her—or versions of her—in movies and TV shows. The critically acclaimed novel *I Was Amelia Earhart* by Jane Mendelsohn imagines Earhart and Noonan falling in love after they're stranded on a deserted island. Maggie Shipstead's *Great Circle* proposes a very different ending to the disappearance of a pilot with a passing resemblance to Earhart—and was short-listed for the Booker Prize in 2021. In 2024, two major pieces of music were released with Amelia as their subject: an elegiac album by performance artist Laurie Anderson and a dreamy exercise in "conceptual pop historiography" by the British band Public Service Broadcasting. For Jennifer Finney Boylan, best-selling author and trans rights advocate, Earhart's disappearance sparked a 2025 multimedia performance addressing liberty, and the lack of it, for women and queer people. "I am haunted by Amelia Earhart," she said. "I'm also haunted by the way she haunts other people."

Earhart's image continues to captivate—and sell. Pop icon Rihanna channeled her timelessness for a *Harper's Bazaar* photo shoot. Major companies such as Apple, Jeep, and Allergan have deployed her image in ad campaigns. Chick-fil-A employed a vague look-alike to market a breakfast sandwich.

McGuire, Mandel, and other fervent fans are far from alone in finding inspiration in Amelia Earhart. "I think it was the spirit of adventure that really distinguished her and the fact that she was determined and courageous and competent enough to do some impressive flights," said Amelia's niece Amy Kleppner. "I don't think she would be as much of a legend and as much of a recurring image in popular culture if it weren't for the disappearance."

Speaking with Earhart's relatives was a reminder that Amelia left behind a grieving family when she disappeared—a family whose mourning would forever be interrupted by people with new theories about how their loved one died. "They had no idea how much pain this caused her," Kleppner said of her mother, Muriel. Kleppner, who died in 2024 at the age of 93, found the searching distasteful. "I don't believe one penny should be spent in that particular way," she said. "There's a lot of misery in the world that can be alleviated by those millions of dollars that have been spent on searching the ocean and digging up graves on various islands and all the rest of it." She believed, as she said her mother did, that the most plausible answer is that the plane crashed into the ocean and sank.

IN THE IMMEDIATE AFTERMATH OF AMELIA and Fred's disappearance, their families had refused to be alarmed. On the first day, George was defiant: "She might have slowed up for any number of causes. She'll make it all right." He'd had scares before—including two weeks earlier, when he'd expected her to arrive in Karachi a day sooner than she did—and Amelia had come through fine.

The next day, newspaper reporters noted with some awe that Muriel seemed to be reassuring *them*. "Amelia always took every precaution on her flights," she said. "I'm not worrying about her." Her mother agreed. "I know Amelia is alright," she said, citing a Navy pilot who had recently been rescued after nine days adrift at sea.

But her mother quickly went into seclusion, and Muriel's face became "drawn ... the circles under her eyes [testifying] to her suffering." Her seven-year-old son, David, cried when told his aunt wouldn't be bringing him the letter covered in international postmarks that she'd promised. A few days later, little Amy, about to turn six, received a birthday present in the mail from her aunt: bangles Amelia had bought for her in Burma less than two weeks before she disappeared.

Both George Putnam and Mary Beatrice "Bea" Noonan, Fred's bride of only three months, were rumored to have collapsed. Bea was under doctor's orders, while George's friends clarified that they'd had to force him to go to bed because he'd been awake since July 2, monitoring the flight and then the search.

Ever the publicist, George later visited Bea at her home in Oakland to put on a show of optimism for the reporters. "I have a hunch they are sitting somewhere on a coral island and sending out their signals," he assured her. "Fred's probably out sitting on a rock now catching their dinner with those fishing lines they had aboard. There'll be driftwood to make fire. Maybe they could rig up a gasoline stove, if there is any gasoline left."

He couldn't sustain the illusion for long, though. "It's this way, Bea," he concluded bluntly. "One of two things have happened. Either they were killed outright—and that must come to all of us sooner or later—or they are alive and will be picked up." He got up to go. "Keep your chin up, Bea," he said. "You, too, Mr. Putnam," she replied.

When, on July 18, the U.S. Navy called off what was then the largest search ever for missing pilots, George's only response was, "I'm deeply appreciative of what the Navy has done. That is all I can say." Six months later, he admitted "hope lingers that the Providence which guarded her so often may still deliver her back in some miraculous manner."

The loss of Amelia shattered George, said Cynthia Putnam, the youngest child of his son George Jr., and another frequent visitor to the festival. "He spent his time and life and funds helping Amelia, providing for Amelia so she could do what she needed to do," she said. When she didn't return, he was left with the debt they'd incurred to repair the Electra after the Honolulu crash.

George tried to continue Amelia's care for her mother and sister—her family still speaks highly of him because of it—but he didn't have the funds. "You see," he wrote to Amy Earhart, "she spent all her money on aviation and on this last flight. You must realize that she expected, properly, to make a great deal of money out of the results of the flight after her return." Now, none of the expenses would be recouped and he'd struggle for money the rest of his life.

On January 5, 1939, after George had filed statements from military and government officials about the thoroughness of the search for Earhart and Noonan, the Superior Court of Los Angeles County declared Amelia legally dead. Five months later, he married Jean-Marie Cosigny James, a bright young woman he met at a Beverly Hills society salon where he was giving a talk. The marriage fell apart between the time he enlisted in the U.S. Army after the attack on Pearl Harbor and when he shipped out to China as an intelligence officer for a bomber squadron. Jean-Marie found life with George too chaotic and volatile—but she regretted the divorce for the rest of her life.

When rumors spread that Earhart was living in Japanese custody as the voice of Tokyo Rose, her sister, Muriel, said that George made a dangerous trek to a Marine Corps post on the coast to listen. "I'll stake my life that that is not Amelia's voice," he stated. "It sounds to me as if the woman might have lived in New York, and of course she has been fiendishly well coached. But Amelia—never." Another biographer claimed that "some time during this period of service," George drove all over the island of Saipan, pursuing rumors of his wife's capture there, but he found nothing.

In 1945, ill health forced George back to the United States; he had developed a kidney ailment, probably due to an infection or poor rations, that would eventually kill him. When he returned, he "very purposefully" started looking for a wife, according to a friend—"GPP was never a loner," another friend said. He found one in Margaret Haviland, an executive at the United Service Organizations he'd met while stationed in Salina, Kansas. They married on June 10, 1945, and retreated to a cabin he'd purchased in the southern Sierra Nevada mountains; later, they also ran the Stovepipe Wells resort in Death Valley. George died of kidney failure on January 4, 1950, at the age of 63.

Amelia's mother, Amy Earhart, died on October 29, 1962. She was 95. She'd moved to Berkeley, California, to be closer to the Pacific Ocean in case Amelia should return. The theory that the Japanese had captured her offered Amy the most hope that her daughter had survived, and so she clung to it. By 1950, though, "she resigned herself," said Muriel, "and came east to live with us." To the end of her life, says great-grandson Bram, Amy kept a bag packed for Amelia "with the stuff she'd need to clean up if she'd been on a desert island for 20 years."

Muriel lived to be 98, dying in Medford, Massachusetts, where she'd spent most of her life. She wrote two biographies of her sister—*Courage Is the Price* and *Amelia, My Courageous Sister*—and a children's book. In the process, she tapped a deep well of grace in her dealings with all the theorists, even the most outlandish ones. "I don't have animosity toward all these people who shatter my feelings," Muriel said late in life. "But Amelia was my beloved sister and we were very close and I think certain people forget that."

If the Electra is eventually found at the bottom of the Pacific or if bones are discovered on Nikumaroro or anywhere else, what will it tell us? That Noonan and Earhart suffered fear and pain in their last moments, that they knew irrevocably that they would never reach home, that their flight had come to an end. The mystery of their deaths may be resolved, but the deaths themselves won't. Sudden deaths never are, as survivors know to their sorrow. Since I first set out on the Earhart quest, I've lost five members of my family—four to the illnesses of old age and one to suicide. I know, as I didn't before, what it is to be tormented by questions, haunted by the feeling that if we only knew the answers, we could bring that person back.

Earhart left legions of survivors—the people who felt they knew her from newspapers and newsreels, the young women who took up flying or started a career due to her example, the mothers who name their daughters Amelia still to give them someone to live up to, and the people who cannot let the mystery go.

Part of mourning is recognizing the questions that can't be answered, that will never be answered. "She was / always leaving, always climbing / up from where we could reach her," writes Gabrielle Calvocoressi in one of the poems from *The Last Time I Saw Amelia Earhart*. In another, this one in George's voice: "Afterwards she was everywhere."

Amelia's closest relatives endured the unresolved nature of her death and their grief for the rest of their days.

Why can't we?

ACKNOWLEDGMENTS

THIS BOOK COULD NOT EXIST WITHOUT the tremendous amount of research of those who came before me. George Palmer Putnam, Amy Otis Earhart, and Muriel Earhart Morrissey gathered the trove of materials Amelia Earhart left behind and generously donated them to Purdue University and the Schlesinger Library at Harvard's Radcliffe Institute for Advanced Study, where they have been assiduously preserved and make delightful, if poignant, browsing. Many of the documents are available online.

Doughty biographers have plumbed Earhart's life in more depth than I was able to do here, especially Mary S. Lovell in *The Sound of Wings* and Susan Butler with *East to the Dawn*. Jean L. Backus captured her lively voice in the collection *Letters from Amelia,* while her sister, Muriel Earhart Morrissey, conveyed details only a family member would know in *Amelia, My Courageous Sister,* cowritten with Carol L. Osborne. Susan Ware's *Still Missing* usefully places Earhart within her culture and contemporary feminism.

The tireless theorists pursuing solutions to the Earhart mystery have produced copious amounts of research. Elgen and Marie Long's *Amelia Earhart: The Mystery Solved* explains their theory of how—and where—the

Electra crashed in great detail. *Amelia Earhart's Shoes* by Thomas F. King, Randall S. Jacobson, Karen R. Burns, and Kenton Spading explores the Nikumaroro castaway theory as it unfolded. Ric Gillespie's *Finding Amelia* breaks down Earhart and Noonan's last flight based on TIGHAR's research. Fred Goerner's *The Search for Amelia Earhart* lays the foundation for the Japanese capture theory. TIGHAR's collection of documents from the world flight and the history of Nikumaroro makes its website invaluable *(tighar.org).* Amelia Earhart: The Truth at Last *(earharttruth.wordpress.com),* a website run by Mike Campbell based on a book he wrote with Thomas Devine, offers an edifying look into the debates surrounding the captured theory. Liz Smith's Date Line Theory site *(www.datelinetheory.com)* provides a cogent explanation of just where Fred Noonan might have gone wrong.

This book has benefited from—and this author has been awestruck by—the researchers' determination to pursue every lead, explore every possibility, and devote so much of their lives to solving this mystery. I am especially grateful to those whose family members have passed away: Bram Kleppner (Earhart's grandnephew and Muriel Morrissey's grandson), Sally Putnam Chapman and Cynthia Putnam (George Palmer Putnam's granddaughters), Ed Akiyama (Josephine Blanco Akiyama's son), Paul Briand, Jr. (Paul Briand's son), Kay Long (Elgen Long's widow), and Gary Zellerbach (Fred Goerner's stepson).

I tapped the considerable expertise of Josephine Akiyama, Jaime Bach, Bob Ballard, John Clauss, Allison Fundis, Ric Gillespie, Dawn Johnson, David Jourdan, Erin Kimmerle, Tom King, Les Kinney, Elgen Long, Andrew McKenna, Tony Romeo, Scott Russell, Liz Smith, Miguel Vilar, Tom Vinson, Frankie West, the many members of TIGHAR on the 2017 cruise, the dog handlers from the Institute for Canine Forensics and the Canine Forensics Foundation, and the science team from the *Nautilus*. Their patience with my ignorance was boundless. Jourdan, especially, provided me with a gold mine: a hard drive full of Elgen Long's interviews.

Margaret Betchart of Betchart Expeditions navigated head-spinningly complicated travel arrangements. During the whirlwind hunt for bones on Tarawa, Kaono Koura and Eria Tebaro demonstrated unmatched equanimity and resourcefulness. The highly competent crews of the *Reef Endeavour* and the *Nautilus* eased this landlubber's anxieties.

But *Lost* never would have been written without a push—two, actually—and for that I owe a debt to former *National Geographic* senior editor Glenn Oeland, a true writers' advocate, for giving me the initial assignment and to agent Susan Canavan for insisting that this story could be a book.

At National Geographic, I was blessed with many exceptionally talented colleagues, including those involved with the Earhart project. Fred Hiebert launched the endeavor, Susan Goldberg graciously granted permission, Patty Edmonds and Debra Adams Simmons smoothed the way, Amy Briggs and Kristen Clark tag-teamed interviews, Kristin Romey remembered the crabs, and Sarah Diamond contributed crucial early research. Corey Robinson and Ben Zupo (2017 Nikumaroro expedition), Chad Cohen and Chris Weber (2019 expedition), and the rest of the film crew welcomed me on their teams and made sure I got the reporting I needed—as long as I stayed out of their shots.

The books team led by Lisa Thomas at National Geographic is small but mighty. Executive editor Hilary Black's enthusiasm gave me heart when I needed it, Tyler Daswick kept me on task, Brad Scriber saved me from countless embarrassments, Heather McElwain and Mary Stephanos burnished my prose, Uliana Bazar scouted amazing images to illustrate the book, Elisa Gibson created a beautiful cover, and Nicole Roberts crafted a compelling interior design.

Claudia Kalb and Dan Stone coached me on the basics of book writing. Eve Conant invited me over for weekly writing sessions, fed me dinner, gave the manuscript a literal stamp of approval—and got me over the final hump.

I am very grateful for the encouragement of family and friends throughout the process of writing this book, which took place during a period of loss, pandemic, and life changes. But sometimes during upheaval, it's steadying to have a project; this book was that for me. It's also helpful to have people around who assume you can do things even when you fear you can't. My mother, Judy, is like that, as was my late father, Frank. So is my son, Will. It's a gift I don't take for granted. I love you all.

SELECTED SOURCES

THIS BIBLIOGRAPHY LISTS THE CHIEF ARCHIVES and secondary publications that provided the source material for this book. It is not an exhaustive list. Sources are grouped by related subject matter: Amelia Earhart's biography, and the three disappearance theories explored in this work—captured by the Japanese, castaway on Nikumaroro, and crashed and sank into the ocean.

BIOGRAPHY

"1919: NC-4 Transatlantic Flight." United States Coast Guard Aviation History. cgaviationhistory.org/1919-nc-4-transatlantic-flight.

"3,000 Women Told of New Trends in U.S." *New York Herald Tribune,* September 27, 1934.

Abbott, Karen. "How the 1904 Marathon Became One of the Weirdest Olympic Events of All Time." *Smithsonian*, August 7, 2012 (updated June 27, 2024, by Ellen Wexler). smithsonianmag.com/history/how-the-1904-marathon-became-one-of-the-weirdest-olympic-events-of-all-time-14910747.

"Amelia Deplores 'Discrimination' Against Her Sex in Aviation Field." *Tulsa World* (AP), November 7, 1935.

"Amelia Earhart Landed in a Field in Ballyarnett in Derry on May 21 of 1932." YouTube, March 21, 2017. youtube.com/watch?v=t7PHJ9jPwRA.

Amelia Earhart's application. Women's Educational and Industrial Union Records. Uncatalogued. Schlesinger Library, Harvard Radcliffe Institute, Cambridge, MA.

"Amelia Earhart's Flight." Mexico Via Airmail, Smithsonian National Postal Museum. postalmuseum.si.edu/exhibition/mexico-via-airmail-nature-and-technology/amelia-earharts-flight.

"Amelia Earhart's Lockheed Vega 5B." Collection Objects, Smithsonian National Air and Space Museum. airandspace.si.edu/collection-objects/lockheed-vega-5b-amelia-earhart/nasm_A19670093000.

"Amelia's Sister Not Worrying, She Says." *The Boston Globe*, July 3, 1937.

Athitakis, Mark. "A 1929 Air Derby Helped Female Pilots Break Barriers." *Humanities* 44, no. 2 (Spring 2023).

Backus, Jean L. *Letters from Amelia, 1901–1937.* Beacon Press, 1982.

Barton, Abbie. "The Poet and the Person." *Flight Paths: Purdue University's Aerospace Pioneers,* April 25, 2016.

Berliner, Don. "The Big Race of 1910." *Air & Space/Smithsonian,* January 2010.

Boylan, Jennifer Finney. "Amelia Earhart, Saved From Drowning." Peggy Downes Baskin Ethics Lecture, The Humanities Institute, University of California, Santa Cruz, March 20, 2025. youtube.com/watch?v=iALk6sG6OYI.

Butler, Susan. *East to the Dawn: The Life of Amelia Earhart.* Da Capo Press, 1999.

Calvocoressi, Gabrielle. *The Last Time I Saw Amelia Earhart: Poems.* Persea, 2005.

Changing Standards: Report of the Fourth Annual New York Herald Tribune *Women's Conference on Current Problems. New York Herald Tribune,* 1934.

Chapman, Sally Putnam with Stephanie Mansfield. *Whistled Like a Bird: The Untold Story of Dorothy Putnam, George Putnam, and Amelia Earhart.* Warner Books, 1997.

"Chick-fil-A Egg White Grill TV Spot, 'Earhart.'" iSpot. ispot.tv/ad/AluX/chick-fil-a-egg-white-grill-earhart.

"Crack Flyers and Planes Here for Winter Show." *Long Beach Press,* December 24, 1920.

Earhart, Amelia. *20 Hrs. 40 Min.: Our Flight in the* Friendship. National Geographic Adventure Classics, 2003. Originally published in 1928 by G. P. Putnam's Sons.

Earhart, Amelia. "Courage," 1927. Published in "Who Is Amelia Earhart?" by Marion Perkins. *Survey Graphic,* July 1, 1928.

Earhart, Amelia. *The Fun of It: Random Records of My Own Flying and of Women in Aviation.* Academy Chicago Publishers, 1977. Originally published in 1932 by Harcourt, Brace and Company, Inc.

Earhart, Amelia. *Last Flight: Amelia Earhart's Flying Adventures.* Trotamundas Press, 2008. Originally published in 1937 by Harcourt, Brace and Company, Inc.

Earhart, Amelia. "My Flight from Hawaii." *National Geographic*, May 1935.

"Earhart Given Up." *The Kansas City Times* (AP), July 19, 1937.

"Fliers' Mates Seek to Cheer Each Other Up." *The Daily Ardmoreite* (AP), July 3, 1937.

Francis, David R. *The Universal Exposition of 1904,* vol. 1. Louisiana Purchase Exposition Company, 1913.

The George Palmer Putnam Collection of Amelia Earhart Papers. Archives and Special Collections. Purdue University Libraries. lib.purdue.edu/aearhart.

Huegerich, Scott, and Bob Miano, dir. *The World's Greatest Fair.* Janson Media, 2004. Documentary.

Jones, Peter, dir. *Blue Sky Metropolis.* Episode one, "Wings." PBS SoCal, July 14, 2019.

Kahanu, Noelle M. K. Y. "Records Reveal the Hidden History of a Pacific Colonization Project." *Ka Wai Ola,* February 1, 2024.

Kindy, Dave. "The Harrowing, Forgotten Journey of the First Transatlantic Flight." *Washington Post,* May 21, 2022.

"Local Aviatrix Is First to Be Given License." *Los Angeles Times,* May 17, 1923.

Lovell, Mary S. *The Sound of Wings: The Life of Amelia Earhart.* St. Martin's Press, 1989.

Maksel, Rebecca. "Wiley Post's Historic Around-the-World Flight." *Air & Space/Smithsonian,* July 16, 2013. smithsonianmag.com/air-space-magazine/follow-path-wiley-posts-historic-around-world-flight-180947934.

McArdle, Kenneth. "Princess Feared Seasickness, Took Up Aviation and Joined the Growing List of Vanished Aviators." *Pittsburgh Press,* December 13, 1934.

Mondor, Colleen. "The Short, Brilliant Career of Alaska's First Woman Pilot." *Anchorage Daily News,* June 19, 2016.

Morrissey, Muriel Earhart, and Carol Osborne. *Amelia, My Courageous Sister.* Osborne Publisher, 1987.

"Mother in Seclusion." *Pasadena Post,* July 3, 1937.

"Mother Sure Amelia Safe." *The San Francisco Examiner* (AP), July 3, 1937.

"Nonsmoker Amelia Earhart Endorses Lucky Strike." *100 Years of Advertising*. American Association of Advertising Agencies. aaaa.org/about/timeline.

"No Word From Mrs. Grayson; Plane 29 Hours Overdue; Air Search Starts Today." *New York Times,* December 25, 1927.

"The Ogontz School 1850–1950." Penn State University Libraries Digital Collections. libraries.psu.edu/about/collections/ogontz-school-1850-1950.

Papers of Amelia Earhart, 1835–1977. Schlesinger Library, Harvard Radcliffe Institute, Cambridge, MA. hollisarchives.lib.harvard.edu/repositories/8/resources/7302.

Papers of Amy Otis Earhart, 1884–1987. Schlesinger Library, Harvard Radcliffe Institute, Cambridge, MA. hollisarchives.lib.harvard.edu/repositories/8/resources/7192.

Papers of Janet Mabie, 1912–1960. Item description. MC 451. Schlesinger Library, Harvard Radcliffe Institute, Cambridge, MA. hollisarchives.lib.harvard.edu/repositories/8/resources/5494.

"The 'Pike' at St. Louis Fair a Marvel." *Minneapolis Star Tribune,* August 21, 1904.

"Prominent Trans Rights Advocate and Bestselling Author Jennifer Finney Boylan Will Deliver Peggy Downes Baskin Ethics Lecture." The Humanities Institute, University of California, Santa Cruz. thi.ucsc.edu/bestselling-author-jennifer-finney-boylan-will-pay-tribute-to-amelia-earhart-at-peggy-downes-baskin-ethics-lecture.

"Publicity Said Flight Object ... Hawaiian Sugar Men Try to Focus Attention on Islands." *Riverside Daily Press* (UP), January 4, 1935.

Putnam, George Palmer. *Soaring Wings: A Biography of Amelia Earhart.* Harcourt, Brace and Company, Inc., 1939.

"Records Relating to Amelia Earhart." National Archives News. archives.gov/news/topics/earhart.

"The Reminiscences of Muriel Earhart Morrissey." Interview by Kenneth W. Leish, September 1960. Aviation project, Columbia Center for Oral History, Columbia University, New York, NY. dx.doi.org/10.7916/d8-y7j6-hv88.

"Rihanna Takes Flight." *Harper's Bazaar,* February 8, 2017.

"Ruth Elder and Pilot Are Rescued From Sea by Dutch Ship, Plane Burns." *New York Times,* October 14, 1927.

Rydell, Robert W. *All the World's a Fair: Visions of Empire at American International Expositions, 1876–1916.* University of Chicago Press, 1987. Originally published in 1984.

Scheinberg, Ellen. "Amelia Earhart in Toronto." Defining Moments Canada. definingmomentscanada.ca/1918-influenza-pandemic/flu-microhistories/amelia-earhart-in-toronto.

"Silence Hides Amelia's Fate on Ocean Hop." *Salt Lake Telegram* (UP), July 2, 1937.

"Sister of Amelia Optimistic; Calm Despite Wearing Ordeal." *Boston Globe,* July 5, 1937.

"The Society's Special Medal Awarded to Amelia Earhart." *National Geographic,* September 1932.

"Thousands Are Thrilled by Aviators' Speed and Skill; Aircraft Exhibition Amazes." *The Daily Telegram* (Long Beach, California), December 27, 1920.

Ware, Susan. *Still Missing: Amelia Earhart and the Search for Modern Feminism.* W. W. Norton, 1993.

"When Amelia Earhart Landed in Derry Field." BBC News, May 31, 2015. bbc.com/news/uk-northern-ireland-32934928.

White, William L. *Slaying the Dragon: The History of Addiction Treatment and Recovery in America.* Chestnut Health Systems, 1998.

Williams, John. "Earhart Plan for Solo Hop Opposed Here." *Honolulu Star Bulletin,* December 29, 1934.

"World's Progress Shown in a New Light by Week's Triumphs at Aviation Meet." *Los Angeles Sunday Times,* January 16, 1910.

CAPTURED

"AF Says Proof of Execution of Aviatrix 'Inconclusive.'" *The Courier-News* (AP), July 7, 1960.

"Amelia Earhart Killed on Saipan." *San Mateo Times,* July 1, 1960.

"Aviatrix Amelia Earhart Disappears Again in Mists." *Siskiyou Daily News* (UPI), July 15, 1960.

Biddlestone, M., R. Green, K. M. Douglas, et al. "Reasons to Believe: A Systematic Review and Meta-analytic Synthesis of the Motives Associated with Conspiracy Beliefs." *Psychological Bulletin* 151 (1). doi.org/10.1037/bul0000463.

Blanco, Juan. "Oral History Interview with Juan Blanco," date unknown. National Museum of the Pacific War/Admiral Nimitz Foundation, Fredericksburg, TX. University of North Texas Libraries, The Portal to Texas History. texashistory.unt.edu/ark:/67531/metapth1604023.

Bower, Barry W. *The Amelia Earhart Saga: Plausible Suppositions.* Self-published, 2015.

Bradsher, Greg. "The Japanese Government's Offer of Assistance to Help Find Amelia Earhart, July 1937." The Text Message, National Archives, July 12, 2017. text-message.blogs.archives.gov/2017/07/12/the-japanese-governments-offer-of-assistance-to-help-find-amelia-earhart-july-1937.

Brenan, Megan. "Decades Later, Most Americans Doubt Lone Gunman Killed JFK." Gallup, November 13, 2023. news.gallup.com/poll/514310/decades-later-americans-doubt-lone-gunman-killed-jfk.aspx.

Brotherton, Rob. *Suspicious Minds: Why We Believe Conspiracy Theories.* Bloomsbury Sigma, 2016.

Brown, Neil. "Earhart Claims Take a Nosedive." *Home News* (New Brunswick, NJ), November 11, 1970.

Burns, Eugene. "Clue Obtained to Mystery of Amelia Earhart." Associated Press, March 21, 1944.

Campbell, Mike. Amelia Earhart: The Truth at Last. earharttruth.wordpress.com.

Coolidge, Frederick L., and Apeksha Srivastava. "Do Conspiracy Beliefs Constitute a New Personality Disorder?" *Psychology Today,* October 25, 2024. psychologytoday .com/us/blog/how-to-think-like-a -neandertal/202410/do-conspiracy-beliefs -constitute-a-new-personality.

Costello, John. *The Pacific War, 1941–1945.* Harper Perennial, 2009. Originally published in 1981 by Rawson, Wade.

Day, Lin. "San Matean Says Japanese Executed Amelia Earhart." *San Mateo Times,* May 27, 1960.

Devine, Thomas E., with Richard M. Daley. *Eyewitness: The Amelia Earhart Incident.* Renaissance House, 1987.

Dwiggins, Don. "Amelia Earhart's Grave Found, AF Officer Says." *Los Angeles Mirror,* July 5, 1960.

"Earhart Mystery Probe Rekindled." *The Spokane-Review* (AP), July 2, 1960.

"Evidence Grows That American Pilots Executed by Japanese." *Lubbock Avalanche-Journal,* July 6, 1960.

"Flier Irene Bolam, 78; Figured in Controversy." *The Daily Register* (Red Bank, NJ), July 12, 1982.

Goerner, Fred. *The Search for Amelia Earhart.* Doubleday, 1966.

Goll, Ralph. "Did the Japs 'Liquidate' Halliburton and Amelia Earhart?" *Detroit Free Press,* January 10, 1943.

Handleman, Howard. "Mystery of Amelia Earhart Revived by Album on Saipan." International News Service, July 12, 1944.

Holbrook, Francis X. "Amelia Earhart's Final Flight." *Proceedings of the U.S. Naval Institute,* February 1971.

"Japan Has a Look at Howland!: Sidelights on the Search for Amelia Earhart." *Pacific Islands Monthly,* August 25, 1937.

Joseph Gervais Papers. "Finding Aid." History of Aviation Archives, Special Collections and Archives Division, Eugene McDermott Library, The University of Texas at Dallas. libarchives.utdallas.edu/repositories/2/ resources/79.

Kinney, Les. Comment, "Marshalls Release Is Latest Twist in Photo Travesty." Amelia Earhart: The Truth At Last, July 28, 2017. earharttruth.wordpress.com/2017/ 07/28/marshalls-release-latest-twist-in -photo-travesty/#comments.

Klaas, Joe. *Amelia Earhart Lives: A Trip Through Intrigue to Find America's First Lady of Mystery.* McGraw-Hill, 1970.

Lipsky, Bill. "Everett Man Disputes Earhart Death Claims." *The Everett* (WA) *Daily Herald,* July 7, 1960.

Maksel, Rebecca. "A Female Aviator in 1926 Needed a Stunt. So She Flew Under the Brooklyn Bridge." *Air & Space/ Smithsonian,* March 9, 2020. smithsonian mag.com/air-space-magazine/flying -cashier-180973963.

Mandel, Alex. "Amelia Earhart's Survival and Repatriation: Myth or Reality?" en.wikisource.org/wiki/Amelia_Earhart %27s_Survival_and_Repatriation: w_Myth_or_Reality%3F.

McCurry, Justin, and Jamiles Lartey. "Blogger Discredits Claim That Amelia Earhart Was

Taken Prisoner by Japan." *The Guardian,* July 11, 2017.

Orth, Taylor. "Which Conspiracy Theories Do Americans Believe?" YouGov., December 8, 2023, today.yougov.com/politics/articles/48113-which-conspiracy-theories-do-americans-believe.

Pasquarella, Jim, Gary Tarpinian, and Paninee Theeranuntawat, exec. prod. *Amelia Earhart: The Lost Evidence.* Morningstar Entertainment, 2017.

Patton, Joseph M. "U.S. Naval Intelligence Investigation Report: Earhart, Amelia; Information re Location of Grave of." Filed December 23, 1960. Reproduced in *With Our Own Eyes: Eyewitnesses to the Final Days of Amelia Earhart* by Mike Campbell with Thomas E. Devine. Lucky Press, 2002.

Paul Briand, Jr. Papers, 1920–1986. MC 120. Milne Special Collections and University Archives, Dimond Library, University of New Hampshire, Durham, NH.

Peattie, Mark R. *Nan'yō: The Rise and Fall of the Japanese in Micronesia, 1885–1945.* University of Hawaii Press, 1988.

"Pilot Claims Photos Reveal Earhart Death." *Oakland Tribune* (AP), July 5, 1960.

PL-Marshall Islands, Jaluit Atoll, Jaluit Island. ONI #14381. Jaluit Harbor. U.S. National Archives, Records of the Office of Naval Intelligence, Record Group 38, Monograph Files Relating to the Pacific Ocean Area, NAID 68141661.

Price, Willard. "Hidden Key to the Pacific: Piercing the Web of Secrecy Which Long Has Veiled Japanese Bases in the Mandated Islands." *National Geographic,* June 1942.

Price, Willard. "Springboards to Tokyo." *National Geographic,* October 1944.

Rust, Nicole C. "Our Memory Is Even Better Than Experts Thought." *Scientific American,* May 25, 2021.

Saudek, Robert, exec. prod. "The Story of Amelia Earhart." *Omnibus with Alistair Cooke,* March 17, 1957. youtube.com/watch?v=70O20KQaGsk.

"U.S.A. Does Australia a Secret Service." *Smith's Weekly,* October 16, 1937.

CASTAWAY

Ballard, Robert. "Mapping Offshore America." *National Geographic,* November 2013.

Ballard, Robert, and Christopher Drew. *Into the Deep: A Memoir from the Man Who Found* Titanic. National Geographic, 2021.

Cohen, Chad, dir. *Expedition Amelia.* National Geographic, 2019.

"Dr. Ballard Endorses TIGHAR." TIGHAR Channel, YouTube, March 27, 2012. youtube.com/watch?v=67qlnUXBdrQ.

The Earhart Project Archives. The International Group for Historic Aircraft Recovery (TIGHAR). tighar.org/Projects/Earhart/Archives/Archives.html.

Gillespie, Ric. *Finding Amelia: The True Story of the Earhart Disappearance.* Naval Institute Press, 2009.

Grebenkemper, John, Adela Morris, Brian F. Byrd, and Laurel Engbring. 2021. "Applying Canine Detection in Support of Collaborative Archaeology." *Advances in Archaeological Practice* 9 (3): 226–37. doi:10.1017/aap.2021.12.

Hartigan, Rachel. "Amelia Earhart Search Crew Shares Personal Theories on Her Disappearance." *National Geographic,* August 23, 2019. nationalgeographic.com/culture/article/amelia-earhart-reflection.

Hartigan, Rachel. "Bones Discovered in 1940 Could Have Been Amelia Earhart's."

National Geographic, March 8, 2018. nationalgeographic.com/history/article/amelia-earhart-bones-forensic-analysis.

Hartigan, Rachel. "Colossal Crabs May Hold Clue to Amelia Earhart Fate." *National Geographic,* August 20, 2019. nationalgeographic.com/culture/article/colossal-crabs-hold-clue-amelia-earhart-fate.

Hartigan, Rachel. "Exclusive: Bone-Sniffing Dogs to Hunt for Amelia Earhart's Remains." *National Geographic,* June 21, 2017. nationalgeographic.com/history/article/amelia-earhart-island-dogs.

Hartigan, Rachel. "Forensic Dogs Locate Spot Where Amelia Earhart May Have Died." *National Geographic,* July 7, 2017. nationalgeographic.com/history/article/forensic-dogs-amelia-earhart-spot-where-died.

Hartigan, Rachel. "Inside Robert Ballard's Search for Amelia Earhart's Airplane." *National Geographic,* August 12, 2019. nationalgeographic.com/culture/article/inside-search-for-amelia-earhart-airplane.

Hartigan, Rachel. "Remembering Two Icons in the Search for Amelia Earhart." *National Geographic,* February 9, 2022. nationalgeographic.com/history/article/remembering-two-icons-amelia-earhart-search.

Hartigan, Rachel. "Robert Ballard Found the *Titanic.* Can He Find Amelia Earhart's Airplane?" *National Geographic,* July 23, 2019. nationalgeographic.com/culture/article/bob-ballard-found-titanic-can-find-amelia-earhart-airplane.

Hartigan, Rachel. "The Searcher of the Deep." *National Geographic,* May 2021.

Hartigan, Rachel. "'Tantalizing Clue' Marks End of Amelia Earhart Expedition." *National Geographic,* August 26, 2019. nationalgeographic.com/culture/article/tantalizing-clue-marks-end-amelia-earhart-expedition.

Hartigan, Rachel. "Why Does Amelia Earhart Still Fascinate Us?" *National Geographic,* October 17, 2019. nationalgeographic.com/history/article/why-amelia-earhart-still-fascinates.

Hartigan, Rachel. "Why This Island Is at the Center of the Search for Amelia Earhart." *National Geographic,* June 20, 2017. nationalgeographic.com/adventure/article/amelia-earhart-search-island-dogs.

Johnson, Dawn. "Forensic Canine Soil Test for Nikumaroro." The International Group for Historic Aircraft Recovery (TIGHAR), August 14, 2015. tighar.org/Projects/Earhart/Niku8/CanineForensicTest.html.

King, Thomas F., Randall S. Jacobson, Karen R. Burns, and Kenton Spading. *Amelia Earhart's Shoes: Is the Mystery Solved?* Altamira Press, 2004.

Mellon v. The International Group for Historic Aircraft Recovery et al. (D. Wyo. 2014). govinfo.gov/app/details/USCOURTS-wyd-1_13-cv-00118/USCOURTS-wyd-1_13-cv-00118-0.

Mellon v. The International Group et al. (10th Cir. 2015). govinfo.gov/app/details/USCOURTS-ca10-14-08062/USCOURTS-ca10-14-08062-0.

"The Object Formerly Known as Nessie." *TIGHAR Tracks: The Journal of the International Group for Historic Aircraft Recovery,* February 2013.

"Part 1, Series G, Section 6: Death of Amelia Earhart: Correspondence, Articles, etc. 1990–93." Harry Evans and Honor Maude Digital Archive. University of Adelaide. hdl.handle.net/2440/115117.

Slon, Viviane, Charlotte Hopfe, Clemens L. Weiss, et al. "Neandertal and Denisovan DNA from Pleistocene Sediments." *Science* 356: 605–608 (2017). doi:10.1126/science.aam9695.

CRASHED AND SANK

Allen, J. Douglas, prod. "A Man, A Plane, and A Dream." 1971. Periscope Film. stock.periscopefilm.com/10044-a-man-a-plane-and-a-dream-1971-round-the-world-flight-by-elgen-marion-long-piper-navajo.

Bartelme, Tony. "Searching for Amelia Earhart." *Post and Courier* (Charleston, S.C.), January 27, 2024.

Boldenweck, Bill. "A Happy Pilot Is Home." *San Francisco Examiner,* December 4, 1971.

Branning, Don. "Pilot Long Loser—Commercially." *San Francisco Examiner,* December 5, 1971.

Dean, Paul. "The Earhart Mystery in Search of a Solution." *Los Angeles Times,* January 14, 1981.

Expedition Report. Eustace Earhart Discovery. Nauticos, September 15, 2017.

"Globe-Circling Pilot Crosses 4th, Last 'Corner' of World." *Los Angeles Times* (UPI), November 29, 1971.

Guidera, Mark. "Joint Venture to Seek Amelia Earhart Plane." *Baltimore Sun,* November 3, 1999.

Jourdan, David W. *The Deep Sea Quest for Amelia Earhart.* Ocellus Productions, 2010.

Liles, Lindsey. "Meet the Adventurer Who Might Have Found Amelia Earhart's Aircraft." *Garden & Gun,* February 20, 2024. gardenandgun.com/articles/meet-the-adventurer-who-might-have-found-amelia-earharts-aircraft.

Long, Elgen M. Amelia Earhart Project Recordings. Courtesy of Nauticos, LLC, Kennebunkport, ME. Also available at the National Air and Space Museum Archives.

Long, Elgen M. "Interview of Elgen M. Long by Brian Shoemaker." May 8, 2001. Byrd Polar Research Center Archival Program, Ohio State University. hdl.handle.net/1811/6510.

Long, Elgen M., and Marie K. Long. *Amelia Earhart: The Mystery Solved.* Simon & Schuster Paperbacks, 2009.

Mills, Bill. "Nauticos Earhart Discovery: Dynamic Aviation & the *Nellie Crockett* Join the Team." Nauticos/BMA Production Services, Inc. vimeo.com/469779444.

Simpson, Joanne Cavanaugh. "Looking for Amelia." *Johns Hopkins Magazine,* June 2002. pages.jh.edu/jhumag/0602web/amelia.html.

Smith, Liz. The Dateline Theory. www.datelinetheory.com.

"Solo Global Pilot to Land at Wake." *San Francisco Examiner,* November 28, 1971.

"Up, Up and Around." *Capital Journal* (UPI), November 4, 1971.

INDEX

Z

ABOUT THE AUTHOR

RACHEL HARTIGAN is a former senior writer and editor with National Geographic, where she focused on culture and history. She has participated in two expeditions to the uninhabited island of Nikumaroro in search of the remains of Amelia Earhart. Previously, she served as editor of *Book World* at the *Washington Post* and as deputy editor for culture and education at *U.S. News & World Report*. She grew up in Reno, Nevada, and lives in Takoma Park, Maryland.